1994

TRANSITION TO DEMOCRACY IN POLAND

Books by Richard F. Staar

Arms Control: Myth versus Reality (*editor*)

Aspects of Modern Communism (*editor*)

Communist Regimes in Eastern Europe, 5th revised edition

East-Central Europe and the USSR (*editor*)

Effects of Soviet Political Fragmentation on the
Energy Infrastructure (*co-author*)

Foreign Policies of the Soviet Union

Future Information Revolution in the USSR (*editor*)

Long-Range Environmental Study of the Northern Tier of
Eastern Europe in 1990-2000

Poland, 1944-1962: Sovietization of A Captive People

Public Diplomacy: USA versus USSR (*editor*)

Soviet Military Policy Since World War II (*co-author*)

Transition to Democracy in Poland (*editor*)

United States-East European Relations in the 1990s (*editor*)

USSR Foreign Policies After Detente, 2nd rev. edition

Yearbook on International Communist Affairs:
Parties and Revolutionary Movements (*editor of 22 volumes*)

TRANSITION TO DEMOCRACY IN POLAND

Edited by
Richard F. Staar

St. Martin's Press
New York

Published in cooperation with
the Hoover Institution on War, Revolution and Peace
Stanford University

First published in the United States of America

Printed in the United States of America

ISBN 0-312-10000-0

Library of Congress Cataloging-in-Publication Data

Transition to democracy in Poland / edited by Richard F. Staar.
    p. cm.
  Includes bibliographical references (p.   ) and index.
  ISBN 0-312-10000-0
  1. Democracy—Poland. 2. Poland—Politics and government—1989-
I. Staar, Richard Felix, 1923-
JN6766.T73 1993
443.805'6—dc20
                                    93-26014
                                    CIP

for Żywieńka

CONTENTS

List of Tables ix

Preface xi

Notes on Contributors xiii

Introduction: The Future of Poland
Richard F. Staar 1

1. Voters, Parties, and Leaders
   Raymond Taras 15

2. Political Activation of Social Groups
   Mirosława Grabowska 41

3. The Presidential-Parliamentary System
   Andrew A. Michta 57

4. Local Government Reform
   James F. Hicks, Jr., and Bartłomiej Kamiński 77

5. Constitutional Reform
   A. E. Dick Howard 97

6. Interaction between Political and Economic Freedom
   Edward P. Lazear 111

7. Privatization Strategy and Its Political Context
   Łucja Świątkowski Cannon 123

8. Product and Labor Markets
   Benjamin H. Slay and Michał Rutkowski 145

9. The Role of Monetary Policy in Market Economies
   Thomas J. Sargent 167

10. Emerging Patterns of Foreign Trade
   Bartłomiej Kamiński 181

11. Prospects for Regional Cooperation
   Sarah Meiklejohn Terry 203

12. National Security Relations
   Arthur R. Rachwald 235

   Index 257

LIST OF TABLES

1.1 Presidential Election Results (25 November 1990) 25

1.2 Parliamentary Election Results (27 October 1991) 27

1.3 Political Orientation of Parties 28

1.4 Political Parties, Programs, and Leaders (April 1993) 30

2.1 The Followers 45

2.2 Voters for Political Parties 46

2.3 Supporters of Major Political Parties 50

8.1 Changes in Gross Industrial Production, 1990-1991 146

8.2 Changes in the Branch Structure of Gross Industrial Output,
1989-1991 148

8.3 Comparison of Employment Structure 153

8.4 Sectoral Profile of Job Losses in Poland 158

8.5 Unemployment Rates (November 1991) 161

10.1 Directions of Poland's Exports and Imports, 1985-1991 182

10.2 Polish Manufactured Product Exports to the EC and Their
Relative Factor Intensities (FI) 190

10.3 Changing Polish Export Orientation from CMEA to OECD,
1988-1991 195

PREFACE

It seemed natural to select Poland for a case study of transition to democracy in East-Central Europe. The country is the largest in both area and population throughout the region, has experienced a long tradition of modern political and social development that dates back to the eighteenth century, and was first to throw off a communist yoke that had been forcibly imposed by the Red Army of the Soviet Union toward the end of World War II.

Another consideration involved the availability of so many United States scholars who know the Polish language and have done on-site research or teaching in Poland. All save one and a half of the chapters were written by such American experts. An attempt was made to pair each of the authors with a respondent from Warsaw, who would critique the draft papers on the basis of firsthand experience at the university or in government agencies or international organizations. This approach proved to be successful.

All participants in the conference owe a debt of gratitude to Dr. Tomasz Gruszecki (European Bank for Reconstruction and Development, London); Mme. Hanna Gronkiewicz-Waltz (president, National Bank of Poland); Professor Krzysztof Jasiewicz (Institute of Political Studies, Polish Academy of Sciences); Senator Andrzej Machalski (president, Confederation of Polish Employers); Dr. Christine Sadowski (Free Trade Union Institute, AFL/CIO), the exceptional American; Dr. Jacek Szymanderski (director, Center for Public Opinion Research at Warsaw); Minister Counselor Jacek Tomorowicz (embassy of Poland in Washington, D.C.); Mme. Halina Wasilewska-Trenker (secretary of state, Central Planning Office, Warsaw); Jan B. de Weydenthal (regional analyst for RFE/RL, Munich); and Justice Janina Zakrzewska (Constitutional Tribunal), who faxed her comments from Warsaw.

The editor expresses his personal thanks to Dr. John Raisian, director of the Hoover Institution, for opening the conference; the Honorable George P. Shultz, former U.S. secretary of state and now distinguished fellow at the Hoover Institution, for his lengthy introductory remarks which provided a stimulus that lasted throughout the proceedings; and also to the following colleagues for having chaired individual discussion panels: Annelise G. Anderson; David W. Brady; Bruce Bueno de Mesquita; John A. Ferejohn; Robert E. Hall; Alex Inkeles; Thomas E. MaCurdy; Charles E. McLure, Jr.; Condoleezza Rice; and Kenneth E. Scott. Professor Charles Wolf, Jr., dean of the Graduate School and director of the Economic Policy Program at the Rand Corporation, delivered a brilliant after-dinner address at the Stanford University faculty club, for which all attendees were grateful.

The generous support of the Hoover Institution and Director John Raisian; the Kościuszko Foundation and President Joseph E. Gore; the American Institute of Polish Culture and President Blanka A. Rosenstiel as well as the United States Information Agency, for allowing us to coopt one of its distinguished visitors from Poland, are acknowledged with thanks.

Finally, the editor wishes to express appreciation to Jadwiga M. Staar for proofreading the text as well as adding the diacritical marks, and to Margit N. Grigory who finalized this book for the press as well as prepared the detailed index.

Richard F. Staar
Stanford, California

NOTES ON CONTRIBUTORS

MIROSLAWA GRABOWSKA (Ph.D., Warsaw) is an associate professor of sociology both at the Institute of Political Studies, Polish Academy of Sciences, and the Institute of Sociology at Warsaw University. Her latest book, *Bitwa o Belweder* (Kraków, 1991), deals with the 25 November and 7 December 1990 presidential elections in Poland.

JAMES F. HICKS, JR. (Ph.D., North Carolina at Chapel Hill) is principal urban development specialist with the World Bank in Washington, D.C. He coauthored most recently a volume, *Poland: Decentralization and Reform of the State* (Washington, D.C., 1992), published by the World Bank in its "Country Study" series.

A. E. DICK HOWARD (LL.B., Virginia) is professor of law and public affairs at the University of Virginia. He was a Rhodes Scholar at Oxford and law clerk to U.S. Supreme Court Justice Hugo L. Black. His most recent books include *The United States Constitution* (Washington, D.C., 1992) and *Democracy's Dawn* (Charlottesville, Va., 1991). He has consulted with drafters of constitutions in Central and Eastern Europe.

BARTŁOMIEJ KAMIŃSKI (Ph.D., Warsaw), a consultant in the International Trade Division of the World Bank and an associate professor of government, directs the Center for Study of Post-Communist Societies at the University of Maryland. His latest book is entitled *The Collapse of State Socialism: The Case of Poland* (Princeton, N.J., 1991).

EDWARD P. LAZEAR (Ph.D., Harvard) is a senior fellow at the Hoover Institution as well as professor of human resource management and economics at the Graduate School of Business, Stanford University. He has published more than 100 scholarly papers in professional journals.

ANDREW A. MICHTA (Ph.D., Johns Hopkins) is an associate professor and holder of the Mertie W. Buckman Chair of International Studies at Rhodes College. His most recent books include *Red Eagle: The Army in Polish Politics* (Stanford, Ca., 1990) and *East-Central Europe After the Warsaw Pact* (Westport, Conn., 1992), the latter coedited.

ARTHUR R. RACHWALD (J.D., Lublin; Ph.D., California at Santa Barbara) is a professor of political science at the United States Naval Academy. His most recent book is entitled, *In Search of Poland: The Superpowers' Response to Solidarity* (Stanford, Ca., 1990).

MICHAŁ RUTKOWSKI (Ph.D., Warsaw), is an associate professor of economics at the Warsaw School of Economics, on leave of absence at the World Bank in Washington, D.C. He has authored numerous articles that have appeared in the Polish and English languages.

THOMAS J. SARGENT (Ph.D., Harvard) is a senior fellow at the Hoover Institution and professor of economics at the University of Chicago. He has published books entitled *Dynamics of Macroeconomic Theory* (Cambridge, Mass., 1987) and *Macroeconomic Theory* (New York, 1987), among others.

BENJAMIN H. SLAY (Ph.D., Indiana) is an assistant professor of economics at Bates College. He spent the 1991-1992 academic year with the RFE/RL Research Institute in Munich, Germany, and has written mostly about the Polish economy.

RICHARD F. STAAR (Ph.D., Michigan) is a senior fellow at the Hoover Institution, from which he took leave of absence for public service as U.S. ambassador to the Mutual and Balanced Forces Reduction talks in Vienna, Austria. He presented a lecture at the Jagiellonian University in Kraków during a visit to cover local elections in Poland at the end of May 1990.

ŁUCJA ŚWIĄTKOWSKI CANNON (Ph.D., Columbia) is a consultant on Poland for the World Bank. Involved with discussions on privatization at the Ministry of Finance during 1989-1990, she has participated in Polish projects related to telecommunications, agriculture, and real estate development reforms.

RAYMOND TARAS (Ph.D., Warsaw) is an associate professor of political science at Tulane University. His interest in Poland stems from a Canada Council doctoral fellowship and a published dissertation, *Ideology in a Socialist State* (Cambridge, England, 1991). A forthcoming book has the title, *Communists and the Polish Road to Socialism* (Stanford, Ca., 1993).

SARAH MEIKLEJOHN TERRY (Ph.D., Harvard) is an associate professor of political science at Tufts University and a fellow of the Russian Research Center at Harvard University. She authored *Poland's Place in Europe* (Princeton, N.J., 1983) and edited *Soviet Policy in Eastern Europe* (New York, 1984).

Introduction:
The Future of Poland

Richard F. Staar

Only one nation in East-Central Europe repeatedly expressed itself through national upheavals against Soviet-imposed[1] communist rule during 1956, 1970, 1976, 1980-1981, and 1989. The Poles must have received some historic inspiration from the two nineteenth-century insurrections within the tsarist-Russian occupation zone of their partitioned country. Poland is also unique within the region in that it remained subject to martial law between 13 December 1981 and 21 July 1983 under Wojciech Jaruzelski, who chaired a military junta comprised of 17 other generals and three colonels.[2]

Yet the Polish people also managed to pioneer revolutionary change throughout the former Soviet bloc, without excessive bloodshed. Indigenous communist leaders at first thought they could remain in power by negotiating with the Solidarity opposition an agreement which guaranteed the ruling party and its client political movements some 65 percent of the seats in the lower house (or Sejm) of parliament after the June 1989 national elections. That situation became rectified in October 1991, when such elections were truly free.

In between, Polish citizens were able to vote for a new president to replace General Jaruzelski, who had agreed to step down before his term expired and not stand for office again. None of the six presidential candidates received an absolute majority, forcing a runoff in December 1990. Solidarity leader Lech Wałęsa won easily over a hitherto unknown emigré of dubious background. The latter had defeated Prime Minister Tadeusz Mazowiecki, who managed to take only 18 percent of the vote in the first round.[3]

Ten main political parties (almost three times that many are represented in the Sejm, although 11 of them have only a single seat each) contend for power in contemporary Poland. Most of them stress traditional values of "God, Family, and Nation" or else neoconservatism and free markets. The former include Christian-nationalists who have support in the industrial working class and among farmers. The latter consist·of technical intelligentsia, private entrepreneurs, and a growing middle class.[4]

Based on such fragmentation of the political spectrum, the first woman ever to become prime minister of Poland crafted a seven-party coalition during July of 1992. Having earlier served as a law professor at Poznań University probably helped Mme. Hanna Suchocka to perform better than any of her four democratic predecessors. This has been exemplified by support at times even from the Alliance of the Democratic Left, as the former communist deputies now call themselves. In late November, President Wałęsa approved a so-called Little Constitution[5] which provides for a presidential-parliamentary system of government.

The cabinet of Prime Minister Suchocka included several former ministers, although all seven parties within the coalition received portfolios depending upon the number of deputies each had in the Sejm. Its 236 seats gave the government an absolute majority of the 460 total. This augurs well for the future. The "Little Constitution" indeed appears to reflect the existing balance of political power. It may even restore public confidence in the evolving democratic system, as a result of the compromise reached between president and parliament.

Politicization of social groups in Poland has not developed commensurately with the rapid growth of a private sector, however. Social consciousness apparently lags behind. One reason may be the low degree of organization found among private entrepreneurs and managers, who mostly socialize at seven clubs. Their membership numbers are even too small for survey purposes.

Employees, by contrast, belong to 14 different labor unions. During the summer of 1992, fewer than one-fourth of those polled had faith in the government; almost two- thirds subscribed to the opposite view. Another public opinion sample gave the government 48, President Wałęsa 41, and parliament 38 percent support—in each case less than half of the adult population. The two largest labor unions, Solidarity with one-third and the former communist All-Polish Trade Unions (*Ogólno-Polskie Związki Zawodowe,* or OPZZ) organization with one-fourth, scored even lower in this survey of popular attitudes.

It is no wonder that voter participation percentages are down—from a high for the 1989 national elections (62), through those in 1990 for local government authorities (42) and the two balloting rounds in 1990 for president (62 and 53), to the 1991 general elections again (43 percent)—all of which suggests that the electorate may have become fatigued from being offered choices so frequently.

The intelligentsia has served as a foundation of the reform program in Poland. Yet only 6 percent of the population holds a university degree, and another 25 percent received a junior college or secondary school diploma. It is not even certain that these two groups can work together. If they should fail to cooperate, the remaining 69 percent of the population might turn to a demagogue. The last one who tried his hand at politics, namely Stanisław Tymiński, forced a runoff in the presidential election as mentioned above.

Nor should one forget that the Roman Catholic Church no longer claims more than nine out of ten Poles as believers, as it did during the late 1980s. Church participation in political life cannot even count for support on a majority of deputies in parliament today. Although some 70 percent of the public wants catechism taught in schools, the same percentage stood against an antiabortion law in 1992. Three years earlier, the response to each question stood at an even 50 percent. The Senate approved by a close 35 to 34 vote a compromise bill on restrictive abortion which the Sejm had passed earlier. It was signed by President Wałęsa and took effect on 16 March 1993. However, a public opinion poll the previous month gave the Church an approval rating of only 46, compared to 67 for the police and 72 percent for the army.[6]

Local government reform, adopted by the Sejm in the form of legislation during March 1990, did not seem to excite successive governments until Prime Minister Suchocka—perhaps because she is an attorney. Local elections, held in May 1990, largely had succeeded in sweeping out the vestiges of former communist appointees from official positions throughout the provinces.

Restructuring at this level in Poland also followed guidelines from the European Charter on Local Self-Government, adopted by the Council of Europe in 1985. Transfer of property rights, or communalization, represented an important feature in the devolution of power from the center in Warsaw. Local government now decides whether to lease, contract out, manage by public corporation, or privatize the assets it controls.[7] Despite the legal framework in place, central bureaucratic structures have continued to block reform of local institutions. On the other hand, local government functions better than anticipated.

More than two centuries ago, Poles adopted a constitution on 3 May 1791. One hundred and twenty-three years of subsequent occupation by Russia,

Prussia, and Austria prevented that document from being implemented. After a brief interwar period of independence, Poland remained subjugated by an alien system for almost 45 years following the German occupation during World War II. However, in December 1989 the new Sejm approved amendments to the former communist basic law. These eliminated the ruling party's "leading role" in society and declared equality for all types of property ownership, including private.[8]

The December 1992 "Little Constitution" received approval from the Sejm, the Senate, and the president of Poland. Each of these authorities had differing ideas concerning future power distribution. In order to achieve agreement, all sides were required to make concessions. The *modus vivendi* is a tribute to the statesmanlike qualities of both legislative and executive leaders. Although incomplete, the transitional basic law has introduced a solid foundation for development of a strong democracy in Poland.

A supplementary Charter of Rights and Freedoms,[9] submitted to the Sejm by President Wałęsa on 21 January 1993, includes a listing of civil rights and liberties as well as minimum social security guarantees. Citizens would have recourse to the court system, if any of these were violated. Nothing will work, however, unless there develops a pervasive acceptance of constitutionalism which includes an independent judiciary. A legal culture and respect for the rule of law had been eradicated by the former communist regime between 1944 and 1989. Hence, it will take time to instill a new generation with traditional Western values after a full-length constitution has been adopted.[10]

In the economic arena, the first democratic government of postwar Poland undertook specific steps in its "shock therapy" program, which commenced on 1 January 1990 by freeing most prices, except for those on housing and energy; launching privatization of state property; supporting individual ownership of agricultural land; demonopolizing; establishing well-defined property rights; introducing an efficient and fair tax system; freeing international trade; bringing about monetary stability; permitting individual enterprises to set wages; attempting to make the state pension system and unemployment compensation adequate.[11]

Privatization is the key to moving from a centrally planned to a market economy. The newly created Ministry of Ownership Transformations, established to implement the July 1990 law on privatization of state-owned enterprises (SOEs), hoped to transform these into joint stock companies or liquidate the bankrupt ones. Surviving enterprises would be offered for sale to domestic and/or foreign investors. About 400 large and profitable SOEs had been selected for privatization already by mid-1991, although little else could be done until after the October national elections. Prime Minister

Suchocka presented her proposal to the Sejm in August 1992. Some 20 national investment funds were to be established in 1993, each holding up to one-third of the stock, an even 30 percent retained by the state, and 10 percent to be given free[12] to employees during 1994.

By the end of summer 1992, about one-fourth of all SOEs (1,841) were in the process of being privatized. Approximately three-fourths of those underwent liquidation, half of them through bankruptcy. One-third of the total (611) were in good enough financial condition so that employee-managed companies could lease them. Dubious property rights contributed to a situation where an enterprise owner remained unable to purchase the land on which his or her business was located. There also reportedly were problems for native-born managers working in foreign-owned companies. Nevertheless, during calendar year 1992, investors from abroad pledged $4 billion or 400 percent more than the previous year.[13]

Despite these achievements, the Sejm rejected Prime Minister Suchocka's mass privatization program on 18 March 1993 by a vote of 203 to 181 with nine abstentions. Parliamentary debate over a revised version began early the following month. The new draft program specifies that the first 200 already operational firms would be taken over by the national investment funds, with shares given to pensioners and government employees as an offset against benefits suspended during 1991. The second phase would involve another 400 companies, whose stock will be distributed among all adult citizens in return for a modest processing fee equal to 5 percent of average wages. Company employees would receive 15 percent of shares free of charge, rather than the earlier proposed 10 percent.[14] The government announced that this new program will be launched on the basis of existing legislation, without parliamentary approval.

Liberalization of labor and product markets has accomplished more in Poland over a brief two-year period than could be achieved by some of the Organization for European Cooperation and Development (OECD) member countries in two decades. By the end of 1992, the private sector produced more than half (58 percent) of the gross domestic product. It had dominated agriculture even before 1989, encompassing three-fourths of all arable land with the remainder held by about 1,500 state farms. Exports of food and agricultural products increased substantially after 1990, and Poland initially announced an overall foreign trade surplus for 1992.[15]

Labor markets have been largely free of arbitrary government interference since the end of 1990. However, employment dropped by some 1.7 million over the 30 months ending with mid-1992. Nine months later, at the end of February 1993, unemployment seemed to have become stabilized at

14.2 percent of the labor force or 2.6 million persons without work. Compensation funds for the jobless had been curtailed successively in 1990, 1991, and 1992. On the other hand, some 30 percent of those claiming benefits were actually employed in the underground economy, making the real figures under 2 million or less than 10 percent without work. As a corollary, inflation declined from 60 percent during 1991 to only 43 percent the following year. The target has been set at 32 percent for 1993.[16]

Much of the foregoing depends for its success on monetary policies. Milton Friedman's seminal article suggests that these cannot be used to control unemployment, real-interest rates, the time path of the price level, inflation, rates of exchange, or to insure bank deposits.[17] Monetary policy is applied through management of the central government's debt. Those who devise the foregoing do not have any influence over its size. That is determined by policymakers on budgetary income and expenditures, namely deputies in the national legislature. The central bank of Poland is responsible for composition of the national debt, which totaled some $45 billion owed to Western governments (Paris Club) and to foreign commercial banks (London Club), requiring 11.1 percent of export revenues to service it. Paris Club debts, amounting to $33 billion will be reduced by half in two stages.[18]

The Sejm approved legislation on new value-added and excise taxes to become effective in July 1993. It rejected two government-supported Senate amendments by lowering from 22 to 7 percent the tax on coal, natural gas, and electricity as well as expanding a preferential 7 percent tax on children's clothing. Despite or perhaps because of such difficulties with parliament, the cabinet had prepared at the end of January 1993 an "urgent" draft bill that will allow it to issue decrees with the force of law. These special powers, if approved, would be restricted to accelerating economic reform, restructuring state institutions, and transforming the legal system in accordance with European Community standards. They were to be discussed by the Sejm in April 1993.

Outside of its borders, Poland has achieved some progress in regional cooperation. Although several attempts had been made to establish the Adria-Alpine and Tisza-Carpathian groups in East-Central Europe, only the Visegrád Triangle has prospered. Founded in February 1991 at a small provincial town, its original members included Czechoslovakia, Hungary, and Poland, which then had a total of 64 million inhabitants. Since 1 January 1993, the triangle has been squared with the establishment of Slovakia and the Czech Republic as independent states. By the year 2001, all national barriers are to be removed for trade purposes in accord with European Community (EC) regulations.[19] This Central European Free Trade Area may be joined by Belarus, Ukraine, the three Baltic states, Croatia, and Slovenia at some future time.

Before any of this happens, the legacy of communist-imposed regionalism with all of its negative aspects must be overcome. Problems include ethnic animosities between Czechs and Poles, Hungarians and Slovaks; minority claims of Germans in Poland, Hungarians in Romania, and Poles in both Lithuania and Ukraine. None of these antagonisms will enhance politicoeconomic cooperation throughout the region. In addition, each country has its own perception of national interests and security.

The future of East-Central European integration depends upon prospects for individual country membership in the EC.[20] If the latter continues to remain ephemeral, then Poland may well choose to deepen its relations with immediate neighbors to the east and south. Such a development would give Warsaw an opportunity to play a leadership role in newly forming post-Soviet regional alignments. The Carpathian Euro-Region Pact signed by Poland, Hungary, and Ukraine (with Slovakia as associate member) in mid-February 1993 is a step in that direction. It provides for regional cooperation by local governments from two Polish, three Hungarian, one Ukrainian, and seven Slovak provinces.[21]

Polish national security policies also center on bilateral relations with its largest neighbors, Germany and Russia, which historically had been Poland's archenemies. Smaller countries, although less important, are not neglected: the Baltic states, other successor republics to the former USSR, as well as the remaining states of southeastern Europe. Obviously, Lithuania, Ukraine, and Belarus merit more attention since they border on Poland. Overseas, the United States represents the most important country to be cultivated. Lech Wałęsa proposed Warsaw as the site for the U.S.-Russian summit during 3-4 April 1993. The decision subsequently was made to hold it in Vancouver, British Columbia.

The Polish government looks toward Germany as its key to becoming a member of the European Community, and perhaps later even NATO. The former may materialize soon after the turn of the century, since Poland already holds full membership in the Council of Europe and has signed an agreement to be an associate member of the EC. At this point, the NATO alliance connection seems remote, even though Poland has been a member of the North Atlantic Cooperation Council since the end of 1991, together with 15 other countries in East-Central Europe.[22]

On the other hand, the Polish defense ministry accepted an invitation to participate in NATO naval maneuvers during 16-18 June 1993 on the Baltic Sea. Lithuania and Russia were also invited, although the latter had not responded immediately. By contrast, however, reports concerning U.S. and Polish air force maneuvers over the Baltic, allegedly scheduled for July 1993, were denied by Warsaw.[23] One informal condition for NATO membership is that Poland's armed forces be placed under full civilian control which has been implemented. Other criteria remain unclear as of this writing.

The border along the Odra and Nysa rivers had been confirmed by treaties with both East (1953) and West (1970) German governments, the agreement on unification of Germany (1990), and the bilateral Polish-German treaty of November 1991. This last document also dealt with the approximately 700,000 Germans (only 2 percent of the Polish population) currently living in Poland. If the "shock therapy" reforms succeed in raising substantially the socioeconomic level of Poles, they will become attractive partners for Germans. However, the most recent dispute between the two countries involves new restrictions on political asylum by Germany scheduled to go into effect during mid-1993. Poland agreed to take back some refugees who had transited the country even though it has no infrastructure to deal with them according to the United Nations.[24]

New links between Poland and Germany appear to have been initiated by some 20 counties in Gorzów province bordering on the state of Brandenburg. The inhabitants intend to develop economic, cultural, and administrative contacts with their German counterparts. If approved by Warsaw, this initiative may lead to an establishment of a "Euroregion." Other communities in Poland have done the same with different German border states, the Czech Republic, and Ukraine.[25]

Russia no longer shares a frontier with Poland, except for Kaliningrad province of former East Prussia. Withdrawal of all but 4,124 Russian troops from Poland as of 1 January 1993 (after having caused an estimated $1 billion damage to the ecology)[26] eliminated one of the irritants in bilateral relations. This had been preceded in May by the state visit to Moscow of Lech Wałęsa, the first noncommunist president of independent Poland ever to have done so. An agreement on economic cooperation, signed at that meeting, should guarantee future supplies from Russia of natural gas and petroleum. During mid-February 1993 the Russian first deputy defense minister, Andrei Kokoshin, visited Warsaw to discuss a military agreement. Moscow is reportedly concerned over Poland's treaties with France, Hungary, Latvia, Greece, former Czechoslovakia, Germany, and Ukraine.[27]

The Russians also appear to be worried about the new Polish military doctrine and subsequent developments. The latter include the largest maneuvers since the collapse of communism, held during the second half of March 1993 in the Mazury lake region just south of Kaliningrad *oblast'*. Furthermore, about 40 percent of Poland's armed forces are being moved toward the country's eastern borders with Ukraine and Belarus. In addition, Polish rapid development forces are being established from among the most combat-ready units available.

When and if the treaty on conventional forces in Europe (CFE) is implemented, Poland's armed forces will be downsized as follows: total manpower (281,400 to 234,000); main battle tanks (2,850 to 1,730); infantry fighting vehicles (2,253 to 2,150); artillery pieces (2,316 to 1,610); and combat aircraft (509 to 460). The one exception will be attack helicopters, which will be increased from 31 to 130.[28]

Early in May 1992, a treaty of friendship and cooperation with Poland had been signed at Warsaw by President Leonid Kravchuk of Ukraine. This implied support for Kiev in its confrontation with Moscow, although Warsaw was careful not to give such an impression. Officially, a policy of equidistance from both Russia and Ukraine has been maintained. Prime Minister Suchocka visited Kiev in mid-January 1993 to negotiate several bilateral accords. A military cooperation agreement was initialed on 3 February 1993 by the two respective defense ministers.

The three years since 1989 have been utilized also to establish bilateral agreements, as well as regional and security structures, with all neighbors. With this as a foundation, Poland will enter the European Community soon after the turn of the century.[29] This appears to be more or less certain in view of the open door for membership that will be offered to Austria, Finland, Norway, and Sweden probably by 1995. The EC special conference at Copenhagen in April 1993 suggested that the date for eventual admission of Poland, Hungary, the Czech Republic, and Slovakia might be decided at the mid-year summit meeting in the Danish capital.

What, then, might one expect regarding future developments in Poland? Much may depend on the situation of neighboring countries, especially on what happens in the Federation of Russia. Should results from early elections for a new parliament and the presidency reject the democratic candidates being presented for popular approval, the so-called creeping revolution may yet succeed in slowing down or stopping Boris Yeltsin's reforms. The military-industrial complex, supported by the new armed forces' High Command, and the former communist party's *nomenklatura,* still entrenched throughout the provinces, could even reverse the Russian transition to a market economy.

Such an outcome is less likely to occur in Poland because its configuration of power differs from that of Russia. No equivalent to the huge military-industrial complex exists anymore,[30] and the former Polish *nomenklatura* has been swept out of local government. Even less conceivable would be a coup d'état by the generals, if the executive-legislative conflict in Warsaw were to make it impossible to govern because of gridlock. It is true that precedent can be found even before the Jaruzelski-led junta during 1981-1983. Not many years after the end of World War I, Marshal Józef Piłsudski seized power in May 1926 and dissolved parliament. Of course, at present nobody even faintly resembles or has the charisma of a *dziadek* (grandfather) Piłsudski—except for Commander in Chief Lech Wałęsa, who is not a general.[31]

An even more remote possibility would involve a return to power of the totally discredited erstwhile three million-strong Polish United Workers' [communist] Party, or PZPR, only 60,000 of whom are currently dues-paying members in the so-called Social Democracy of the Republic of Poland, or SdRP, whose new label fools nobody. During the May 1990 local elections, this writer observed campaign posters on Warsaw streets that had been defaced with SdRP crossed out and PZPR written above it. One should not anticipate that indigenous communists will return to power in Poland,[32] as they did in Lithuania with the 25 February 1993 inauguration of Algirdas Brazauskas as president after he had won 60 percent of the popular vote.

More plausible for Poland is a scenario that results in new national elections, which will remove many of the minuscule political movements, strengthen current coalition partners, and cut down the inflated number of communist deputies to the fringe they truly represent. Only then will a reconstituted government be strong enough to carry through its popular mandate for transition to democracy without undue delay.

On 28 May 1993, the coalition government led by Hanna Suchocka lost a no-confidence motion in the Sejm concerning its tight fiscal policies by one vote. The following day, President Wałęsa dissolved parliament and called for new elections. He refused to accept the prime minister's resignation and requested that she remain in office during the transition period.

Just prior to its dissolution, the Sejm adopted an election law that should eliminate fragmentation. It stipulated that a total of 3,000 signatures must be collected to register a list of candidates in each electoral district. The new law also requires that a political party attain at least five percent of the vote nationwide to receive representation in the legislature.

President Wałęsa signed this law and announced that elections for a new Sejm would be held on Sunday, 19 September 1993. He promised that the leader of the political party receiving the largest number of votes would be designated prime minister and asked to form a government.

NOTES

1. See, for example, Richard F. Staar, *Poland 1944-1962: The Sovietization of a Captive People* (Westport, Conn.: Greenwood Press, 1975), for the imposition of communist rule.

2. Józef Kozłowski and Tomasz Paluch, *Stan wojenny: Przekaz codzienny* (Łódź: Verbum, 1992).

3. Mirosława Grabowska, "Nowa scena polityczna," in Piotr Łukasiewicz and Wojciech Zaborowski, eds., *Szanse i zagrożenia polskich przemian* (Warsaw, PAN, 1992), pp. 39-40.

4. Jacek Wasilewski and Włodzimierz Wesołowski, eds., *Początki parlamentarnej elity* (Warsaw: Wydawnictwo IFiS PAN, 1992).

5. *Ustawa konstytucyjna z dnia 17 października 1991 roku* (Warsaw: Wydawnictwo Sejmowe, 1992), printed text in 79 articles as sent to President Wałęsa for his signature.

6. "Political Roundup," *RFE/RL Daily Report,* 9 February 1993, p. 5. However, the Sejm restored tax breaks for religious denominations. Some 169 deputies petitioned that a cross be placed next to the state seal in parliament, and a room is being converted into a chapel. Ibid., 8 March 1993, p. 4.

7. Janusz Fiszer, *Financing Local Government in Poland* (Warsaw: Friedrich Ebert Foundation, 1991); Economic Policy Series. On 23 January 1993, the Sejm voted to restore the *powiat*, or county, which had been abolished as a centralization measure by the former communist regime in 1975.

8. See Marian Pawlak, ed., *200 lat konstytucji 3 maja* (Bydgoszcz: Wydawnictwo Uczelniane WSP, 1992); Marian Kallas, comp., *Projekty konstytucyjne, 1989-1991* (Warsaw: Wydawnictwo Sejmowe, 1992).

9. *Karta praw i wolności* (Warsaw: Office of the President, 1993), mimeograph; a 49-article document submitted to the Sejm.

10. See Andrzej Ajnenkiel, *Polskie konstytucje* (Warsaw: Wydawnictwo Szkolne i Pedagogiczne, 1991); Komisja Konstytucyjna, *Konstytucja: projekt* (Warsaw: Wydawnictwo Sejmowe, 1992), pp. 21-95, for the Sejm draft document, with an introduction by Bronisław Geremek.

11. Irina Demchenko, "V Pol'she udalas' 'nasha' reforma," *Izvestiia* (Moscow), 26 February 1993, p. 4, states that "Russian reforms" have succeeded in Poland after three years.

12. "Enterprise Pact for Poland," *The Wall Street Journal,* 23 February 1993, p. A-15; Christopher Bobiński, "Poles sign enterprise pact," *Financial Times* (London), 23 February 1993, p. 2.

13. Christopher Bobiński, "Pol'skie menedzhery razocharovany rabotoi na inostrantsev," *Finansovye izvestiia* (Moscow), 24-29 December 1992, p. V; Daniel Michaels "Foreign Investment Pledges of $4 billion . . . ," *The Wall Street Journal,* 8 February 1993, p. A-10.

14. John Darnton, "Polish Parliament Rejects Bill . . . ," *The New York Times,* 19 March 1993, p. A-3.

15. Linwood Hoffman and Michał Kisiel, "Market Reform and Poland's Grain Sector," *Economies in Transition* (Washington, D.C.: U.S. Department of Agriculture, October 1992), pp. 10-21; Central Office of Planning, *Poland 1992: The Social and Economic Situation* (Warsaw: February 1993), pp. 1-18. According to the Polish foreign trade ministry, an unfavorable balance of payments had been registered for 1992. See "Polish trade view worsens," *Financial Times,* 15 March 1993, p. 3.

16. Central Office of Planning, *Poland 1992.* Industrial production had increased by 5.7 percent and labor productivity by nearly 11 percent during the year ending 31 January 1993. "Polish Growth Continues," *RFE/RL Daily Report,* 17 February 1993, p. 5.

17. Milton Friedman, "The Role of Monetary Policy," *American Economic Review* 58, no. 1 (March 1968): 1-17.

18. "Basic Tendencies of the Polish Economy in 1992" (Warsaw: Central Office of Planning, December 1992), p. 2; mimeograph. See also "Poland moves back on track with debt talks," *Financial Times,* 10 March 1993, p. 3.

19. "Porozumienie o strefie wolnego handlu pomiędzy Polską, Węgrami, Czechami i Słowacją," *MSZ dalekopisy* (Warsaw: January 1993); mimeograph.

20. See the draft program to adapt Poland's economy to EC requirements in Urząd Rady Ministrów, *Program działań dostosowujących gospodarkę polską do wymagań Układu Europejskiego* (Warsaw: November 1992).

21. Nikolai Ermolovich, "Karpatskii region Evropy," *Izvestiia,* 16 February 1993, p. 3.

22. Manki Ponomarëv, "Dubler NATO v Vostochnoi Evrope," *Krasnaia zvezda* (Moscow), 20 October 1992, p. 3. See also Theresa Hitchens, "NATO Tightens Military Links to East Europe," *Defense News* (Washington, D.C.), 1-7 February 1993, p. 6.

23. Aleksandr Os'kin, "Pol'sko-amerkanskie manevry. Protiv kogo?" *Rabochaia tribuna* (Moscow), 20 January 1993, p. 3; ITAR-TASS, "Amerkano-pol'skie manevry VVS ne sostoiatsia," *Krasnaia zvezda,* 12 February 1993, p. 3.

24. Judy Dempsey, "Poland agrees to take back refugees," *Financial Times,* 10 February 1993, p. 2; "What's News World-wide," *The Wall Street Journal,* 5 March 1993, p. A-1.

25. "New Links Between Poland and Germany?" *RFE/RL Daily Report,* 18 March 1993, p. 5.

26. "Sovetskaia armiia nanesla ushcherb prirode Pol'shi v odin milliard dollarov," *Izvestiia,* 6 March 1993, p. 3.

27. See Michał Dobroczyński, *Pomiędzy Rosją a zachodem* (Toruń: Wydawnictwo Adam Marszałek, 1992); Valery Masterov, "Russia and Poland: forging a military agreement," *Moscow News,* 18 February 1993, p. 8.

28. Iurii Kostin and Dmitrii Shepelov, "U byvshikh soiuznikov po OVD," *Krasnaia zvezda,* 11 March 1993, p. 3.

29. Mark N. Nelson, "Into Its Own," *The Wall Street Journal,* 3 February 1993, p. R-5; *RFE/RL Research Bulletin* 10, no. 3 (2 February 1993): 4-5.

30. Only about 90,000 workers are employed in producing weapons. Conversion should proceed rapidly because of the skilled labor force and up-to-date technology. "Protest in Polish Arms Industry," *RFE/RL Daily Report,* 25 February 1993, pp. 4-5. For the sale of $300 million worth of T-72 tanks, see "Pol'sha sobiraietsia prodat' tanki Pakistanu," *Krasnaia zvezda,* 9 February 1993, p. 3.

31. See Zbigniew Zaborowski, *Osobowość Lecha Wałęsy* (Warsaw: Ośrodek Badań Społecznych, 1992).

32. Nikolai Ermolovich, "Grozit li Pol'she kommunisticheskaia opasnost'?" *Izvestiia,* 18 December 1992, p. 7; for PZPR and SdRP figures, see Arthur R. Rachwald, "Poland," in Richard F. Staar, ed., *1989 Yearbook on International Communist Affairs* (Stanford, Calif.: Hoover Institution Press, 1989), p. 335, and ibid. (1991), p. 316.

1

Voters, Parties, and Leaders

*Raymond Taras**

Poland ended 1992 as it had ended a decade earlier—in economic crisis. New leaders today press for a free-enterprise system to solve economic problems with as much determination as, ten years ago, the martial law leadership had championed the command economy. During the intervening period, the political landscape has changed beyond imagination. Where elite-focused research by political scientists had its own rationale in 1982, today's research agendas concentrate on politics of the electorate.

This chapter begins, accordingly, with analysis of a political group that remained conceptually vacuous a decade ago—the voters. Following the tradition of Western political science research, the behavior of the electorate serves as the starting point for the study of politics in a democracy. The next focus is on political parties—aggregators of individual preferences. Finally, leaders and executives are discussed.[1] If the parameters of the chapter are extensive, they are limited longitudinally to four years, from 1989 through the end of 1992. Among the issues considered here are national and local election results, electoral laws, formation of political parties, their policy programs and leaders, and, finally, their coalition-building and schismatic tendencies. The chapter begins with an assessment of the transition process.

* The author is grateful to Professor Krzysztof Jasiewicz, Institute of Political Studies, Polish Academy of Sciences, for his valuable comments on an early draft of this chapter.

REGIME TRANSITION AND POLITICAL FRAGMENTATION

Politically, Poland has not perfected the institutions crucial to stable democratic practice. The "Little Constitution," the first draft of which had been vigorously supported by President Lech Wałęsa, was passed by parliament in much-amended form during November 1992. The powers of the president, the prime minister and her or his cabinet, and the parliament or Sejm were balanced off, giving satisfaction to no institution. Poland had five prime ministers between 1989 and the end of 1992—more than any European country. From the inevitable and welcome "positive disintegration"[2] of the catchall Solidarity movement, a surfeit of personal ambitions and a deficit of coalition-building skills have produced splintering within large (the Democratic Union, or UD) and minor (Polish Beer Lovers' Party, or PPPP) political parties alike.

In Brazil, another state undergoing a democratic transition, one of every three Congress members changed parties during the 1987-1991 legislature, and a comparable figure was recorded in Poland since semifree elections were first held in June 1989. Indeed, creating rather than switching parties was especially popular in Poland during this period. As in Brazil, an increasing perception on the part of the public that politics were being forced upon the country has led to the emergence of "civic fatigue"—public disenchantment with the political and electoral process.[3] Political competition seems to be outstripping the institutionalization of democracy which, for University of Chicago political scientist Adam Przeworski, is "the devolution of power from a group of people to a set of rules." If the party system is treated as an integral part of a system's institutional framework, then its instability is a sign of unconsolidated democracy. Przeworski holds that "democracy is consolidated when compliance—acting within the institutional framework—constitutes the equilibrium of the decentralized strategies of all the relevant political forces."[4]

It is debatable whether party fragmentation, and the associated civic fatigue that followed, were inevitable in Poland. Some have argued that a structural determinism was at work which produced both results. Thus, Przeworski hints at the nature of the transitional moment as pivotal. In the bid to end authoritarian rule, "the struggle for democracy always takes place on two fronts: against the authoritarian regime for democracy and against one's allies for the best place under democracy."[5]

The socially heterogeneous nature of the postcommunist leadership group in Poland may also help explain why political centrifugalism has dominated. In a number of ways this group resembles what one writer described in a different context as a "living museum."[6] It consists of 1950s maverick intellectuals, 1960s student leaders, 1970s trade unionists, 1980s quasi-legal entrepreneurs, and 1990s quacks (e.g., Stanisław Tymiński). Though not with equal force, these diverse groups have shaped the country's emergent democracy and have embedded flaws in it. Finally, an increasingly popular position is to hold that fragmentation of new political elites behaving myopically has been the outcome. Politics have been personalized, as illustrated by Wałęsa choosing to forgo a strong presidential party and opting instead for antiparty rhetoric. In this view, what makes the new elite a political class apart is its unrestrained self-interest in power and its trappings.

Poland's political *skansen* is not as heterogeneous as it could have been, were former communists permitted to play a role. Even without them, it is remarkably fragmented. Career paths alone do not explain the propensity toward fragmentation. James Madison must have had an earlier experience of Poland in mind when, in 1788, he wrote for *The Federalist*: "So strong is this propensity of mankind to fall into mutual animosities, that where no substantial occasion presents itself, the most frivolous and fanciful distinctions have been sufficient to kindle their unfriendly passions and excite their most violent conflicts."[7]

Noncooperation can also be interpreted as a rational strategy in a period of transition. Polish political fragmentation may be viewed through the prism of the prisoners' dilemma, facing political actors in Argentina: "In this game of collective action, high levels of uncertainty concerning macroeconomic policy, combined with doubts about the stability of the new democratic regime, structure the expectations of the principal protagonists—state elites, party leaders, business interests, and organized labor—in such a way as to maximize the incentives to pursue strategies of noncooperation."[8] An escalating spiral of political conflict is the product of the prisoners' dilemma, then. But more optimistically, the above writer concludes about Argentina in transition that "democratic consolidation will, to a large extent, hinge on the ability of elected politicians and policymakers to defuse the distributional struggle by forging rules, based on consensus, backed up by strong, autonomous social and political institutions." In Argentina, as in Poland, an ideology of neoliberalism that empowers private capital while it simultaneously limits the power of the state to regulate the economy is designed to serve as a rule-making and institution-building mechanism. The emerging institutional order is likely to become elitist and socially regressive although, at the same time, competent and growth-inducing.

Indeed, postcommunist political fragmentation and the institutions it creates can be treated as a success indicator of the transition. Because competition now occurs over voters, among parties, between leaders, the battle for the "minds of men" is not joined. Transition implies a hybrid of oldness and newness contained in provisional structures, but it is difficult to exaggerate the obstacles that stood in the way of such "cohabitation." *Ancien régime* officials decided to forgo confrontation, that is, political polarization (as opposed to more benign fragmentation), when it became rational for them to do so.

One of many illuminating analyses of this rational choice approach is presented by a Polish economist who has used a property rights analysis to highlight the pivotal position of the *nomenklatura* in the transition to a free market economy.[9] Communist apparatchiks were the principal beneficiaries of rent-seeking activities under the old system and, confronted with the prospects of transition, asked: "Isn't it possible that the expected benefits within the framework of the new regime, or new structure of property rights, were larger for the major groups of rent-seekers than the rents they could acquire within the existing property rights structure?"[10] We need not subscribe to a conspiracy theory of secret deals having being struck at Magdalenka—the site outside Warsaw where communists and oppositionists hammered out a compromise Roundtable agreement to increase political pluralism in the country—to reach an affirmative answer. As long as we agree that some of the major beneficiary groups of the old system were able now to join the new system as net economic gainers, transition from communism was a perfectly rational choice for communists themselves to make.

In addition to rent-seekers' benefits, what other general factors were at work in encouraging cooperative behavior between communists and oppositionists in 1989? One was the calculation by the incumbent coalition of securing Solidarity's coresponsibility for austerity policies at a perceived low risk to the ruling party. Survey data[11] available to communist leaders at the time suggested the communist party could expect to gain no less than 25 to 30 percent of the vote, Solidarity only 20 percent, with the remainder of the electorate uncommitted. In addition, reformists in the ruling party and moderates in the opposition increasingly agreed on the principle of extrication from the authoritarian regime.[12] They shared certain fears: impending economic disaster; a return to the social anarchy of late 1981, when even Wałęsa could not rein in wildcat strikes throughout the country; a plunge into violence as immigrant groups from the disintegrating USSR and organized gangsters drew Poles into a struggle over diminishing resources.

Authorities and opposition also shared the same generalized vision of how to get out of this impasse: the urgency of profound structural change, going beyond fine tuning of the extant system, and a shared recognition of the interconnectedness between economic and political reform. By 1989 communist leader General Wojciech Jaruzelski needed a partner more influential, or at least more dynamic, than the reformist wing of the ruling movement with which he was allied. The opposition, in turn, was prepared to obtain institutional guarantees for itself. Many opposition activists sensed a loss of will and a crisis in confidence within the communist party leadership and sought to seize the moment. Further, memory of martial law also haunted the dissidents, and they were determined to avoid the over-confidence that had cost Solidarity deeply during 1981-1982. The impress-ive resources they had marshaled by 1989 could, theoretically, be lost as suddenly as in December 1981 under martial law, thereby inclining the opposition to dialogue.

In 1989, then, communist reformists together with the "constructive" opposition were drawn to each other and could mobilize, together, sufficient power to implement an antimonocratic breakthrough. Both increasingly defined their identity in terms of serving as prime agents of change. Once negotiations were completed on the size of the handicap (as in golf) to be given to the ruling party, both expressed willingness to abide by the verdict of the electorate.

VOTERS

Two American authors have described three basic types of political orienta-tions among voters: (1) psychological involvement—the importance voters assign to politics, (2) strength of partisan identification—the degree of attachment to a political party, and (3) sense of contribution to the general welfare—the effort to expand collective goods.[13]

It is ironic, then, that the largest single bloc of the electorate is comprised of nonvoters—those formally not involved in, identifying with, or contrib-uting to the public sphere at election time. During the 1991 parliamentary elections in Poland, 56.8 percent of eligible voters did not cast their ballots, about the same level of abstention as in the May 1990 local elections. While there may be traditional class explanations for this group—they consist largely of the less educated, poorer sectors of society resembling nonvoters in Western countries—such an answer is not helpful in explaining the high rate of abstention during the politically charged transition process.

Other factors may be advanced: the lack of clear and consistent political orientations and commitments by postcommunist parties may produce equivocalness among voters, difficulty with partisan identification, and a sense of not being offered clear-cut choices despite the range of parties competing for office. Further, the general consensus among parties favoring a market economy, accompanying public sector sell-offs, and austerity measures was either not supported or not understood by a substantial proportion of the electorate. Accordingly, abstention was a form of protest for these voters. Variations in levels of abstention in Poland could also be understood in the terms presented by Western psephology—studies of electoral behavior—such as regional (industrial versus agrarian), generational (older versus younger), and psychological (organization joiners versus nonjoiners) factors.

Among reasons why Poles have voted the way they have are also motivations prevailing within Western democratic electorates. Voters are concerned with pocketbook issues and support the party that is perceived to be committed to expanding benefits available for a specific group. Choice voting behavior seeks to maximize expected utility, then. Voter calculations are also based on utility accruing to individuals from their party's holding power in the legislature. Solitary benefits may be more important to certain social groups than others, although they seem especially valued in a society making the transition from command to market economy. Here opportunities for individual benefits are tantalizing, since widespread perceptions exist that: (1) the playing surface is level, and (2) one begins with a tabula rasa.

Thus businesspersons, actual and prospective, seek solitary benefits more energetically than a social class more conscious of its collective interests and of threats to them, such as industrial workers at large plants threatened with closure. Expectations about individual and group benefits from a particular party are, therefore, an underlying source for voting preference. As examples from Polish politics, members of the intelligentsia largely viewed Tadeusz Mazowiecki—Poland's first postcommunist prime minister—as the best guarantor of individual benefits, while peasants and workers saw their class interests protected best by their respective class-oriented parties (Wałęsa's original Citizens' Committees—*Komitety Obywatelskie,* or KO—still umbilically linked to Solidarity, or the Polish Peasant Party—*Polskie Stronnictwo Ludowe,* or PSL).

An electoral factor related to expectations is identity. As in Western democracies, voters use elections to affirm self-identity or group identity. In the case of an emergent market economy and liberal democracy, voters seek to create *new* identities for themselves as prospective entrepreneurs, independent journalists, larger-scale farmers, and so on. The Liberal-Democratic Congress (*Kongres Liberalno-Demokratyczny,* or KLD) party appeals to voters who are or want to be businesspersons.

Voting can be based on personalist politics—support for or opposition to individual politicians regardless of party ticket. Without a presidential party of his own, Wałęsa has become more than ever a leader who is supported or opposed on personalist grounds. More subtle evidence of personalist voting behavior in Poland came from the 1991 Senate elections: only five of 49 constituencies returned members of the same party, while 44 split their tickets. This indicates that voters were choosing among individuals rather than lists.

Voting can be issue-oriented too. In the formative period of a new regime, this represents potentially a key source of electoral behavior. There is a plurality of alternative futures, as voters and leaders select from a menu of choices: role of government, fate of the welfare state, changes to social legislation, economic priorities, status of minority and disadvantaged groups, foreign policy. Despite this inherent potential for issue-driven voting, the party system has provided deceptively little choice, as noted earlier and as depicted in Table 1.4. Single-issue voting, on privatization, the Leszek Balcerowicz economic program, or state interventionism, has not been possible as parties across the spectrum, from the right-wing Confederation for an Independent Poland (*Konfederacja Polski Niepodległej,* or KPN) to the quasi-communist Social Democracy of the Republic of Poland (*Socjaldemokracja Rzeczypospolitej Polskiej,* or SdRP), concur on the fundamental principles while disagreeing on methods or pace. Nevertheless, issue salience in voting is likely to increase as parties develop specific policy programs and their voting patterns on legislation before parliament become more consistent.

As a result, then, party ideology may play a role in influencing voting. This ideology is very different in form from the comprehensive, inflexible set of canons that characterized Marxist parties, although it is, nevertheless, visible through its broader strokes. In the 1991 parliamentary elections, the most graphic case of partisan voting was the electoral allegiance to the communist successor party by beneficiaries of the *ancien régime.* The SdRP still retained enough Marxist ideology to elicit voting in its favor and, more commonly, against it. Partisan allegiance in the case of the Solidarity opposition—expressed so dramatically in the June 1989 elections—disappeared with the breakup of the Solidarity coalition, although the second round of presidential elections seemed momentarily to reconstruct the broad alliance. Competition among parties to claim the honor of Poland's authentic Christian Democratic movement, which is seen as of immense strategic benefit in its own right, involves ideological tacking, as well as a good deal of posturing. The claim to be the most important party serving the interests of medium and small entrepreneurs also entails ideological as well as practical dimensions. By contrast, catchall parties with ephemeral ideological identity (projected as being anticommunist, accelerating decommunization, serving as Solidarity's successor, embodying peasant leader Stanisław Mikołajczyk's legacy) are at present ineffective electoral machines, although the KPN may prove to be the exception in the future.

One should add that "stolen rhetoric" abounds in today's party system. With malleable identities and programs, it is easy for one political group to appropriate the arguments of another for its own. As examples, the economic liberalism of the Democratic Union (*Unia Demokratyczna,* or UD) borrowed from the KLD, the nationalism of the Christian National Union (*Zjednoczenie Chrześcijańsko-Narodowe,* or ZChN) had been a consistent feature earlier of the KPN, the concern about a strong presidential system advanced by the Center Accord (*Porozumienie Centrum,* or PC) was identified previously with the first anti-Wałęsa parties. However, such stolen rhetoric only confirms the importance attached by parties to developing electorally appealing identities and ideologies.

As in the West, Polish voters now express differing types of consent about their parties and leaders. Prospective choice entails deciding which party can be trusted to govern the country most effectively for the next term. In the 1991 parliamentary elections, the public clearly made no prospective choice other than to deflate the UD's status as a governing party. Retrospective choice is passing judgment on incumbents: do we want another term of this? The next elections in Poland will offer voters such a retrospective evaluation for the first time. Selecting a benevolent, enlightened, charismatic, or strong leader is another consideration of voters. The 1990 presidential contest was essentially a referendum on Wałęsa. Finally, voting itself is a symbolic act supporting the new system, while nonvoting provides evidence of a sense of political inefficacy, irrelevance, or bewilderment. At times, it also signifies a rejection of those actors who have urged people to vote, as in the case of Wałęsa and the Roman Catholic Church's combined exhortation in the 1991 parliamentary elections.

ELECTIONS

Results of four elections held in Poland since the Roundtable agreement—the parliamentary ones of June 1989, at local levels in May 1990, for president during November-December 1990, and again parliamentary ones in October 1991—will be discussed next.

The elections to the Sejm (lower house of parliament) in June 1989 were to be "competitive but not confrontational," as agreed at the Roundtable. The competitive aspect would apply only to 35 percent of Sejm seats, and all 100 seats of the reconstituted Senate. The governing "coalition," thus, received patronage over 65 percent of lower chamber seats, locking in a majority. Considering the stakes, the campaign was brief, lasting only two months.[14] The Solidarity camp sought to depersonalize elections and projected an image of offering a highly competent alternative team of policymakers. By contrast, the governing coalition campaigned on the basis of personalist politics, urging electors to "choose the best." The turnout for the first round of these historic elections was just 62.7 percent of eligible voters. All but one of Solidarity's candidates won the contested seats, while only a few communist party candidates were returned in the first round. About 40 percent of the voters struck off the names of all government "coalition" candidates and slightly fewer (35 percent) crossed out all candidates from the coalition's national list. Only two national list candidates won the necessary 50 percent of the votes in the first round, creating a crisis affecting both camps. After all, Solidarity had acquiesced to the communist party's national list and had not anticipated holding a second round. The Senate results showed an even more spectacular Solidarity victory: it captured 99 of the 100 seats. Its share of the vote was considerably less. About two-thirds of all votes went to Solidarity candidates, up to one-fourth for ruling party candidates, and the remainder for independents.[15]

An unintended consequence of the 1989 elections—the formation of a Solidarity government by September—overshadowed the planned result of political pluralism and power-sharing. Ramifications of these elections were felt throughout the Soviet bloc. No communist leader in the region felt safe any longer from electoral devastation. Indeed, Poland's pioneering elections were soon regarded as timid compared to what was to follow elsewhere.

The May 1990 local elections produced another victory for a still relatively unified Solidarity camp, campaigning as Citizens' Committees (KO). The electoral law provided for proportional representation in cities and large towns (the Saint-Lague method), and simple majority results in all other areas. Turnout was only 42.3 percent and, in some localities, dropped below 15 percent. Even with an emerging split between Wałęsa and Mazowiecki in the Solidarity camp, just over two-thirds of voters in large towns supported the Citizens' Committees. And while this figure was somewhat lower in smaller towns, the simple majority system created an even more one-sided representation for the KO. The successor communist party, the SdRP, obtained only 8.6 percent of votes; the once procommunist peasant party, renamed PSL, captured just over three percent. Among new parties contesting elections for the first time, only KPN and ZChN made inroads. In fact, after KO candidates, the independents polled best.[16]

A discernible change in the collective mindset took place during the period between January and November 1990, as opinion polls indicated. Approval of the government, Sejm, and Senate fell from 85 to 55 percent. The proportion of respondents asserting that living standards were bad increased from 65 to 80 percent. Under these conditions, direct presidential elections were held. The Solidarity movement (still organized as the KO) and the embryonic PC (the first group to have demanded Jaruzelski's immediate resignation) were Wałęsa's organizational pillars in his run for the presidential office. As campaign strategist he named Jacek Merkel, who shortly was to become a KLD member and thus able to tap its constituency on Wałęsa's behalf. Finally, a political movement that was quickly growing in strength, the ZChN, also gave its endorsement to Wałęsa from the outset.

By contrast, Prime Minister Mazowiecki lacked a prior organizational base for the presidential campaign and depended on his Citizens' Movement for Democratic Action (*Ruch Obywatelski Akcja Demokratyczna*, or ROAD) to create campaign committees spontaneously. The SdRP, postcommunist although with organizations throughout the country and a relatively large membership (about 60,000), selected Włodzimierz Cimoszewicz as its nominee. The largest party in terms of membership (about 400,000) was the PSL, still seeking to shake off its former communist satellite status. Its candidate was Roman Bartoszcze, then party leader, subsequently removed in June 1991. Longtime KPN head Leszek Moczulski announced his candidacy. In total, 13 individuals ran in the election.[17]

Early opinion polls showed greater public confidence in Wałęsa than Mazowiecki (by a margin of about 2 to 1) to resolve such issues as improving living standards, limiting unemployment, freezing foreign debt, and securing the country's western border with Germany. Some 60 percent of the electorate voted in the first round of the presidential contest (see Table 1.1). Interestingly, the highest turnout was in the southern provinces that had once been part of Austria.[18] Wałęsa topped vote-getters but was far short of the 50 percent needed to avoid a runoff. The greatest shock provided by the elections was the second-place showing of outsider Stan Tymiński and the elimination of Prime Minister Mazowiecki.

The second round of elections on 9 December 1990 brought 7.2 percent fewer voters to the polls, despite exhortations from the Catholic Church. Indicating the volatility of the electorate, some 12 percent of those who cast ballots in the first round did not do so in the second. However, this was

Table 1.1
Presidential Election Results
(25 November 1990)

Name	Party	Votes	Percent
Lech Wałęsa	Solidarity KO	6,569,889	39.96
Stanisław Tymiński	"X"	3,397,605	23.10
Tadeusz Mazowiecki	ROAD	2,973,264	18.08
Włodzimierz Cimoszewicz	SdRP	1,514,025	9.21
Roman Bartoszcze	PSL	1,176,175	7.15
Leszek Moczulski	KPN	411,516	1.49
invalidated ballots			1.01
Totals		16,042,474	100.00

Source: Jacek Raciborski, ed., *Wybory i narodziny demokracji w krajach Europy środkowej i wschodniej* (Warsaw: Uniwersytet Warszawski, Instytut Socjologii, 1992), p. 146.

compensated for by 9 percent of the voters, who took part for the first time in the second round. Second-round abstainers were primarily Tymiński supporters—and not those of eliminated candidates—embarrassed, perhaps, by his good showing and now heeding calls by all establishment political leaders not to vote for him in the runoff; as many as 34 percent of first-round Tymiński supporters may have abstained in December.

During first-round voting, the Tymiński constituency correlated positively with former communist party members, the newly unemployed, those having lower educational levels, and the weaker presence of clergy in a region. Whether it correlated with small town or rural Poland, as many observers (especially bitter Mazowiecki supporters) asserted, remains an open question.[19] In these presidential elections, the voting behavior of women did not markedly differ from men, although SdRP candidate Cimoszewicz benefited somewhat from his pledge to leave the liberal communist abortion law untouched. The runoff produced expected results: Wałęsa received 74.25 percent (10,622,696) of votes cast against Tymiński's 25.75 percent (3,583,098).

Following local and presidential elections, it was the voters' turn again in October 1991 to elect a parliament that would be completely untainted by the former compromise reached with communists. Controversy flared over changes in the electoral law, however. Legislation governing elections for the upper chamber or Senate was simple compared to that for the Sejm. Similarly to the United States, voters would choose two senators by plurality vote in each of the country's 47 provinces, and three each from the densely populated metropolitan areas of Warsaw and Katowice, for a total of 100 seats. For the Sejm elections, 37 constituencies would provide anywhere from 7 to 17 deputies each, depending on size, for a total of 391 seats.[20] The remaining 69 deputies would be elected indirectly. Parties would provide national lists of candidates and would be apportioned seats, based on the number of votes they received in the constituencies.[21]

The electoral law was hypersensitive to voter support given even the smallest parties, especially since there was a minimum threshold required to obtain Sejm representation (see Table 1.2). While Polish politics had been fragmenting anyway, as noted above, the law institutionalized this fragmentation. Yet it should come as no surprise that such a law was adopted. The architects of the new system wished to ensure that no political force went unrepresented and was bound to the fledgling democracy. Phrased another way, small political groups had more to lose from opting out of democracy than staying in, winning some representation, and hoping for a better showing next time.

PARTIES

Professionalization of politics has taken place in Poland since 1989, and there has been a return to narrow national and religious loyalties, as one author[22] has noted: "The new parties in Polish politics are Catholic, nationalistic, and right wing. They claim for themselves a continuity of resistance against communism, and they reject dissident intellectuals as left wing and cosmopolitan, elitist and alienated." Furthermore, as two other observers have written, "all perceptions are dominated by a supersensitivity to Western reactions."[23] This applies to parties across the political spectrum, the notable exception being SdRP.

The ten main parties listed in Table 1.2 are torn by the ambition to hold power, caution about entering into alliances in which they may become junior partners, and fear of being dominated by Wałęsa. While the majority of parties is conservative, differences do exist among them. Western Europe

Table 1.2
Parliamentary Election Results
(27 October 1991)

Party	Percentage	Sejm (N=460)	Senate (N=100)
Democratic Union (UD)	12.31	62	21
Alliance of the Democratic Left (SLD)	11.98	60	4
Catholic Election Action (WAK)	8.73	49	9
Center Accord (PC)	8.71	44	9
Polish Peasant Party (PSL)	8.67	48	8
Confederation for Independent Poland (KPN)	7.50	46	4
Liberal Democratic Congress (KLD)	7.48	37	6
Peasant Accord (PL)	5.46	28	7
Solidarity	5.05	27	12
Friends of Beer Party	3.27	16	0
19 other parties	11.86	43	20
Totals	*91.02	460	100

Note: *Nine additional parties received the remaining 8.98 percent of the vote and have no representation in the Sejm.

Source: Marek Łaziński, "The First Free Parliament," *Uncaptive Minds* 4, no. 4 (Winter 1991-1992): 116.

has produced two general variants on political conservatism: (1) a traditionalist approach that has stressed family, God, the nation, and has very often been populist in form; and (2) neoconservative views stressing economic individualism as well as free markets, and associated with urban professional groups. In Poland, also, conservative parties range from the tradition-oriented like ZChN or PSL to the laissez-faire ones like KLD and the Union of Political Realism (*Unia Polityki Realnej,* or UPR).

Table 1.3
Political Orientation of Parties

Center	Right
Western	nationalist
secular	clerical
urban	rural
business	agrarian
civil rights	social order
social liberalism	conservatism
political liberalism	authoritarianism
metacommunist	anticommunist
interdependence	national defense

Source: prepared by the author

A cluster of political orientations that distinguishes conservative parties from centrist ones can be identified.[24] The dichotomy presented in Table 1.3 is designed to underscore substantive differences between two ideal-type political orientations. In practice, however, contemporary Polish parties pick and choose from both lists, thereby producing the schismatic tendencies observed in the party formation process since 1989.

Mapping differences between constituencies of political parties requires a separate framework. One can apply the notion of political fields, developed by Hungarian sociologists, to the Polish case.[25] The liberal field includes the intellectual elite, especially the technical intelligentsia, as well as the new entrepreneurial and incipient middle class.[26] This is the political space disputed by UD and KLD, among others. The Christian-nationalist field is located among the emergent entrepreneurial (capitalist), working (above all, the labor aristocracy), and peasant classes. This center-right field is represented by ZChN, the PC, and a plethora of peasant parties. The social democratic field pulls together part of the working class and the intelligentsia. SdRP is theoretically the major force within this field, although more respectable groups operating here include the Democratic Social Movement (*Ruch Demokratyczno-Socjalny,* or RDS) of Zbigniew Bujak, *Solidarność '80,* and Labor Solidarity (*Solidarność Pracy*).

Table 1.4 identifies the main political parties and their leadership, and provides a notional understanding of their policy orientations.[27] At the outset one must stress that in recent years parties have not just splintered frequently, but, conversely, have entered electoral pacts with other parties to capture votes and seats. They have adopted different names when contesting elections. Their elected members have also joined other forces to establish clubs within parliament. As examples, ZChN ran in the 1991 parliamentary elections under the label Catholic Electoral Action (*Wyborcza Akcja Katolicka,* or WAK). Offshoots of the former communist party joined with SdRP to constitute an Alliance of the Democratic Left (*Sojusz Lewicy Demokratycznej,* or SLD). The numerous peasant parties have regularly organized parliamentary blocs as well as electoral pacts. In short, individual parties and party alliances are both fluid and inextricably linked in contemporary Poland.

The strongest electoral showing of any party in 1991 could be claimed by the Democratic Union (UD). Its leaders have asserted that UD has no ideology or program,[28] although it has been divided for some time precisely over matters of principle. UD consisted of a recognizably left-wing ROAD group, centrist Mazowiecki supporters, and, until 1992, a right-wing faction under Aleksander Hall. The last group largely comprised fellow travelers of KLD and finally broke away to form, at the end of 1992, the Conservative Party (*Partia Konserwatywna*) under Hall's leadership. Given the diversity of views within UD, it had been able to hold together for such a long time by serving as a movement that was liberal on social issues yet monetarist on economic ones. The first postcommunist government of Mazowiecki had been a precursor of UD, officially founded in December 1990.

The government of Prime Minister Hanna Suchocka, in power from summer 1992, also represented primarily a UD prodigy. A carefully crafted coalition based on a UD alliance with the right-wing nationalist ZChN, it also received support from KLD; the Polish Economic Alliance business lobby; two Solidarity farmers' parties—the Peasants' Accord, or *Porozumienie Ludowe* (PL), and the Christian Peasant Party, or *Stronnictwo Chrześcijańsko-Ludowe* (SChL)—and the small Christian Democratic Party (*Partia Chrześcijańsko-Demokratyczna,* or PChD). In sum, the Suchocka government comprised a seven-party coalition that commanded 200 of the 460 Sejm seats. It was occasionally threatened by the defection of a minor party or two yet, in turn, received overtures from nongovernment parties about joining the coalition.

The right-wing Christian National Union (ZChN) formed one of the backbones of Prime Minister Jan Olszewski's government in power from late 1991

Table 1.4
Political Parties, Programs, and Leaders
(April 1993)

Party (Acronym)	Policy Orientation	Leaders (Prime Ministers)
Democratic Union (*Unia Demokratyczna,* or UD)	centrist, market-oriented, intellectual	(Hanna Suchocka)
Split into:		
Liberal wing	State intervention, anticlerical	Jacek Kuroń
Moderates	ethical, antipopulist	(Tadeusz Mazowiecki)
Right wing	nationalist	Aleksander Hall broke away in 1992 to form the Conservative Party (*Partia Konserwatywna*)
Social Democracy of the Polish Republic (*Socjaldemokracja Rzeczypospolitej Polskiej,* or SdRP)	part of the Alliance of the Democratic Left (SLD); third way welfarism, secular	Aleksander Kwaśniewski, Leszek Miller
Christian National Union (*Zjednoczenie Chrześcijańsko Narodowe,* or ZChN)	in Catholic Election Action (*Wyborcza Akcja Katolicka,* or WAK); right-wing, nationalist, clerical, corporatist, economic interventionist	Wiesław Chrzanowski, Jan Łopuszański
Center Accord (*Porozumienie Centrum,* or PC)	capitalist, Christian Democratic, formerly pro-Wałęsa, interventionist	Jarosław Kaczyński, Jacek Maziarski
Polish Peasant Party (*Polskie Stronnictwo Ludowe,* or PSL)	combines former communist satellite party with postwar PSL; protectionist, interventionist, secular	(Waldemar Pawlak)
Confederation for an Independent Poland (*Konfederacja Polski Niepodległej,* or KPN)	anticommunist, anti-Russian, ultranationalist, law-and-order, Keynesian, anticorruption	Leszek Moczulski, Krzysztof Król
Liberal Democratic Congress (*Kongres Liberalno-Demokratyczny,* or KLD)	laissez-faire, supply-side, libertarian, secular	(Jan Krzysztof Bielecki), *Donald Tusk*

Party (Acronym)	Policy Orientation	Leaders (Prime Ministers)
Peasant Accord (*Porozumienie Ludowe*, or PL)	*in alliance with Christian* Peasant Party (Stronnictwo Chrześcijańsko-Ludowe, or SChL) and rural Solidarity; Catholic, farm subsidies	Henryk Bąk, Józef Ślisz
Solidarity (*Solidarność*)	syndicalist, interventionist, mixed economy	Marian Krząklewski
Movement for the Republic (*Ruch dla Rzeczypospolitej*, or RdR)	postelection group for accelerated decommunization	**(Jan Olszewski):** alliance with Antoni Macierewicz

Source: prepared by the author

to spring 1992. This party, too, had internal tensions which eventually resulted in expulsion of one of its leaders, Antoni Macierewicz. Its present head, Wiesław Chrzanowski, was implicated in past secret police work by files released during June 1992. The ZChN receives considerable support from older women.

The controversial Olszewski administration had been propped up by support from other parties as well. These included a number of peasant organizations—the PSL, PL, and the Polish Peasant Party "Solidarity" (*Polskie Stronnictwo Ludowe "Solidarność"*, or PSL "S"). Most importantly, Olszewski was backed by the PC—an increasingly nationalist party which at the time still enjoyed "most-favored party" status in the eyes of President Wałęsa.

The Liberal-Democratic Congress (KLD) served as a critical mass for the government of Prime Minister Jan Krzysztof Bielecki, which spanned the period between Mazowiecki's resignation and Olszewski's nomination. It is a neoconservative grouping that fosters a "yuppie" image and enjoys particular strength in the Gdańsk region, where its leadership originated. It has been accused of using American-style "pork barrel" tactics to increase its popularity.

The rightist Confederation for an Independent Poland (KPN) has been determined to remain in opposition, hoping in this way to form a government in the future. It has been critical of the International Monetary Fund (IMF)-driven government economic policy and opposed the 5 percent ceiling on the 1992 budget deficit. Especially popular among men, it has pushed for early national elections so as to capture the protest vote of an increasingly disaffected electorate.

The Polish Peasant Party (PSL) has become the strongest among smaller scale farmers, whose number remains large given that the rural population in Poland still accounts for 37 percent of the electorate. The nomination of its leader, Waldemar Pawlak, to form a government in early summer 1992 gave the PSL added visibility, although it was also criticized as an offshoot of the *ancien régime.*

Even more so, the Alliance of the Democratic Left (SLD) can not expect to be invited into a government coalition for doctrinal reasons. It has provided informal support to governments like that of prime ministers Olszewski and Suchocka, in order to postpone parliamentary elections. The protest vote it hopes to attract may grow in the meantime, or so the SLD hopes. Its electoral performance has been consistent, and it possesses traditional "red" bastions like the industrial centers of Sosnowiec and Łódź. SLD also is by far the most internally disciplined of all parties. It has been defended from ultrarightist attacks by UD and, in turn, has supported the Suchocka coalition.

During late 1992, several additional political groups gained widespread attention. Former Defense Minister Jan Parys set up a new organization, Movement for the Third Republic (*Ruch dla Trzeciej Rzeczypospolitej,* or RTR), asserting that Poland's democracy and even sovereignty were being threatened by Wałęsa's dictatorial "soft-on-communists" approach. In turn, ex-Prime Minister Olszewski, also upset by Wałęsa, organized the Christian Democratic Forum (*Chrześcijańsko-Demokratyczne Forum,* or ChDF) and received support from the former ZChN leader and interior minister, Macierewicz. This led to the emergence of a new umbrella organization, Movement for the Republic (*Ruch dla Rzeczypospolitej,* or RdR, distinct from RTR). At the beginning of 1993 these political figures, all disenchanted with Wałęsa's presidency, campaigned vigorously throughout the country on a platform of eradicating all remaining communist influence. This had become a euphemism, paradoxically, for attacks on the president. Wałęsa was becoming perceived, incredulously, as part of the *ancien régime*'s establishment and a politician who had outlived his usefulness.

EXECUTIVES AND LEADERS

A strong executive is an unlikely outcome of transitions from communist rule. Indeed, the *raison d'être* for extrication from authoritarianism is to create institutional pluralism under which many parties and government agencies share power with checks and balances. Keeping actors committed to democracy means dispersing power widely. However, political leadership remains pivotal during transitions. One writer described how behavior of political elites could stabilize or undermine democratic government in a plural society. Where socioeconomic cleavages are deep and easily converted into political cleavages, adversarial politics within the elite may deepen political fragmentation. Consensual elite behavior can, by contrast, counterbalance societal cleavages and produce consociational democracy.[29] Popular perceptions of leadership in Poland today stress adversarial relations, although the daunting task of coalition-building to form governments has hinged more on consensual politics.

There are a number of interrelated aspects to leadership, then, that merit attention: (1) structure of the executive branch; (2) personalities and political styles, such as risk-averse and risk-taking behavior; (3) leadership skills, such as bargaining and brokerage abilities; and (4) serendipitous events involving noncontrollable factors, such as timing.

The balance of power between executive and legislative branches of government has had particular importance in Poland. The powerful personality and alleged ambitions of President Wałęsa are commonly held to be the main reason for concern about the extent of executive power. Cynics in Poland describe Wałęsa as seeking to establish a dictatorship of the proletariat which the communists had failed to accomplish (reference is to Wałęsa's working-class origins). A sequence of largely ineffectual and unstable government coalitions, together with bickering among the many parties represented in the Sejm and the fact that parliament is virtually in continuous session, have drawn further attention to the problem of executive-legislative relations. Wałęsa himself described this conflict in May 1992 as a "Bermuda triangle" that had pulled in himself, the Sejm, and the government.

Wałęsa has, arguably, proven to be a weak president. He lost to the Sejm on the key issue of the electoral law, which legislators had insisted should be hyperproportional rather than limit representation of minor parties as Wałęsa had preferred.[30] He failed to obtain approval from the Sejm for his version of the "Little Constitution," which would have redefined the powers of the executive. His political style—populist forays into factories and dairy cooperatives—has been attacked for bringing the dignity of the presidency into question. His response was that he had no interest in becoming a champagne-drinking president; instead, "I pull, I push, I initiate." Concern about the emergence of a political mafia prompted Wałęsa to oppose the rise of a strong party in parliament, wage "war at the top" within the former Solidarity leadership, and regularly purge close associates within the PC (with which he had identified for a time) as well as from his own Office of the President. The fear of an emergent hegemonic power was given by Wałęsa as his reason for dismissing such individuals: "That is why I am merciless. My price is losing friends; theirs, losing their posts."

Not surprisingly, then, former colleagues like Jarosław Kaczyński turned on Wałęsa after they had lost their positions. In January 1993 renewed charges were made that the president had once been "Agent Bolek" of the communist secret police (*Urząd Bezpieczeństwa,* or UB). Wałęsa's top advisor, Mieczysław Wachowski, secretary of state in the president's chancellory, was accused of having undergone field training at a UB camp. Not even Wałęsa's one-time confessor was spared charges of earlier collaboration with communist security organs. The president came under attack at the same time that the Sejm had approved his draft Charter of Rights and Freedoms, intended as an annex to a future constitution. What should one make, then, of Wałęsa's power in Poland's Third Republic? A look at the country's "Little Constitution" can provide some answers.

In November 1992 the Sejm finally gave approval to the "Little Constitution" project, as amended by the Senate. The final version seemed to formalize the gridlock within Polish politics. The country was to have "a presidential-parliamentary system of government." The president's powers to form governments were enhanced, and the Sejm was no longer designated as the highest organ of state power. The president could initiate legislation, veto it (which the Sejm may override with a two-thirds majority), dissolve the legislature if it did not pass a budget within a three-month period, and provide stewardship over defense and national security matters. By contrast, the government was now empowered to rule by decree. However, even here, the president could veto a decree, in which case it would go to the Sejm for resolution. Certain subjects remained off-limits for decrees: budget matters, constitutional issues, personal freedoms, and, as a concession to left-wing parties, social security measures. It appeared that in early 1993 Poland was still feeling the awesome pull of "the Bermuda triangle."

Apart from the chief of state, political leadership also falls to the head of government. Five prime ministers have been asked to form governments since General Czesław Kiszczak's failure to forge the last communist cabinet. They have included individuals of differing sociooccupational backgrounds—a Catholic intellectual, a businessman, a lawyer, a 33-year-old farmer, and a woman who previously had belonged to a communist satellite party. This complements the background of the president—an electrician by trade.

Relations between president and prime ministers have varied. Mazowiecki was originally selected by Wałęsa to serve as prime minister because he promised to rein in the Warsaw intelligentsia (about which the future president always had harbored deep suspicions). Soon Mazowiecki proved to be his own man, while Wałęsa's stature as national leader began to erode.[31] The schism between the future president and his former Solidarity advisors was formalized when Mazowiecki decided to run for president. He was then replaced by Prime Minister Jan Krzysztof Bielecki of the KLD, a private businessman, who promised to retain Leszek Balcerowicz (a doctrinaire monetarist and architect of market transition) in his government. Despite the foregoing, Bielecki's government ran up an enormous deficit and, following the October 1991 parliamentary elections in which the KLD made a poor showing, President Wałęsa felt obliged to replace the prime minister. When longtime Wałęsa advisor Bronisław Geremek's candidacy appeared not viable in the new parliament, the president was forced to ask Jan Olszewski to form a new government. This man was determined to enhance the power of prime minister, and he quickly replaced Wałęsa's appointee as defense minister—even though the still operative, much-amended 1952 constitution gave the president broad constitutional authority over security and defense policies. The showdown between Olszewski's defense ministry and Wałęsa's national security bureau represented more than a clash of personalities: it brought into question the fundamental question of executive-legislative relations and of who was responsible for what policy.

In February 1992, frustrated by what he saw as an obstructionist parliament and a meddling president, Olszewski asked the Sejm for emergency powers to govern by decree. This, he was unable to secure. Several months later, a number of sealed envelopes were presented to President Wałęsa by the interior minister. They contained names of some 60 people who, it was alleged, had been collaborators and agents of the former communist regime. These "revelations" included copies of Wałęsa's alleged loyalty pledges to the communist secret police after the 1970 political unrest. Olszewski had decided to disclose these secret police dossiers on prominent officials, though he may have been unaware that some files contained forged documents. A few days later, his government was removed.

The leader of the largest among the peasant parties, but one that in an earlier incarnation had supported the communist regime, was entrusted by President Wałęsa to form a new cabinet in summer 1992. Waldemar Pawlak could not shake off his party's pedigree and, instead, the country obtained its first woman prime minister. Hanna Suchocka's career path, arguably, had been even more tainted than Pawlak's. Before joining ROAD she previously belonged to the Democratic Party, a satellite of the communists before 1989. Furthermore, she had only abstained rather than voted against the critical

1981 martial law decree. Charges of "recommunization" were leveled at her and UD, to which she belonged. Having survived attacks on her character, Suchocka was able to establish a relatively firm parliamentary coalition while maintaining a working relationship with the president. Success in stabilizing the government, coupled with a flurry of visits she made to West European states that enhanced Poland's stature, earned her high popularity ratings in the country.

The diversity of political leaders is suggestive of a decline in the status of intellectuals. As with *Polonia Reconstituta* of 1918, so now, too, intellectuals who had struggled alongside other social groups for an independent country have been largely marginalized with the task accomplished. Dissident intellectuals are sometimes seen today as political amateurs and new leaders, less well known than the dissidents, need only a respectable past to launch a political career. However, that is not so different from established democratic systems.

CONCLUSION

Individual voters, parties, and leaders have shaped Poland's transition from communist rule. They will also determine the enduring features of the Third Republic. Which political actors will exert greatest influence on longer-term developments depends on the respective resources and the issue salience they bring to bear on the electorate.

It is important, then, to measure resource types for each set of actors. These include: (*a*) incumbency, i.e., electoral seats; (*b*) nonelective incumbency and influence, i.e., control over the bureaucracy, share of wealth, media access, and public opinion support; and (*c*) coercive potential, should the going become difficult, i.e., mass mobilization. Also significant is the value of actors' resources—the utility of different types of resources under changing political circumstances and how effectively they are mobilized.[32]

Assessing prospects for individual political actors must also involve a study of issue distance: (*a*) how they identify the major issues; and (*b*) their estimates of the distance between preferred outcome and the positions held by rivals. Issue salience—the relative importance different contenders attach to issues—is crucial in determining the electoral fortunes of contending parties. These are calculations that leading actors in consolidated democracies must make regularly, and they are even more important to those in a less consolidated democratic system, where actors' fortunes and that of the emergent system are closely interconnected.

NOTES

1. The approach taken here is patterned on a widely used textbook of British politics: Jean Blondel, *Voters, Parties, and Leaders* (Harmondsworth, Middlesex: Penguin Books, 1974).
2. This notion is borrowed from the pioneering psychiatric work of Kazimierz Dąbrowski.
3. See Timothy J. Power, "Politicized Democracy: Competition, Institutions, and 'Civic Fatigue' in Brazil," *Journal of Interamerican Studies and World Affairs* 33, no. 3 (Fall 1991): 96. Part of the following account is based on Power's analysis of Brazil under the New Republic.
4. Adam Przeworski, *Democracy and the Market* (Cambridge: Cambridge University Press, 1992), p. 26.
5. Ibid., p. 67.
6. Charles Anderson, *Politics and Economic Change in Latin America* (Princeton, N.J.: Van Nostrand, 1967).
7. James Madison, "The Size and Variety of the Union as a Check on Faction," *The Federalist,* no. 10 (1788). Reprinted in Alexander Hamilton, James Madison, John Jay, *The Federalist,* Benjamin F. Wright, ed. (Cambridge, Mass.: Belknap Press, 1966), p. 131.
8. William C. Smith, "State, Market and Neoliberalism in Post-Transition Argentina: The Menem Experiment," *Journal of Interamerican Studies and World Affairs* 33, no. 4 (Winter 1991): 51.
9. Described by Jan Winiecki, *Resistance to Change in the Soviet Economic System: A Property Rights Approach* (London: Routledge, 1991). See also Winiecki's extensive self-references in his "The Polish Transition Programme: Underpinnings, Results, Interpretations," *Soviet Studies* 44, no. 5 (1992): 834-835.
10. László Urbán, "Hungarian Transition from a Public Choice Perspective," in András Bozóki, András Körösényi, and George Schöpflin, eds., *Post-Communist Transition: Emerging Pluralism in Hungary* (New York: St. Martin's Press, 1992), p. 92. For Urbán, the answer in the Hungarian case was a clear affirmative.
11. Cited in Mieczysław Rakowski, *Jak to się stało* (Warsaw: BGW, 1991).
12. See Guillermo O'Donnell and Philippe Schmitter, *Transitions from Authoritarian Rule* (Baltimore, Md.: Johns Hopkins University Press, 1986); Przeworski, *Democracy and the Market,* pp. 66-79, for a study of extrication from authoritarianism employing four actor types: hardliners and reformers inside the authoritarian bloc, and moderates and radicals inside the opposition bloc.

13. Norman H. Nie and Sidney Verba, "Political Participation," in Fred Greenstein and Nelson W. Polsby, eds., *Handbook of Political Science: Nongovernmental Politics* (Reading, Mass.: Addison-Wesley, 1975), p. 17.

14. For a detailed sociological analysis of the 1989 elections, see L. Kolarska-Bobińska, P. Łukasiewicz, Z. Rykowski, eds., *Wyniki badań, wyniki wyborów* (Warsaw: PTS, 1990); also, R. Kałuża, *Polska: wybory '89* (Warsaw: Wydawnictwo Andrzej Bonarski, 1989).

15. Stanisław Gebethner, "Wybory do Sejmu i Senatu 1989 r.," *Państwo i prawo*, no. 8 (August 1989).

16. Jacek Raciborski, "Wybory samorządowe 1990," Instytut Socjologii, Uniwersytet Warszawski; typescript.

17. Frivolous candidacies included Jerzy Bartoszewski (a lawyer), Edward Mizikowski (locksmith), W. Trajdos (claiming to be editor of a nonexistent newspaper), and Bolesław Tejkowski (anti-Semite).

   Three serious candidates, who were unable to obtain the 100,000 signatures (0.4 percent of the electorate) to run, included Janusz Korwin-Mikke (Union of Political Realism), Władysław Siła-Nowicki (Party of Labor), and Kornel Morawiecki (Party of Liberty/Fighting Solidarity).

   Stanisław Tymiński rose successively from frivolous candidate to one who obtained sufficient signatures to enter the election, and sufficient votes to participate in the runoff contest against Wałęsa.

18. For a detailed statistical analysis of voting behavior as well as turnout during the presidential election, see Jerzy Bartkowski and Jacek Raciborski, "Wybory prezydenta RP: kampania, wyniki," in Raciborski, ed., *Wybory i narodziny demokracji w krajach Europy środkowej i wschodniej* (Warsaw: Instytut Sociologii, Uniwersytet Warszawski, 1991), pp. 125-167.

19. Raciborski claims that no correlation existed. See ibid., pp. 147-149. In a personal communication, Krzysztof Jasiewicz from the Institute of Political Studies, Polish Academy of Sciences, contends that they did correlate.

20. Each party would receive a certain number of seats for a constituency based on (1) number of seats available multiplied by votes received; (2) the product divided by total votes cast. Remainders were used to distribute the balance of seats.

21. To be eligible for national representation, a party had to win seats in at least five separate constituencies or to have polled five percent of the countrywide vote. Alliances between party lists were permitted.

22. Irena Grudzińska Gross, "Post-Communist Resentment, or the Rewriting of Polish History," in *East European Politics and Societies* 6, no. 2 (Spring 1992): 147.

23. Judith Gentleman and Voytek Zubek, "International Integration and Democratic Development: The Cases of Poland and Mexico," *Journal of Interamerican Studies and World Affairs* 34, no. 1 (Spring 1992): 72.

24. This is adapted from András Körösényi, "Revival of the Past or New Beginning? The Nature of Post-Communist Politics," in Bozóki, Körösényi, Schöpflin, *Post-Communist Transitions*, p. 117. The term "center" is used where Körösényi uses "left", in deference to the self-designation of Polish parties; the only left movement is the one that calls itself that.

25. These fields are adapted from Tamás Kolosi, Iván Szelényi, Szonja Szelényi, and Bruce Western, "The Making of Political Fields in Post-Communist Transition," in Bozóki, Körösényi, Schöpflin, *Post-Communist Transition*, pp. 134-139. In this framework, peasants are seemingly absorbed into the "new petty bourgeoisie" and do not stand as a class. Such an approach fails to explain the proliferation of parties aiming specifically to pick up the peasant vote.

26. On this class, see Krzysztof Jasiewicz, "Czy istnieje polska klasa średnia?" *Więź* 32, nos. 7-8 (July-August 1991): 16-24.

27. For a wider spectrum of political parties, yet also a somewhat dated one, see Tadeusz Mołdowa, Ludzie władzy, 1944-1991 (Warsaw: Polskie Wydawnictwo Naukowe, 1991), pp. 266-306.

28. Indeed, an earlier incarnation of UD questioned the importance of having any party system in Poland. See Antoni Szwed, "Czy partie polityczne są Polsce potrzebne?" *Tygodnik powszechny,* 10 February 1991.

29. Arend Lijphart, *Democracy in Plural Societies* (New Haven, Conn.: Yale University Press, 1977).

30. On the law, see Frances Millard, "The Polish Parliamentary Elections of October 1991," *Soviet Studies* 44, no. 5 (1992): 838-840.

31. For the origins of the Mazowiecki government, see Zbigniew Domarańczyk, *100 dni Mazowieckiego* (Warsaw: Andrzej Bonarski, 1990); on the role of intelligentsia, see Voytek Zubek, "The Rise and Fall of Rule by Poland's Best and Brightest," *Soviet Studies* 44, no. 4 (1992): 579-608.

32. This framework is adapted from Gabriel A. Almond, Scott C. Flanagan, Robert J. Mundt, "Crisis, Choice, and Change in Retrospect," in *Government in Opposition* 27, no. 3 (Summer 1992): 366.

2

Political Activation of Social Groups

*Mirosława Grabowska**

It was not long ago—in February 1989—that the Roundtable negotiations took place. As a result of agreements achieved there, four months later parliamentary elections were won—to the extent possible—by Solidarity. Tadeusz Mazowiecki, the first post-World War II noncommunist prime minister, formed a new government. Opportunities thus created led to the proliferation of socially active forces, articulation of programs, and organization of political parties. Sweeping economic reforms have already confronted society with hitherto unknown problems, which perhaps had never appeared before on this scale in recorded history. They shook all areas of economic life: enterprises as well as households, production as well as consumers' habits, the work ethic as well as lifestyles. So much has changed and is still changing that one should determine in what areas, and to what extent, the changes will be treated. The following analyses are offered:

- The economic realm, including privatization of the ownership structure and attitudes of society toward those transformations.
- The political realm, encompassing creation of a new institutional order (along with a party system and citizen participation in politics as well as people's attitudes toward politics).

* The author wishes to thank Dr. Christine Sadowski (Free Trade Institute, AFL/CIO) for her comments on this chapter.

- The cultural realm, centering above all on the problem of the church-state relationship and questions pertaining to it.

THE ECONOMY

In the economic realm, three phenomena are most important: (1) a long-lasting and deep economic recession, which perhaps will at least slow down in 1993 (production, which had been declining after 1989, has been growing since April 1992, and it is estimated that by December it will reach up to a 1 percent increase as compared with 1991); (2) the budget deficit (as of 6 November 1992 the budget for that year had reached an 81.8 billion złoty deficit, comprising 21 percent of expenditures), limiting the state's implementation of important welfare and social functions which until recently were believed to constitute its obvious duties; (3) ownership transformations introduced by the government. Subsequent administrations—except perhaps for the one under Prime Minister Jan Olszewski—placed their hopes in the privatization process for establishment of a sector which would be more effective economically (and therefore more abundantly fill the budget in the future), and more dynamic and flexible than the noneffective, difficult-to-steer or transform, state sector. The liberal politicians assigned to the privatization process hope for the emergence of a middle class.

What is the current state of ownership transformation, after nearly three years of activity? From among 7,500 existing state-owned enterprises, some 1,714 had been in the process of privatization by 30 April 1992—nearly 23 percent. Of that number, only 207 (fewer than 3 percent of the total 12 percent of all privatized enterprises) already have a private owner, and 78 (1 percent of all and 4.6 percent of those privatized) have been liquidated. One can see, then, that the process of eliminating noneffective enterprises from the Polish economy, and of creating private economic entities, has barely begun.

Despite the above, transformations in the economic realm have been taking place. They are visible in the form of two phenomena: unemployment and change in employment structure. In June 1990, there were 568,000 unemployed; in December, about 1,126,000; in June 1991 the number reached 1,574,000; in December, some 2,156,000; in June 1992, up to 2,297,000; and in September, almost 2.5 million. During the same period of time, unemployment rose from 3 percent to 13.6 percent. A further increase is expected, supposedly reaching the level of three million. Although these figures are lower than in some EC countries, such as Ireland or Spain, Polish society is not accustomed to this phenomenon. Some 46 percent of the people believed in September 1992 that unemployment was the most serious problem in the country.

As far as employment structure is concerned, the data are not the same. Before the formation of a democratic government by Prime Minister Tadeusz Mazowiecki in 1989, about 13 percent of all wage earners worked in the private sector outside of agriculture. At the end of that year, the percentage had risen to 31. This change did not indicate, however, any sudden increase of unemployment in the private sector. It can be explained simply by exclusion of the cooperative sector from the state administration. In September 1992, according to the Main Statistical Agency, about 41 percent were employed in the private sector outside of agriculture. Sociological surveys[1] offer more modest estimates, at 36 percent. However, the GNP share of this sector rose dramatically from 28 in September 1989 to 30 percent in September 1990 and 40 percent in September 1991. One should not have any doubts concerning the direction of change.

The foregoing transformation has not been accompanied by an equal change in social consciousness. The newly formed class of entrepreneurs is organized only to a minute degree. Although seven separate organizations for businessmen and managers of state enterprises exist, they have a socializing purpose rather than any sociopolitical meaning. The largest is said to be the Business Center Club, numbering about 600 private entrepreneurs and managers. It was at this club that establishment of a special fund was discussed, because of legal problems affecting big business. The fund was supposed to help finance 40 to 50 individuals running for parliament from several different political parties. Such candidates would work in the interests of private business.[2] One can see the beginning of an organized lobby.

Private businessmen are in a category insufficiently large for their voting behavior or preferences to be analyzed by means of representative sociological surveys. It is known that in the 1991 parliamentary elections, they supported various political parties. At the same time, voting preferences by employees of the private sector barely differ from their counterparts in the state sector. The above takes into consideration only larger parties, i.e., those having at least 4 percent support on a national basis.

It seems that employees are better organized than businessmen. There exist 14 labor unions, including two large ones: the former communist OPZZ and NSZZ Solidarity. They pose a problem of extralegal union activities, with far more radical demands and operations than their counterparts in Western Europe. The two-month strike during the summer of 1992, organized by the labor union Solidarność '80, which shut down the Fiat automobile plant, was against the law. And *Samoobrona* (self-defense), a union of farmers in debt, organized by Andrzej Lepper, openly called for nonrepayment of loans and organized roadblocks.

Social attitudes, full of enthusiasm and trust in politics after the 1989 victory, quickly began to deteriorate. In the period between June and August 1992, only 23 percent of those surveyed held to the belief that the government was moving in the right direction, about 64 percent believed the opposite, and 13 percent had no opinion. The dominant view about change, then, appeared negative. Attitudes toward privatization—the process which is claimed to be the engine of reform—at first favorable, started to worsen and are today unfavorable.

It can be seen that, with an economy in a state of crisis, changes are taking place which nevertheless do not automatically generate—perhaps they will—either social groups supporting those changes or favorable attitudes.

POLITICS

The political opposition emerging during the 1970s had the objective of building a civic society, not to fill nor even to supplement state structures, but rather to position itself outside the reach of communist authority. This movement wanted, in a way, to lead the people out of the communist state, or at least to deprive the state of as many functions as possible and manage without it. Solidarity was the perfect product of such a mentality and strategy. The underground opposition constituted its continuation.

The situation changed radically after the Roundtable negotiations, elections of 4 June 1989, and appointment of Tadeusz Mazowiecki as prime minister. These developments did not proceed smoothly. Both the Roundtable compromise as well as the elections were fiercely criticized, and even the future prime minister at first spoke out against his own Solidarity movement being in the government. These criticisms could be refuted by pointing out that most of them came from those who "did not make it to the top." See Table 2.1.

It is true, however, that Solidarity negotiators and candidates for parliament in the 1989 elections were selected by narrow circles unauthorized to perform such functions and not controlled by anyone. Roundtable negotiations between the opposition and the government represented an historic opportunity and had to be exploited. This did not mean that these talks had a constitutional basis or were generally seen as valid or legitimate. The opportunity was seized, although its legal elaboration and transformation into a law-abiding democratic mechanism has proceeded at a slow pace.

Table 2.1
The Followers
(in percentages)

Parties	State Employees	Private Employees
KPN	11.0	11.0
KLD	6.5	6.0
"S"	4.0	3.0
PSL	9.0	9.0
SdRP	5.0	4.0
UD	22.0	23.0
ZChN	3.0	4.0
Other	16.5	18.0
Nonvoters	*22.0*	*22.0*
Totals	100.0	100.0

Compiled by the author

Notes:

KPN=	Confederation for an Independent Poland
KLD=	Liberal Democratic Congress
"S"=	parliamentary representation of NSZZ Solidarity
PSL=	postcommunist Polish Peasant Party
SdRP=	Social Democracy of the Republic of Poland (former communist party)
UD=	Democratic Union
ZChN=	Christian National Union, which ran under the label Catholic Electoral Action in parliamentary elections.

For more than three years, since the transfer of political power from communists to the opposition, Poland has had no new basic law. (The so-called Little Constitution, a temporary solution, was adopted toward the end of November 1992.) The country does not even have a postcommunist electoral law, and the future political order—parliamentary or presidential—has yet to be decided upon.

What are public attitudes toward state and government institutions? In August 1992, the Demoskop public opinion polling agency asked about the

Table 2.2
Voters for Political Parties

Organization	Trust	Do not trust
Army	ZChN, NSZZ "S"	not voting
Police	UP	KPN, NSZZ "S"
Prosecutors and courts	KLD	SdRP
Television	ZChN	not voting, SdRP, NSZZ "S"
Church	ZChN, NSZZ "S", KLD	SdRP
OPZZ	SdRP	UP, UD, KLD, KPN, NSZZ "S", not voting
NSZZ "S"	NSZZ "S"	SdRP, not voting
Political institutions	KLD, ZChN, UD, NSZZ "S"	SdRP, not voting

Compiled by the author

degree of trust in various institutions. There was a high degree of faith in the army (78 percent) and quite a high degree in the police, courts, and prosecutors (64, 55, and 53 percent, respectively). People trusted the Roman Catholic Church; they had faith in the mass media (television, 54 percent; press and radio, 53 percent). The lowest percentages were scored by labor unions— OPZZ, established by the communist regime under martial law, registered only slightly below Solidarity (26 and 34 percent, respectively). Although the scores were less than favorable for all political institutions (the president, 41 percent, the Sejm and the Senate, 38 percent each)—they were somewhat better for the government (48 percent).

Supporters of various parties trusted or distrusted the above institutions unequally. A comparison is given on Table 2.2. It should be noted that supporters of post-Solidarity parties trust the institutions of public life. Those who distrust them are either the ones who would not vote (they trust the mass media to only a slight degree, so it is difficult to change their minds), or the communist SdRP electorate, which accepts only the OPZZ trade union established by the martial law regime and its own press.

In order to participate actively in institutionalized political processes (voting in elections, membership in parties), an individual must meet certain criteria, for example, being at least to a minimum degree interested in politics. This interest—according to surveys by the Center for Public Opinion Research and Demoskop during 1992—includes 30 percent or, at most, half of all adult citizens. Those more often interested in politics are usually men, people between 30 and 49, and educated city dwellers; those less interested are people aged 15 to 29. The rest do not care about politics.

How does participation in elections present itself against this background? In West European countries, one can observe a high participation in parliamentary elections. During the 1980s this did not drop below 75 percent, usually reaching over 80 percent in France, Great Britain, Italy, the Netherlands, and Sweden. However, for the United States, the turnout of voters in congressional races has been only half of that in Western Europe. A higher turnout can be observed every four years during American presidential elections. At least this example suggests that there is no direct relationship between the level of electorate mobilization and stability of the democratic system.

In Poland, some 62 percent of those having the right to vote participated in the June 1989 general elections; only 42 percent came out to choose local government officials in May 1990; and 61 percent during the first round of presidential balloting on 25 September 1990, which dropped to 53 percent in the second round; and only 43 percent took part in general elections on 27 October 1991. If one were to treat participation over these two years as symptomatic of a permanent phenomenon, one could deduce that between 40 and 60 percent of the electorate exercises its vote. This means that two-fifths of all citizens exclude themselves permanently from voting, and about one-fifth will vote only every other time. Those not participating appreciated and trusted democratic institutions to a lesser degree than those who voted. The former were uninterested in politics and did not support promarket reforms of the economy or privatization.[3] More important is the fact that half did not have any party preference at all.

At the beginning of 1991, only a few percent of the adult population recognized the then existing parties. The electoral campaign and the election itself resulted in a breakthrough in terms of ability to recognize political parties. Some 43 percent of those who participated in the elections knew the range of movements and also in some way identified themselves with the party for which they had voted. According to Demoskop data from the period between January and September 1992, more than 60 percent of the potential electorate held precise party preferences, that is, could identify the party for which they would vote. Nothing teaches democracy better than practicing it.

However, participation in elections and the expressed acceptance of democracy do not automatically translate into support for the realized process of reform. As mentioned above, in the summer of 1992, only 23 percent of those surveyed actually believed that the affairs of Poland were proceeding in the right direction, some 64 percent thought that they were going in the wrong one, and 13 percent lacked any opinion. The negative view, therefore, prevailed.

One among every four Polish citizens, positively viewed the changes taking place. Every fourth person (26 percent) votes for UD, every tenth for KPN or KLD (each 11 percent) or for PSL (10 percent). Some 12 percent have no intention to vote at all.

The largest group among those negatively viewing change consists of people who have said they will not vote (26 percent); followers of UD (16 percent), of PSL (14 percent), and of KPN (10 percent). These groups, then, are politically different, although the differences are of degree rather than of basic quality.

A closer look at attitudes toward reform, the attitudes of social groups distinguished by education and place of work, in state or private enterprises, is warranted.

First, one should remember that 45 percent of the Polish population has an educational level not higher than elementary school, some 24 percent completed a trade school or dropped out of high school, 25 percent received high school diplomas or have an incomplete higher education, and 6 percent have university degrees.

Among people with only an elementary school education, some 22 percent perceive changes positively; among those with a higher education, 37 percent. Negative perceptions dominate among 64 percent of elementary school graduates, and 52 percent with a completed higher education. Even in the last group, the majority believes that Poland is following the wrong direction in its policies. Only those people with a higher education have distinct views; all of the other groups share views in these matters that are almost identical with people who have only an elementary school education.

Among those who completed their higher education, the followers of UD make up 29 percent (which means that almost one out of three intends to vote for UD); some 14 percent would vote for KLD, some 12 percent for SdRP, and those who do not want to vote comprise 11 percent.

Among people with a completed elementary education, one out of four does not intend to vote. Of these, followers of PSL make up 17 percent, those of UD comprise 15 percent, and those of KPN, 9 percent.

People with a higher education can be distinguished by their lesser suscepti-bility to prejudice and resentment. In September 1992, Demoskop asked people whether they agreed with the statement about "the influence of Jews in our cultural, economic, and political life being too great." Among those with a higher education, one out of ten accepted the statement in the three indicated areas; and 66 percent consistently disagreed with the statement. Among those with an elementary school education, the percentages were 24 and 39, respectively; the percentages for all remaining educational levels were almost identical.

The division between those employed in state-run enterprises and those in private enterprise will become more and more important. Whether and how to differentiate between these two social categories, working under different conditions, is an important question. The structure of employment for those between 15 and 69 years of age, according to survey data by Demoskop, is the following: 31 percent (two-thirds of those employed outside of agriculture) work in state enterprises, 17 percent (one-third of those employed outside agriculture) in private enterprise, 7 percent on their own farms, and 45 percent do not work at all.

One out of five people, employed in a state-run enterprise or institution, believes that the country's affairs are going in the right direction; two-thirds (68 percent) believe the opposite. At the same time, almost one out of three in the private sector (31 percent) believes that the country's affairs are moving in a good direction, while 58 percent are of the opposite opinion.

Among those with state jobs, 22 percent would vote for UD; the same percentage would not vote at all; 11 percent would vote for KPN; and 9 percent for PSL. Almost identical voting preferences were declared by people employed in the private sector: 23 percent would vote for UD, 22 percent would not vote, 10 percent favor KPN, and 9 percent, PSL.

Both groups differ in their susceptibility to prejudice and resentment. Some 22 percent of those employed in the state sector consistently agree with statements about the influence of Jews being too great, while 43 percent consistently reject that statement. Quite different are the reactions of private sector employees: 28 percent accept the statements, and 39 percent reject them. They are, therefore, more susceptible to prejudice and resentment. These attitudes are not related to differences in education.

What follows from the foregoing? First, the institutional sphere does not excite enthusiasm. Neither is it an object of social disrespect, although it becomes such for the mass media. However, there is the mark of a division— the electorates of post-Solidarity political parties trust the institutions of public life, while those who refused to vote, as well as the SdRP constituency, reject these institutions.

Second, contrary to beliefs being spread by the mass media, between 40 and 60 percent of adults are interested in politics. They are inclined to

Table 2.3
Supporters of Major Political Parties
(percentages)

Parties	EDUCATION LEVEL			
	Elementary	Trade school	High school	University
KPN	9	14	7	8
KLD	3	6	8	14
"S"	5	3	2	3
PSL	17	11	9	3
SdRP	4	2	4	12
UD	15	17	26	29
ZChN	4	4	3	4
Other	18	21	19	16
Nonvoters	25	22	22	11
Totals	100	100	100	100

Compiled by the author

participate in elections and, to some extent, accept the political institutions of the Third Republic. One could agree that this is not much, although it does not compare unfavorably with the situation in many other countries. They are people of fundamental sociopolitical attitudes and party preferences, in this writer's opinion.

Third, within society, the group standing out is the intelligentsia, those people with a completed higher education. Although the private sector of the economy is growing, it is the intelligentsia rather than the middle class which constitutes the basis for sociopolitical reforms. Almost one-third of the votes go to UD, which can be seen as the beginning of a political representation; other parties are much weaker (see Table 2.3).

Where, then, should one look for dangers to the emerging democratic order? Between 40 and 60 percent of the electorate still does not want to participate in the political process. Yet, these people do have their own interests and their own beliefs. This means that their articulation is not registered in the democratic system. Either this articulation will improve, or it will take place sporadically through such "media" as Stanisław Tymiński and Andrzej Lepper. And that is always socially unfavorable and dangerous.

It is not certain how long the intelligentsia will remain the foundation of Polish reforms, considering how lightly the so-called budget sphere is treated by successive governments. Another problem is that the new categories and social groups, enlarging the basis for Polish reforms, are developing so slowly.

One also cannot see an emerging agreement concerning the basic institutional order in Poland, that is, an order founded on a full-length constitution (not the "little" one). Such an order requires a consensus among all political forces which would ensure a smooth functioning of that complex machinery we call modern democracy. At the same time, this would make it clear to all citizens how democracy functions.

THE CHURCH

Over the past several years, quantitative and qualitative changes have been taking place in the Polish Catholic Church. First, the quantitative changes. The lowest indicators for religiousness were noted during the 1960s and 1970s. Within all of Polish society, about three-fourths comprised believers and two-thirds practicing Catholics. However, in youth and academic circles, these figures were much lower. For example, among Warsaw high school graduates in 1972, some 48 percent were believers and 46 percent regularly attended church. Since about the mid-1970s, there has been a growth in numbers of the faithful and support for the church.[4] The percentage of believers approached 90, then reached 93 and even 95 percent during the late 1980s. The process of revival took place with the greatest intensity in intelligentsia circles. During the early 1970s, only 52 percent declared their faith and 39 percent its absence; in the late 1980s, faith was declared by 89 percent of the intelligentsia, and absence thereof by only 11 percent; in 1977 some 28 percent prayed daily, while in 1983 already 78 percent did so.

The process of religious revival, therefore, started before the election of Karol Cardinal Wojtyła as Pope John Paul II and his first pilgrimage to Poland; before the period of Solidarity, when faith and the church participated so prominently in public life; even before martial law, although the political situation had created a certain "juncture for faith." Intergenerational studies are convincing about that. During the early 1970s, the absence of faith was passed on within families most effectively; in the 1980s, religious faith could be transmitted in the same manner. These results are confirmed in church statistics as well as from the common observation about acquiring faith and joining the church by people from nonbelieving families. Other church statistics attest the religious revival as well. For instance, since 1974 there has been an increase of participation in pilgrimages to Jasna Góra; the number of calls to priesthood also rose.[5]

Were such quantitative changes accompanied by qualitative transformations? These are difficult to measure. Studies of religious knowledge, acceptance of religious truths or of a religiously motivated morality show that more people declare their faith than know what they believe in; that different truths of faith meet with different levels of believer approval (more people believe in God than in the resurrection of bodies); and that religiously motivated moral commands are accepted selectively. This is what has happened in the whole Christian world, and the religiousness of Polish society does not differ from the religiousness, for example, of American society.

One could argue further that the high level of church attendance, motivations notwithstanding, cannot remain without influence on practicing Catholics. The evidence of systematic, consistent, and clear influence is overwhelming.

One could finally point to the new phenomena in Catholicism. During the second half of the 1970s (before the election of the Pope!), new religious communities appeared. In Poland, there had been no tradition of such communal forms of religious practice. Most of the currently active renewal groups were "imported" to Poland. In less than a decade, they have been adopted and are still developing. Over the past two or three years, one could notice the beginning of their institutionalization. Although in relation to the size of the Catholic Church these renewal communities are marginal, they represent an important point of reference for the believers. The more so because the ethos character of their faith, the striving to live a life based on one's belief, results in their being visible in parishes and in everyday life.

How, then, is the position of the Catholic Church in democratic Poland being shaped? Will the situation described above endure, or will there be a violent breakdown of religiousness? Or will the result perhaps be more powerful church control over the whole of social life, in its Khomeinization?

As to the social dimension and the church as a community of faithful, the forceful process of laicization of society probably will not take place. There is no reason to believe that there exists a reverse relationship between the "amount" of democracy or the condition of the economy and the level of religiousness. The case of American society contradicts such interpretations. Faith not only provides answers to historical circumstances. Its vitality is not directly dependent on economic crises and political circumstances. Moreover, according to the analysis presented above, the increase in religiousness was not that of juncture only. It represented qualitative changes of faith. If someone is counting on the miracle of laicization in Poland, he or she must be warned that such a miracle will not happen.

There are, however, signs of a decrease in religious involvement. Since 1987 the number of men entering the priesthood and some other church activities has been declining. It is difficult to decide whether this will become a permanent trend and to what extent. Such indicators, however, show that at the margins of this social giant—the Catholic Church community—traces of erosion are visible, and the mechanisms of social support are weakening.

In the economic dimension, two facts should be considered. The first one is the struggle of the church to fit into the new economic reality. As an organization, the church adapts itself. By undertaking initiatives of reprivatization and other economic activity (e.g., by renting rooms to retail and service companies), it makes budget cuts and asks poorer parishioners to increase their donations. This "market" behavior of the church under conditions of self-financing is understandable.

The second fact, more serious, is the absence of an economic dimension that would attempt to meet new challenges in the social teaching of the church. People's economic beliefs have nothing to do with their religious attitudes. This does not mean that they do not differ in that respect, but their economic beliefs are not founded upon either religious or lay attitudes. The unprecedented restoration of the Polish economy is taking place with a mute disinterest of the church, even though it is theoretically prepared to take up the subject through the encyclical *Centesimus annus*. Although the position of John Paul II on abortion is widely known, his position on the market economy and democratic order is not.

The relationship between economic views and faith is complex. These are ideological concepts, shaped over decades, being passed on from generation to generation within social circles rather than institutions. Only recently and in part have they been institutionalized in programs of political parties, whose main representatives are members of the intelligentsia. Their views constitute a crystallization of more dispersed ideological concepts. The author has studied these political elites—delegates to congresses of three political movements (PC, UD, KLD) which held five such meetings during 1991 and 1992. The economic outlook of such political elites does not depend on religious views either, even though one of them calls itself a Christian-Democratic party.

In its political dimension, the role of the church has changed radically. During the June 1989 elections, half of the Citizens' Committees—according to an analysis by Krzysztof Koseła[6]—had their first quarters in parish buildings. The church did not ask at that time about religious orthodoxy of candidates for either house of parliament, spontaneously taking the opposition-Solidarity side. No criticism was heard at that time of church involvement in politics. However, during the first free and democratic Sejm elections of October 1991, the church played a different role. Despite episcopal statements that it would not support specific political groups, there appeared a so-called instruction which proposed five lists that a Catholic could/had to choose from. This instruction helped, for example, Catholic Electoral Action. For the others, it did not matter.

So far the church, at least formally, has not participated in any direct political activity. Yet through its trusted lay groups, it takes part in political life, aiming at realization of its social values and ideals. Even such indirect practice of politics has precipitated serious social resistance. In surveys conducted during the spring of 1992, the church was identified as the power governing Poland more often than state institutions. The majority of respondents also wished to limit the political influence of the church. Trust in the church as an institution, as well as the prestige of the Primate, are declining. Among various institutions of public life, the church is not in last place, but neither is it anywhere near to the position of unquestionable authority it held during the 1980s. Meanwhile, the church influences politics in an inconsistent and chaotic manner. Just as there is no economic dimension to its teachings, neither is there a political dimension, except for church-state relations.

The most serious political problem is and will be the arrangement of church-state relations. In emotional public debates, positions are both extreme and moderate. Moderation on the part of the church means calling for a model close to the American one: division between state and church institutions, with simultaneous presence of faith in public life. Lay groups call for the French model, in which the division of institutions goes along with a separation of public from religious life. Faith would have to fit into an appropriate place and time, beyond which it would have no right to exist. The American model does not separate so strictly the lay from the sacred, faith from life, or religion from politics.[7]

The cultural-moral dimension also undergoes change. The church, demanding space for itself in public life, wants to influence the cultural-moral rather than the economic or political realm (although it needs political empowerment). This sphere consists of religious instruction in schools and the struggle for a law prohibiting abortion or a change in divorce legislation.

In that sphere there are relationships between the lay and religious world view and the attitude toward the presence of religion and of the church in public life, both at the popular and the elite levels. It should be expected that believers will call for the presence of religion in public life, for consideration of religious norms in legal regulations, and for participation of the church in political life. It is interesting, however, that religiousness influences people's positions of this sort with a different force, depending on the group. Some 96 percent of deeply religious PC members, 60 percent of KLD, and 47 percent of UD Sejm deputies called for the antiabortion law. About 43 pecent of regularly church-attending PC, 20 percent of UD, and only about 15 percent of KLD parliamentarians wanted a church presence in political life. This means, for example, that the postulate of church participation in political life does not have the support even of a majority among the most religious of those surveyed in the PC environment.

Opinions about that matter not only differ in various social circles, but they also change dynamically over time. In 1989, attitudes toward teaching catechism in schools and toward the antiabortion law were more or less balanced: half were for religion in schools and antiabortion legislation; half opposed both. Three years later, 70 percent were for teaching religion in schools, and the same percentage were against the antiabortion law. This means that people feel free, at least to a certain degree, to shape their own views on questions about which the church has its own position. They also feel free to act: they send children to Catholic schools and establish Catholic associations. At the same time, they have founded lay and anticlerical associations like *Neutrum* and do not hesitate to criticize publicly church authorities. And this is a normal, unstable situation in a vital, changing society.

NOTES

1. Data by Demoskop: Market and Social Research, from the period June through August 1992, computed and analyzed by the author.
2. Piotr Najsztub, "Obrona biznesmenów," *Gazeta wyborcza,* 4 November 1992, p. 3.
3. See Centrum Badania Opinii Społecznej, *Kto nie poszedł na wybory? Komunikat z badań* (Warsaw: November 1991), pp. 4-5.
4. In the years 1980-1984, there were more baptisms than births. See "Kościół katolicki w Polsce, 1918-1990," *Rocznik statystyczny* (Warsaw: Główny Urząd Statystyczny 1991), p. 246.
5. Ibid., pp. 229 and 246.
6. Krzysztof Koseła, "The Polish Catholic Church and the Election of 1989," *Religion in Communist Lands* 18, no. 2 (Summer 1990): 124-137.
7. What is believed in Poland to be an inappropriate prayer when said by President Lech Wałęsa is commonplace in America; it is not only possible but even considered traditional for President William J. Clinton to repeat "God Bless America."

3

The Presidential-Parliamentary System

Andrew A. Michta*

Since the historic 1989 Roundtable compromise agreement between the communists and Solidarity trade union, Poland has been in the forefront of democratic change throughout East-Central Europe. The country was the first among the USSR's former client-states to embark in 1990 upon an ambitious program of economic reform that has laid the foundations for a market system. It acted jointly with Czechoslovakia and Hungary, partners within the East-Central European "triangle," to dismantle the military and political structures of the Warsaw Pact, while restructuring the Polish armed forces.[1]

In the foreign affairs arena, Poland negotiated two vital agreements with Germany: the October 1990 border treaty and the June 1991 treaty on good neighborly relations between the two countries. Next, following dissolution of the Soviet Union at the end of December 1991, Warsaw moved to improve relations with its eastern neighbors, hosting an official visit by Ukraine's President Leonid Kravchuk in May 1992. It also began negotiating with Moscow to improve trade and state-to-state relations, and to finalize withdrawal of Russian troops from Poland.

In sharp contrast to these economic, security, and foreign policy achievements, the process of creating an effective democratic system has proven an arduous task. During 1991 and most of 1992, the country's political elites were often deadlocked over the question of constitutional reform, specifically the

* The author wishes to thank Dr. Jacek Szymanderski, director of the Center for the Study of Public Opinion in Warsaw, for his careful critique of this chapter.

extent and precise definition of presidential, parliamentary, and governmental authority. Paradoxically, the democratically elected president and parliament continued to function within the confines of the largely irrelevant 1952 communist constitution which had only been amended.

By mid-1992, it was clear that lack of constitutional reform and failure to address adequately the division of powers between executive and legislative branches of government were paralyzing the country's ability to govern itself. The "war at the top" among President Lech Wałęsa, the government, and the Sejm over the ultimate shape of Polish democracy was brought into focus during the debate over the wording of the so-called Little Constitution (*Mała Konstytucja*), a temporary replacement for the 1952 basic law. Political paralysis during 1991 and 1992 became compounded by progressive fragmentation of the Solidarity movement and attendant weakness of nascent political parties, as well as growing disenchantment and apathy among the electorate.

By mid-1992 a hybrid presidential-parliamentary system began to emerge as a compromise solution for Polish democracy. The four landmarks in this process were the following: (1) the 1990 presidential election; (2) the 1991 parliamentary election; (3) the subsequent "war at the top" over the powers and responsibilities of the president, parliament, and government; and (4) adoption by the Sejm and subsequent endorsement by President Wałęsa of the Little Constitution, outlining Poland's presidential-parliamentary system of government.

THE 1990 PRESIDENTIAL ELECTION

In December 1990, the Polish people elected Lech Wałęsa their first democratic president. He won a landslide victory in a runoff against Stanisław Tymiński, by receiving close to three-fourths of the vote. This constituted a powerful popular mandate for the president, and it placed Wałęsa in a strong position vis-à-vis the Sejm, which was still composed of deputies elected before the end of the communist era.

During the presidential campaign, Wałęsa ran against the parliament, repeatedly attacking the legitimacy of the "contract Roundtable" Sejm in which the communists and their fellow travelers retained a 60 percent majority. The challenge to Lech Wałęsa by Stanisław Tymiński, an emigré businessman who attracted more votes than Prime Minister Tadeusz Mazowiecki (the third major presidential candidate), served as a warning about the degree of popular discontent throughout the country. It also demonstrated that the electorate remained quite susceptible to manipulation through populist appeals. During the final days of the campaign in December

1990, Wałęsa charged that Tymiński's candidacy represented a counterattack by the ousted communist *nomenklatura* and pointed out that his opponent's staff included a number of former secret police officers.[2]

At the time, there was considerable concern among the opposition to Wałęsa, centered around the Democratic Union of Mazowiecki, that the new president might attempt to exploit his popular mandate to dominate the country's political scene. This allegedly would be done by forming a "presidential party," built around the Center Alliance, which had strongly supported his candidacy. The opposition charged that Wałęsa was interested in setting up an "imperial presidency," with the objective of undercutting the Sejm's oversight powers vis-à-vis the executive. These concerns decreased significantly after the inauguration, when Wałęsa both reaffirmed his commitment to the market economic program of the Mazowiecki government and distanced himself from leaders of the Center Alliance.[3]

Wałęsa asked Jan Olszewski, a lawyer close to Solidarity, to become prime minister. Two weeks later, Olszewski withdrew his candidacy, alleging "significant differences of opinion between the president-elect and himself on the composition of the government."[4] Early on, Olszewski became opposed to the continued presence in the cabinet of Leszek Balcerowicz, former finance minister and author of the IMF-endorsed economic reform program. Wałęsa's next choice was Jan Krzysztof Bielecki, a young businessman strongly committed to continuing the program of currency stabilization and market liberalization. This signaled the president's willingness to continue the Balcerowicz economic reform program, notwithstanding his past criticism of the Mazowiecki government's economic performance. Still, the protracted negotiations which preceded Bielecki's appointment represented a harbinger of an increasingly confrontational relationship between president and parliament.

Poland now had its first chief of state since World War II with a popular mandate to govern, while the Sejm still lacked such legitimacy. The new presidential assertiveness became apparent when President Wałęsa called for creation of a political council attached to his office. It would function as a consultative body to ensure continuation of the government's reform program.[5] The Sejm leadership expressed fears that the new council would become Wałęsa's shadow cabinet and would encroach upon executive authority of the prime minister. The issue did not become an immediate point of contention, in part because of the good working relationship between Wałęsa and Bielecki. The question of powers and responsibilities of the Sejm, the prime minister, and the president had come to the fore of Polish domestic politics already in December 1990, however.

The foregoing suggested that a new parliamentary election to give the Sejm a popular mandate was imperative. Sejm speaker Mikołaj Kozakiewicz, in February 1991, called for a speedy dissolution of the legislature and elections within three months. This position was backed by the parliamentary constitutional commission chairman, Bronisław Geremek. He argued that a fully legitimate parliament would represent a necessary precondition for constitutional reform. The same opinion was expressed by Wałęsa's twelve-member advisory committee, which recommended 26 May as the day for the new election. Wałęsa submitted a draft electoral law to the Sejm, naming the above date.

The argument over timing of the election became joined when Mazowiecki, chairman of the Democratic Union, came out against the president's proposal. He accused the Bielecki government (and indirectly Wałęsa himself) of trying to manipulate the political process through local Solidarity and Citizens' Committee organizations. Arguing that postponement of the election was necessary to give Poland's nascent parties time to organize, Mazowiecki called for the election to be held in the fall. He also charged that the government was purging the state administration of "people not associated with the present ruling camp." The election date issue was resolved on 9 March 1991 when the Sejm voted 314 to 18, with 40 abstentions, to continue working through the summer and to hold the election in October.

Wałęsa's defeat intensified the confrontation between president and parliament. It also meant that, in effect, key policy decisions would have to be postponed until Poland had a new democratically elected parliament in place. Most of all, this would result in more delay on the urgent issue of the new constitution to replace the 1952 basic law of the former communist regime.

On the positive side, the confrontation reaffirmed a commitment to democracy by both president and Sejm, regardless of their differing visions as to how democracy should actually work. Despite charges and counter-charges over the timing and procedures of the election, President Wałęsa accepted the Sejm vote, vowing that he would not "break the laws" and would not attempt to dissolve the parliament, as had been suggested by one of his aides from the Center Alliance.[6]

THE 1991 PARLIAMENTARY ELECTION

The national election of October 1991 came late in the cycle of Poland's transition to democracy. Paradoxically, the country, whose 1989 revolutionary Roundtable agreement between Solidarity and the communists had set in motion the democratic transformation throughout East-Central Europe, postponed the business of electing a truly representative legislature until almost two years after launching the January 1990 radical economic reform program and ten months after the December 1990 presidential elections. The campaign for a new parliament would demonstrate how divided the original Solidarity movement and the electorate had become during that short period.

On the eve of the Sejm election, Poland had more than 100 registered political parties.[7] In addition to the more established groups, they included such bizarre organizations as the Owners of Video Cassette Recorders "V," the Polish Erotic Party, and the Polish Friends of Beer. Some of these organizations would have an impact on the nation's political scene; for example, the last movement listed above managed to obtain 16 seats in the new parliament.

The new electoral law itself had proven a bone of contention. The proposal had been vetoed twice by President Wałęsa before the final version was agreed upon, after several protracted debates in both Sejm and Senate.[8] The voter turnout on 27 October was disappointingly low, estimated at about two-fifths of the 27.6 million Polish electorate. Voters chose from among some 7,000 candidates for the 460 seats in the Sejm and 612 candidates for the 100 Senate seats. No party received more than 13 percent of the Sejm vote. Moreover, the fact that almost two-thirds of the Polish electorate did not vote raised a disturbing question about the strength of popular support for any government put together by the new parliament.

Final election results were published on 31 October by the State Electoral Committee. The report set the voter turnout at 43.2 percent and announced that 29 of the 69 political groups contesting the elections won seats in parliament. The scope of fragmentation was best symbolized by the fact that 11 of the 29 victorious political parties won only one seat each. See Table 2 in Chapter 1. From among the 200 deputies who ran for reelection, the voters returned only 115 to the Sejm.[9]

The Democratic Left Alliance (former communists) carried 11 of Poland's 37 electoral districts; the Democratic Union only ten; the peasant parties jointly won nine; the Catholic Electoral Action and the Center Alliance, two districts each; the Confederation for an Independent Poland, the Liberal-Democratic Congress, and the German Minority Party had one district each. The two biggest winners, the Democratic Union (UD) and the Democratic Left Alliance (SLD), represented clearly different constituencies. Most electoral support for Mazowiecki's UD was concentrated in large cities throughout central and southern Poland; the SLD remained strongest in northern and northwestern regions, in formerly German areas settled after World War II by Poles from eastern territories annexed by the USSR.[10]

The 100 Senate seats were divided up as follows: Democratic Union (21), Solidarity (11), Center Alliance and Catholic Electoral Action (9 each), the Polish Peasant Party (8), Rural Solidarity (7), Liberal-Democratic Congress (6), and the Democratic Left Alliance or former communists (4).

If the Poles looked to their first free and democratic parliamentary election since World War II as a means to accelerate reforms and to end weak government, they were bound to be disappointed. The single most important result of the October 1991 election involved fragmentation of the Sejm. With 29 political parties represented, not even one had the prospects of building a strong majority government. Furthermore, splintering of parliament reflected a growing ideological division and polarization of the Polish electorate, making passage of an entirely new constitution (including a bill of rights) a truly formidable task.[11]

WAR AT THE TOP

The period between October 1991 and July 1992 became characterized by intense confrontation among Wałęsa, the Sejm, and the prime minister over competing claims to executive and legislative authority. Results included constitutional paralysis, a slowdown of the economic reform program, and a growing perception abroad that Poland was moving toward political instability to a degree that endangered its prospects for continued foreign investment. Described by the media as the "war at the top," constitutional paralysis was evidenced by collapse of two consecutive governments, led by Jan Olszewski and Waldemar Pawlak. The deadlock appeared to have been finally broken by a majority coalition government under Prime Minister Hanna Suchocka. This was followed on 1 August 1992 by Sejm adoption of the Little Constitution which, upon Wałęsa's approval in late November, superseded the 1952 basic law. In the process, the outline of a compromise on the formula for Polish democracy that would combine elements of presidential and parliamentary systems began to emerge.

OLSZEWSKI'S GOVERNMENT AND PROGRAM

The process of selecting a new cabinet after the 1991 parliamentary election became symbolic of the growing legislative paralysis and the conflict between president and Sejm over their respective prerogatives. Wałęsa's initial decision to give the Democratic Union the option of naming three candidates for prime minister (because that party had won the most seats in parliament), and his selection on 8 November of Bronisław Geremek from the Democratic Union as his candidate to form the new cabinet, were opposed by the center-right parties. The Center Alliance put forward the candidacy of Jan Olszewski. Wałęsa's refusal to accept this proposal set the stage for a stalemate between president and prime minister which would plague Polish politics for months to come.

The impasse over the selection of a new government continued through 25 November 1991 when the resignation of Prime Minister Jan Krzysztof Bielecki (despite President Wałęsa's request that he remain) forced the issue. With the presidential call for constitutional reform to break the impasse and strengthen the executive unheeded, the center-right coalition mustered sufficient support in parliament for the appointment of Olszewski. On 5 December, President Wałęsa yielded and formally nominated the man as prime minister, in order to "respect the principles of democracy." Even while doing so, he described the new government as inappropriate for the country's needs. President Wałęsa's concerns centered on Olszewski's criticism of Poland's economic austerity program, as well as his promise of a "breakthrough" in economic policy—presumably through repudiation of the Balcerowicz plan.

The new government was confirmed on the following day, with 250 votes in favor, 47 against, and 107 abstentions. The cabinet originally had been based on a coalition of the five center-right parties: Confederation for an Independent Poland, Center Alliance, Liberal-Democratic Congress, Peasant Alliance, and Christian National Union. However, this coalition proved tenuous from the start, with the Liberal-Democratic Congress walking out a week after the government's confirmation on the grounds that the "five" could not agree on a coherent economic program or the budget.[12] Also, the Confederation for an Independent Poland—an original sponsor of Olszewski—found itself excluded from the government when its composition was presented to the president.

Wałęsa's continued disapproval of the new cabinet led to Olszewski's resignation on 17 December and his charge that the president was trying to prevent his government from taking office. Further negotiations, including Olszewski's agreement to retain Krzysztof Skubiszewski as foreign minister (Skubiszewski accepted the offer after consulting with President Wałęsa) as well as several expressions of support for Olszewski by the chairman of the Polish Peasant Party (PSL), Waldemar Pawlak, brought about another effort to form a government. On 21 December, almost two months after the parliamentary election, Olszewski finally presented his cabinet and its program to the Sejm. In his speech, Olszewski attacked Bielecki's economic policies as based on a flawed theory of "building a healthy economy on the ruins of state industry." The government was finally approved two days later by a margin of 235 votes in favor and 60 votes against, with 139 abstentions.

In sharp contrast to Bielecki's tenure as prime minister, from the start Wałęsa and Olszewski failed to develop a working formula for collaboration. Considering that the 1952 constitution did not provide any guidance for the process, nor did it reflect the new political reality in the country, a working relationship between president and prime minister was the *sine qua non* for effective government. As personal animosity between Olszewski and Wałęsa grew, the lack of a precise constitutional division of power proved debilitating.

Political deadlock at the top was further compounded by the fact that the Olszewski cabinet consisted in large part of relatively unknown nonparty experts; only eight representatives of Olszewski's original center-right coalition remained as well as four previous members of the Bielecki government. The eclectic composition of the cabinet often led to erratic policies, especially on the question of economic reform. For instance, shortly after taking office, Olszewski reversed himself on an earlier pledge to bring about a "breakthrough" in economic policy, refused to increase government spending, and moved instead toward a dramatic reorganization of the ministerial bureaucracy. The theme that would set Olszewski's administration apart from his predecessors was his call for the "settling of accounts" with the past and for the "beginning of the end of communism in Poland." The government's policy-making process became, to a large extent, dominated by personnel decisions.

Olszewski's move to "decommunize" the country's politics increased the division between former Solidarity activists and politicians tainted by their past association with the communists. The prime minister's strong and unequivocal opposition to continued participation of ex-communists in the country's administration and in the military forced the Polish population to confront its most recent past to a much greater degree than had been the case during the Mazowiecki and Bielecki governments. Olszewski's criticism of Mazowiecki's decision to defer the issue became especially effective once the Russian and Polish press published accounts detailing the financial assistance channeled after 1989 by Moscow to the communists in Warsaw.[13]

Other reports on past collaboration of various politicians, as well as release of police files kept by the communists on the opposition (including allegations about Wałęsa himself), polarized the parties and made it increasingly difficult for Olszewski to retain a base of support in the Sejm.

In February 1992, the prime minister presented his government's economic program for that calendar year, which called for financial help to state enterprises, increasing money supply, boosting investment, reducing taxes and interest rates, and guaranteeing prices for agricultural products. The program was widely criticized by the opposition in parliament as inflationary (Finance Minister Karol Lutkowski resigned his post in protest, warning that the proposed policies would wreck the economy). The plan also seemed to have confirmed President Wałęsa's original fears that Olszewski would abandon the economic austerity program of the Mazowiecki and Bielecki governments that had commenced on 1 January 1990. The prime minister's request for special powers to allow him to govern by decree while he attempted to stabilize the economy (a sentiment echoed by his new finance minister, Andrzej Olechowski), reopened once more the constitutional issue of division between legislative and executive authority and brought up the urgent need for constitutional reform.

Olszewski's position became considerably weakened when the Sejm rejected his economic program in a vote on 5 March. The base of support for his coalition had eroded beyond repair. If his government were to retain even a modicum of effectiveness, the only solution for the prime minister was to seek a new coalition arrangement. Olszewski's efforts to broaden his coalition would continue through the end of April, by which time even he would recognize that the government had failed.

PRESIDENT VS. PRIME MINISTER: THE "PARYS AFFAIR"

Attempts at cooperation between Wałęsa and Olszewski remained tenuous at best. The relationship was not helped by the president's occasional hints that he stood ready to take over the premiership if necessary. Wałęsa also openly expressed preference for the French constitutional model, whereby the president has substantial executive powers as well as the right to appoint and dismiss the cabinet.

Early signs of an impending all-out confrontation between the two men came in January 1992 concerning the question of overall supervision over the armed forces. The new civilian defense minister, Jan Parys, forced the issue by pensioning off his predecessor (Rear Admiral Piotr Kołodziejczyk). The forced retirement of an officer whom Wałęsa had proposed at a June 1991 session of the National Security Council for the position of armed forces inspector general, the highest position envisioned in the proposed military reform program, was reportedly perceived by the president as a personal attack against his authority as commander in chief. The conflict escalated on 27 February when Olszewski appointed a 29-year-old journalist,

Radosław Sikorski, as deputy defense minister, without seeking Wałęsa's advice. At issue was the question whether the president or the government had the ultimate authority to control the armed forces, including key personnel decisions. The confrontation quickly escalated to symbolize the extent of presidential prerogative versus powers of the government.

The dispute occurred against the background of a concerted effort by Olszewski to purge the senior military establishment of officers compromised by their past close collaboration with the communist regime, in line with his overall objective to "decommunize Polish politics."[14] The purge was announced by Deputy Defense Minister Romuald Szermietiew in a speech at Szczecin to officers of the Pomeranian Military District. In another move, expressive of the government's determination to assert its authority over military matters, Defense Minister Jan Parys rejected the plan presented on 7 February (with Wałęsa's approval) to the National Security Council meeting. It proposed to reduce the armed forces by an additional 50,000 men. The confrontation between president and prime minister reached its denouement on 6 April 1992, when Defense Minister Parys charged in a speech to the General Staff that the army was being used by "some politicians" to bring down democracy in Poland. Two days later in a newspaper interview, Parys implied that Chief of Staff Mieczysław Wachowski was one of the key conspirators and that General Wachowski had acted on President Wałęsa's orders.[15] Parys alleged that high-ranking army officers had been approached by the president's advisors with a promise of promotions if they joined the conspiracy. Wałęsa denied the allegations and countercharged that, as the commander in chief of the armed forces, it was natural for him to have frequent contact with the military.

Parys was also attacked in parliament, where leaders of the opposition parties blamed the government for spreading disinformation about the military being involved in politics. The Democratic Union of Mazowiecki was particularly vocal in its criticism of statements by Parys. Amidst the gathering political storm, Olszewski was compelled to set up a special commission to investigate his minister's comments. The uproar caused by the "Parys affair" in parliament and the media forced Olszewski to place his defense minister on leave of absence.

At the same time, Olszewski raised the stakes in the confrontation by remarking to the press that the "Parys affair" reflected "a struggle among the president, the government, and the parliament for leadership of the Polish army." Subsequent newspaper reports alleging that the National Security Bureau was working in secret on martial law plans further fueled the crisis. A report in the newspaper *Nowy świat* on 9 April 1992 implied that such plans were being drafted without proper notification of the government or parliament. These allegations prompted an official denial by Jerzy Milewski, director of the National Security Bureau.

None of the previous confrontations between Wałęsa and Olszewski had cost the latter politically as much as did the "Parys affair." Determined to remove Olszewski, President Wałęsa addressed parliament on 8 May and called for creation of a strong presidency based on the French system as a necessary step to overcome the paralysis of government. Reportedly, the day after that speech, Olszewski met with Sejm speaker Wiesław Chrzanowski to discuss his government's resignation. Nine days later, Defense Minister Parys officially resigned after the parliamentary commission appointed to investigate his charges of conspiracy in the army had declared them to be unfounded and recommended his dismissal.

The remnants of Olszewski's power base in the Sejm began to crumble. Leaders of various political parties, ranging from the opposition Democratic Union to his own Center Alliance, called for the government to resign. On 26 May, Wałęsa submitted a letter to the speaker of the Sejm in which he formally withdrew his support for Olszewski and asked parliament to replace him. Three days later, 65 deputies from the so-called little coalition of the Democratic Union, the Liberal-Democratic Congress, and the Polish Economic Program submitted a motion calling for a vote of no-confidence in the government. The last act of the drama involved release of police files that implicated a number of prominent politicians as former communist collaborators, possibly in an attempt to raise questions about President Wałęsa's own fitness to remain in office.

THE "COALITION OF SEVEN"

After less than six months in office, the Olszewski government was dismissed on 5 June 1992, when parliament also accepted President Wałęsa's nomination of Waldemar Pawlak from the Polish Peasant Party (PSL) as prime minister. The latter pledged to end the strife between government and presidency that had bedeviled the previous administration. However, his efforts to build a broad coalition in cooperation with the Democratic Union, the Liberal-Democratic Congress, the Polish Economic Program, and the Confederation for an Independent Poland failed, in part because the last party withdrew from the talks citing irreconcilable differences over the budget. President Wałęsa's attempts to assist Pawlak's coalition by turning to the Christian National Union (ZChN) also failed, because ZChN refused to participate in a government headed by the PSL chairman. Unable to form a working coalition, Pawlak resigned on 2 July after a month of fruitless efforts. Wałęsa's remaining alternatives were either to approach the Democratic Union of Mazowiecki or to push for dissolution of the Sejm and a new parliamentary election.

In a speech on 3 July, President Wałęsa warned that he might resort to extraordinary measures (possibly even dissolving parliament), unless a working coalition government were presented to him within the next few days. The tripartite "little coalition" (UD, KLD, PPG) and five Christian-Democratic and peasant parties responded two days later by presenting the candidacy of Hanna Suchocka, a lawyer and a Democratic Union deputy to the Sejm from Poznań, as prime minister-designate to form a new government.

The eight parties in this majority coalition represented the entire spectrum of the Solidarity movement. The agreement gave 11 portfolios, including foreign affairs, privatization, finance, and defense, to the "little coalition" (Democratic Union, Liberal-Democratic Congress, and Polish Economic Program) which jointly holds 112 Sejm seats. The remaining "group of five" parties, with 115 deputies, received 15 portfolios, which included two deputy premierships. The Center Alliance, one of the original "five," walked out at the last moment in protest, thus reducing Suchocka's majority coalition to seven parties.

The new prime minister proved extraordinarily adept in forging consensus on the question of appointments and rapidly completed her cabinet list. Within one day, she announced that the ministers-designate had promised to leave ideological battles to the parliament. In an interview with the newspaper *Gazeta wyborcza*, Suchocka pledged to seek a middle ground in her dealings with President Wałęsa.

The new cabinet included members of the previous Solidarity governments, such as Jan Krzysztof Bielecki (EC integration), Jacek Kuroń (labor), Janusz Lewandowski (privatization), Jerzy Osiatyński (finance), Janusz Onyszkiewicz (defense), Krzysztof Skubiszewski (foreign affairs), and Gabriel Jankowski (agriculture). The liberal "little coalition" won the key economic and political posts it had demanded, while justice, education, and culture were given to the right-wing Christian National Union.

In addition to these veteran ministerial appointments, Suchocka brought in deputy ministers with experience from the Mazowiecki and Bielecki governments. Her choice of advisors on the economy reflected a commitment to reaffirm the austerity market economic program, as symbolized by the appointment of Karol Lutkowski (an advisor to Leszek Balcerowicz in the Mazowiecki government and briefly the finance minister in Olszewski's cabinet until his resignation in protest over Olszewski's economic program).[16]

Before endorsing Suchocka's cabinet, President Wałęsa demanded a written statement from all coalition parties accepting the new prime minister and her nominations. The government could count on 236 from a total of 460 votes in the Sejm. With Prime Minister Suchocka's confirmation, Poland acquired a majority government based on a democratically elected parliament.

THE LITTLE CONSTITUTION

The paralysis of government during the last two months of 1991 and first half of 1992 brought home the urgent need for a new constitution. According to a poll taken by the Center for the Study of Public Opinion (CSPO), some 65 percent of the respondents expressed dissatisfaction with the process of democratic transformation in Poland, while only 27 percent were pleased with the changes.[17] The high initial social cost of economic reform, as well as increased popular expectations after the collapse of communism, contributed to a growing sense of popular alienation from politics. As one critic charged, the two years of the postcommunist experiment had "failed to develop national goals" and in the process "demoralized both society and [political] elites."[18]

The growing disenchantment of the electorate was accompanied by general confusion over the division of governmental authority in the country. One month after the election, another CSPO poll revealed a popular perception of chaos in the country's administration. When asked who in their view was in charge of Poland, the following responses were given by percentage: President Lech Wałęsa (24), the government (15), the Catholic Church (11), the Sejm (6). Thirteen percent of the respondents stated that they did not know who was in charge, and 9 percent thought that nobody was really in control.[19]

Shortly after the parliamentary election, the Sejm made an effort to bring about constitutional reform. It set up an extraordinary commission to recommend revisions to the 1952 constitution. For his part, President Wałęsa submitted to the Sejm his draft proposal for constitutional changes, the so-called Little Constitution, which called for strengthening the presidency and the government. This proposal would have given the government special legislative prerogatives; specifically, the authority to issue decrees with the force of law. At the same time, it would have created a strong presidency modeled after the French system.

President Wałęsa's plan collapsed when the extraordinary Sejm commission insisted that the vote of no-confidence in the government (which could be initiated by a minimum of 46 deputies) represented a necessary check to guard against abuse by the executive of these special legislative powers.

Toward the end of the year, the president sent a letter to the speaker of the parliament, Wiesław Chrzanowski, withdrawing his draft proposal for the Little Constitution.

In addition three other draft proposals were reviewed, having been submitted by the Sejm, the Senate, and University of Warsaw lawyers. The principal differences among them concerned authority to form and dismiss a government (President Wałęsa had insisted that this should be among his powers), procedures for a no-confidence vote in the Sejm, and the scope of special legislative prerogatives of the government.[20]

The proposal submitted by the Senate granted the president the right to form a government; the Sejm and University of Warsaw proposals left this authority in the hands of parliament (although the president would retain the right to designate the candidate for prime minister), while the Sejm proposal would give the president a two-week deadline for submitting his choice, after which the power to name a new prime minister would move to the Sejm. In order to guard against the abuse of the no-confidence vote provision, the Sejm proposal required a petition by 60 deputies before the motion could be brought to the floor; the Senate version required 46, whereas the university would require only 25 names.

Work on the Little Constitution continued in parliament under Mazowiecki's leadership, as the "war at the top" between Wałęsa and Olszewski dragged on. The change of government and growing realization among legislators that a democratic constitutional framework remained absolutely essential for Poland's future helped to craft a document acceptable to a Sejm majority. The formula finally adopted on 1 August 1992 by the required two-thirds majority of votes was subject to approval by the Senate and by the president.[21] Three and a half months later the new constitution was ratified by the Senate and, on 17 November 1992, signed into law by President Wałęsa.

The Little Constitution describes a hybrid presidential-parliamentary system, a compromise solution that accommodates the present political reality in Poland. It seeks a middle ground between the Sejm's insistence on overall supervision of the government and Wałęsa's demand for greater presidential powers, while also strengthening the government. It offers the best opportunity to date for a break in the constitutional deadlock and replacement of vitriolic arguments over the preceding three years with a compromise rooted in practical politics. The new document may in fact prove to be a breakthrough in Poland's postcommunist reconstruction, for it can function as the country's new basic law until the Large Constitution is adopted.

In a remarkable development during the debate over the Little Constitution, an amendment from the floor was introduced to declare that "the 22 July 1952

Constitution is abolished."[22] (A clause stating this is included in Article 78 of the new document.) Hence, rather than modifying the old constitution, the Little Constitution has replaced it, with only chapters on the judiciary and civil rights retained from the 1952 basic law. These are to be redefined in the future Large Constitution. The principal contribution of the new legislation lies in its clear division of power among parliament, president, and government.

THE PARLIAMENT[23]

In a concession to President Wałęsa, the Little Constitution dropped the previous description of the Sejm as supreme authority. Instead, Chapter 1 on "General Principles" identifies the legislature (Sejm and Senate), executive (president and Council of Ministers), and independent judiciary as the three branches of government.

Parliament has the power to dissolve itself after a two-thirds majority vote. It may also be dissolved by the president, if it fails over a three-month period to pass the budget or approve the government (Articles 4 and 21). At the same time, the president no longer has the authority to dissolve parliament even if the Sejm passes a law which (contrary to constitutional provisions) limits the chief of state's authority.

Legislation can be initiated by the Sejm, Senate, president, and Council of Ministers (Article 15). In a departure from previous practice, a special "fast track" legislative process has been established to accelerate parliamentary procedure, with the Sejm deciding which bills qualify for such review (Article 16). In an attempt to control government spending, all legislative amendments introduced in the Senate will be accompanied by a clear statement as to how they will be financed without increasing the budget (Article 17). Most importantly, the Sejm will empower the government to issue decrees with the force of law, except in the areas of constitutional change, presidential and parliamentary election laws, regional government, the budget, civil rights, and ratification of international treaties (Article 23). As in the case of parliamentary legislation, all such decrees must be signed by the head of state.

THE PRESIDENT

The Little Constitution reaffirms the election of a president through direct popular vote for a five-year term (Article 30). The president remains the head of state and the commander in chief of the armed forces (Articles 29 and 36).

As such, and upon consultation with the defense minister, he appoints the chief of the general staff, heads of the services, and commanders of military districts. Under previous practice, the defense minister nominated the chief of the general staff, while the president made the actual appointment. The old procedure was not mentioned in the 1952 constitution.

The president has the authority to introduce martial law for a period of up to three months, with one three-month extension, provided it has been authorized by the Sejm (Article 38). However parliament may not be dissolved while martial law is in effect, nor can the constitution be amended during that time.

The Little Constitution reaffirms the president's leading role on foreign policy and national security affairs (Articles 33 and 35). This particular prerogative of the presidency became a source of contention in 1992 between Wałęsa and Prime Minister Olszewski during the "Parys affair." In effect, reaffirmation of presidential control over foreign policy and national security is an explicit victory for the president.

The basic law places a new constraint on presidential powers by requiring the prime minister or another minister's countersignature under the president's decisions. Exceptions include dissolution of parliament, calling a national election, submitting new legislation, presidential legislative veto, nominating a prime minister, calling a meeting of the Council of Ministers, initiating a referendum (provided the Senate approves), judicial appointments, nominating the president of the Polish National Bank, and calling for an investigation by the Constitutional Tribunal (Articles 47 and 48). The president can be impeached for violating the constitution or for other crimes by a two-thirds majority in both houses of parliament, after which he will be tried by the Constitutional Tribunal (Article 51).

THE GOVERNMENT

The Little Constitution gives the president the right to appoint the prime minister and, upon his or her recommendation, the cabinet (Article 58). This is a significant change from past practice, whereby the government was approved by parliament after nomination by the president. However, under these new rules, the government appointed by the president must present its program to the Sejm within 14 days and subsequently win an absolute majority vote. If the government fails to win such a vote of confidence, the Sejm has the right within 21 days to appoint a new government, which then again must win an absolute majority of votes (Article 59). Should this attempt to form a government fail, it is the president's turn to appoint a government, which now would have to win only a simple majority of votes in the Sejm (Article 60). If this fails, the Sejm has 21 more days to appoint yet another government which also need only win a simple parliamentary majority for approval. If these four attempts by president and parliament to appoint a government all fail, the president has a choice: either dissolve parliament or, within 14 days, appoint a government which then must win a vote of confidence within six months. Should that also fail, the president must dissolve parliament and call a new election (Article 63).

Another limitation on presidential powers (and, conversely, an increase in the prime minister's authority) introduced by the Little Constitution is a clause which requires the premier to win the president's approval only for appointments of internal affairs, national defense, and foreign ministers, regardless of the manner in which the government is being formed. Previously, the prime minister-designate had to receive presidential approval for all appointments to his cabinet. The government may be dismissed by the Sejm which then can form a new cabinet. If that cabinet fails to win a vote of confidence, it is up to the president to appoint a replacement (Article 65). Under the new constitution, the president may no longer ask for the government's dismissal as was the case under the old system. However, the president may change individual ministers in the cabinet, provided the prime minister requests the change (Article 69).

QUO VADIS POLISH DEMOCRACY?

While the Little Constitution compromise has not dramatically changed the distribution of political power in postcommunist Poland, it nevertheless clarified and institutionalized the existing presidential-parliamentary system of government. In broad strokes, it reaffirms the division of power between legislative and executive branches of government while recognizing the special role of the presidency that had become apparent after the 1991 parliamentary election.[24] In effect, it represents an attempt at a mediated compromise between Lech Wałęsa's desire to build a system centered on the president and the Sejm's insistence on primacy of the legislature. The only clear winner seems to be the government, which will have executive authority strengthened. Its right to issue decrees with the force of law should go a long way toward accelerating economic reform in Poland, especially the stalled privatization of state property.

In the course of constitutional debate, the Sejm also moved to strengthen its legislative procedures. The new parliamentary rules of order limit the number of parliamentary caucuses by setting the minimum requirement of 15 rather than only three deputies required to form one. This change has reduced the number of parties in the Sejm which can decide on procedural questions from 18 to ten. In addition, the quorum needed for committee meetings was brought down from 50 to 33 percent. Delinquent committee members will be fined for unexcused absences and their names publicized. The new rules also forbid last-minute changes to the agenda and impose tighter limits on speeches, with the goal of accelerating parliamentary debate.[25]

The struggle over division of powers in postcommunist Poland may not yet be over. It appears that, from Wałęsa's point of view, the Little Constitution strengthens authority of the Sejm and the government at the expense of the presidency. According to Lech Falandysz, presidential spokesman on the issue, the only concession made by parliament was removal of the clause designating the Sejm as the supreme authority. In an interview, Falandysz argued that in practice the new constitution retains the supremacy of parliament. As proof of continued limitation on presidential authority, he pointed to the new requirement for countersignature on certain presidential decisions by the premier or a minister. Falandysz also expressed Lech Wałęsa's doubts whether "Sejmocracy" is indeed the best option for Poland.[26]

At the other end of the spectrum, staunch proponents for supremacy of parliament over the president and the government have objected that the Little Constitution preserves the lion's share of presidential powers. Jarosław Kaczyński, leader of the Center Alliance which voted against the new law, has continued to argue that the agreement would eventually lead to a dictatorial presidency or, if the government and the president find themselves at odds, to a perpetual deadlock within the executive. Still other critics of the law, including Leszek Moczulski from the Confederation for an Independent Poland, have opposed the new constitution on the grounds that it imposes excessive limits on the powers of the president.

It appears, on balance, that the Little Constitution is a realistic reflection of the existing distribution of political power in Poland. It also expresses a growing awareness in the Sejm that the country badly needs to strengthen the government if it is to continue on the path to democracy and reintegration with Europe. The Little Constitution is clearly a compromise, arguably the best one that current political conditions in Poland could produce. As such, it goes a long way toward dispelling the fears at the time of the October 1991 parliamentary elections that the country could become ungovernable.

The Little Constitution may also represent badly needed reassurance to the public that parliamentary democracy in Poland can work after all. The executive deadlock in the country following the 1991 Sejm election badly undermined public confidence in the system. According to a poll taken by the Center for the Study of Public Opinion, which compared the change in popular attitudes toward democracy between September 1991 and July 1992, a disturbing trend away from the popular acceptance of parliamentary democratic government has begun to emerge. In July 1992 more than 60 percent of respondents believed that Poland needed a "strong-handed government," while 72 percent thought that the government was unable to rule because it was prevented from doing so by the excessively fragmented Sejm.[27] Even considering the 2.8 percent margin of error, these numbers reflect the growing fatigue of the population with the protracted constitutional deadlock.

For now, the compromise over the Little Constitution is also an expression of willingness on the part of the Democratic Union, one of the key parties in parliament and the principal supporter of the Suchocka majority government, to accommodate some of Wałęsa's demands for greater presidential powers. The draft of the basic law finally adopted was prepared by the Democratic Union. According to Bronisław Geremek, leader of that party's parliamentary caucus, the goal of the compromise was to overcome governmental deadlock and to define clearly the powers and prerogatives of the three branches of government. Geremek expressed the emerging consensus in parliament that, while being far from perfect, the Little Constitution was "better than the pre-existing situation."[28] In light of the fact that an alternative to the new law is continued chaos, the Little Constitution may indeed become a watershed in Poland's transition to democracy by demonstrating for the first time since 1989 the willingness of all sides to compromise in the name of a common national interest.

NOTES

1. See "Struktury cywilne i wojskowe," *Życie Warszawy,* 16 April 1991; "Czym się bronić?" *Wokanda,* 12 May 1991.
2. Radio Free Europe/Radio Liberty (RFE/RL), *Daily Report,* 3 December 1990; henceforth, *Daily Report.*
3. Ewa Rosolak, "Sukces—to prezydent, porażki—to my," *Trybuna,* 16 November 1991.
4. Quoted in *Daily Report,* 19 December 1990.
5. Ibid., 3 January 1991.

6. Ibid., 14 March 1992.

7. *Informator o partiach politycznych w Polsce* (Warsaw: Polska Agencja Informacyjna, October 1991), pp. 1-2.

8. "Wybory 91: Scena po pierwszym starciu," *Życie Warszawy,* 20-21 July 1991.

9. "Ze starego do nowego Sejmu," *Rzeczpospolita,* 6 November 1991.

10. "Polska geografia polityczna," *Gazeta wyborcza,* 7 November 1991.

11. According to Bronisław Geremek, floor leader for the Democratic Union, ideological polarization on issues such as abortion virtually precluded a majority vote on key civil rights guarantees. Conversation with the author in Warsaw on 25 May 1992.

12. Małgorzata Subotić and Kazimierz Groblewski, "Liberałowie opuszczają 'piątkę,' " *Rzeczpospolita,* 12 December 1991.

13. Tomasz Rogulski, "Poparcie dla Jana Olszewskiego," *Rzeczpospolita,* 18 November 1991.

14. For an insight into the government's motivation, see the account of his tenure as deputy defense minister by Radek Sikorski, "My Hundred Days," *National Review* (20 July 1992), pp. 30-34.

15. Dariusz Fikus, "Incydent wojskowy," *Rzeczpospolita,* 9 April 1992.

16. Kazimierz Groblewski, "Wiceministrowie odchodzą i wracają," *Rzeczpospolita,* 20 August 1992.

17. "Polacy niezadowoleni z rozwoju demokracji," *Rzeczpospolita,* 19 December 1991.

18. "Polską rządzą królewienta (rozmowa z Jerzym Gedroyciem)," *Spotkania,* 19 October 1991.

19. "Polacy niezadowoleni z rozwoju demokracji," *Rzeczpospolita,* 19 December 1991.

20. Stanisław Podemska " 'Mała Konstytucja': koślawa szachownica," *Polityka,* 14 December 1991.

21. For the draft text of the Little Constitution, see *Rzeczpospolita,* 7 August 1992.

22. Janina Paradowska, "Święta nie było," *Polityka,* 8 August 1992.

23. The following discussion is based on the draft document in Note 21 above; Piotr Zaremba, "Równowaga władz," *Życie Warszawy,* 3 August 1992; and Louisa Vinton, "Poland's 'Little Constitution,' " RFE/RL *Research Report* 1, no. 35 (4 September 1992).

24. Senator Andrzej Celiński, interviewed by Ewa Szemplińska, "W stronę silnej prezydentury," *Życie Warszawy,* 8 November 1991.

25. Vinton, "Poland's 'Little Constitution' . . . ," p. 25.

26. Eliza Olczyk, "Równowaga czy dominacją?" *Rzeczpospolita,* 4 August 1992; Danuta Frey, "Prezydent nie może być dekoracją," ibid., 10 August 1992.

27. "Nużąca demokracja," *Gazeta wyborcza,* 11 August 1992.

28. Eliza Olczyk, "Coś za coś, czyli sztuka kompromisu," *Rzeczpospolita,* 10 August 1992.

4

Local Government Reform

James F. Hicks, Jr., and Bartłomiej Kamiński*

The dominant theme of the commentary on transition from communism to a market-based democracy emphasizes privatization, liberalization of prices, and establishing a multiparty political system. The task of dismantling communism tends to be conceptualized in terms of removing the state from economic and political realms: in order to emphasize it, a new word, "deetatization," has been coined. According to this approach, the key to a successful transition is the ejection of the state from the economic system through privatization of state assets and from the political realm by providing citizens with instruments to control its activities.

Although this conceptualization captures some aspects of the transition, it suffers from two major intertwined deficiencies. First, it fails to highlight the role of the state, both during the transition and in the final shape of the institutional design that is to emerge. The problem is not to "kick out" the state from the economy, but to reorganize it so as to make the state compatible with changing requirements of the transformation process. As one author noted in a different context, the problem is ". . . the quality, not the size of the state."[1] The challenge consists in finding the best mix between activities controlled by the state and the market. The major role of the state during the

* The writers are grateful to Daniel Davidson for useful suggestions. They also thank Mme. Halina Wasilewska-Trenker (secretary of state, Central Planning Office) for her comments on a draft of this paper. The views expressed here are the authors' own. They should not be attributed to the World Bank or any of its member countries.

transition is to supply new institutions that would create an environment enabling competition and development of private activities. There is no other actor that could perform this task.

Second, the dominant approach pays only lip service to changes needed at a microlevel. Drawing on the experience of postcommunist countries so far, one may observe that the easiest measures to implement have been liberalization of prices and establishing democratic institutions, including free elections, at a macrolevel. A much more difficult task, calling for considerable innovative thinking, is to provide an institutional basis for a viable market economy and consolidation of democracy. While one may argue that the state will respond to pressures triggered by restraints on its economic activity by reforming itself, this situation will unnecessarily increase the costs of transition and may produce political instabilities, which could otherwise be avoided. In fact, the contraction in aggregate economic activity throughout the postcommunist world, much greater than anticipated by most observers, and grim prospects for a quick recovery can be attributed to the neglect of microfoundations, both political and economic, of the transition.[2]

Governmental decentralization is crucial to addressing the political and economic foundations of transition. The key to a successful transformation lies in finding a good match between macroactivities and their microfoundations, both political and economic. While a number of authors have addressed the issue of incompatibility between Western-sponsored stabilization programs and the postcommunist economic institutional environment, little attention has been paid in both scholarly literature and transformation strategies of postcommunist governments to decentralization of governance. The preoccupation with "de-etatization" has pushed aside the problem of reforming general government. It is surprising, because both consolidation of democracy and economic prosperity critically hinge upon decentralization.

This chapter addresses the problem of local self-government in the postcommunist transition of Poland during the 1990-1991 period.[3] Our focus is on one aspect of the transition-cum-decentralization reform: devolution of power to subnational units of the central government in the context of dismantling communism.

DECENTRALIZATION AND DISMANTLING OF COMMUNISM

Decentralization, broadly conceived as the divestiture of central government responsibility to outside organizations (local governments, private enterprises, and quasi-governmental organizations), is crucial for efforts to dismantle the communist politicoeconomic order. Transition to a market-based democracy is a process of decentralization, encompassing all spheres of public activity. In the economy, it involves transfer of property rights to economic actors in order to create an environment enabling competition and enhancing efficiency. In the political sphere, it entails transfer of power to the people. It also creates an environment protecting individuals against the state as well as protecting the state from being captured by narrow-interest groups or by a dictator. Thus, decentralization performs in a postcommunist society a wide variety of functions going beyond assuring a match between local preferences and public services or improving the implementation of centrally designed policies.

Strong local governments may contribute to consolidating democracy and fostering economic development in postcommunist societies. By erecting a barrier between central government and citizens, decentralization provides a much needed cushion between central politics and developments directly affecting individuals. Political uncertainty at the top will not percolate down once the state's power is meaningfully decentralized and subjected to the rule of law. Otherwise, citizens will tend to blame central government for all shortcomings, which—as the history of communist rule clearly shows—is politically destabilizing. Local governments also offer opportunities for individuals to learn how to operate in a democratic environment, and they provide a springboard for future careers in national politics.

The strengthening of local governments, as a component of modernizing the public sector, is also important to economic prosperity. Developments throughout the world during the 1980s buried the notion that centralization is the key to industrialization. The collapse of communism in 1989 demonstrated the economic and political nonviability of institutional arrangements based on the rejection of markets and democracy. Centralization destroys the institutional diversity which is necessary to sustain public debate and legitimize decisions. It crushes incentives to elicit ingenuity and innovativeness from individuals, and deprives central authorities of information about outcomes of implemented policies. It leads to excessive employment in the central administration, as the government seeks to manage activities which are virtually impossible to control from the top. Last but not least, centralization makes difficult the provision of many services to local communities and raises their costs.

Decentralization also may yield less tangible gains. In postcommunist countries, local governments are instrumental to establish and sustain an environment supportive of private-sector development. This can be accomplished through privatization of local government-owned assets and providing—directly or in partnership with the private sector—investments, operation and maintenance of inputs to human capital (education, health, social assistance), physical infrastructure essential as intermediary inputs to directly productive activities, and a regulatory framework that promotes public health and safety, private-property rights (primarily land-based property), and private-sector productivity.

LEGACIES: CONTINUITIES AND DISCONTINUITIES

Poland has made impressive strides in establishing a market-based democracy. Impartial rules for all citizens have replaced negotiable rules characteristic of governance in Poland during the 1980s. Legal constraints on arbitrary action by authorities have been significantly strengthened. In a dramatic break with the communist past, citizens may now remove incompetent elected officials through the ballot. Property rights have been more clearly delineated, and economic powers somewhat decentralized. In brief, power has devolved considerably from a narrow group of people to a set of rules. This impressive progress was the result of developments preceding the collapse of communism and of actions taken by the first noncommunist government established after the communists' defeat during the limited free elections in June 1989.

On the eve of the collapse of communism, Poland was better prepared to move to a market-based democracy than most other communist-ruled countries. The disintegration of communism was much more advanced than elsewhere. In an ironic twist, the various political and economic reforms implemented to prevent the disintegration of communism, instead of prolonging its existence, created an environment conducive to the development of democracy and markets. The evolutionary potential of communism was exhausted throughout the 1980s, creating conditions for a radical departure from past arrangements, that is, for the emergence of discontinuities in earlier trends of the politicoeconomic evolution.

The departure point of Poland's transformation program was a crumbling communism, markedly different from the pure Stalinist version of the 1950s. While disintegration of communism went farthest in Poland among communist-ruled countries, it fell short of generating real democracy and a competitive economy. Political and economic reforms in the 1980s reached limits of what could be done without completely overhauling communism. They reached the point where they could improve neither economic efficiency nor governability without destroying the identity of communism. Market-oriented reforms could not work without markets, that is, price liberalization and competition. Political reforms had limited meaning when citizens were denied the right to choose their government. Yet, in retrospect, the reforms left a mixed legacy: on the one hand, by decentralizing some spheres, they created an institutional environment more conducive to establishing a viable market-democracy; on the other hand, they were deeply implicated in the devastation of Poland's economic developmental potential. They may have made political transformation easier than in other postcommunist countries, but they have proven to be costly in the economic sphere.

In the late 1980s, Poland's political and economic system was a caricature of both communism and a market-based democracy. Although economic powers had been significantly decentralized and SOEs (state-owned enterprises) enjoyed substantial autonomy, property rights were not clearly defined and SOEs were not exposed to competition and hard budget constraint. Although the party-state had unlimited formal powers, in fact these were greatly diluted. The state was significantly deconcentrated during the 1980s, with voivodships (districts) enjoying a substantial financial autonomy.[4] The central government's "weight," as proxied by the share of total state budget revenues in GDP, was not extravagant by Western standards (it was lower than in Great Britain under Margaret Thatcher) and the subnational level of government had significant own source revenues accounting for around one-third of total state revenues and between 13 and 15 percent of GDP during the 1980s.[5]

Voivodships had considerable independence vis-à-vis the central government: central government intervention was de facto circumscribed by information and political constraints. They were responsible for providing numerous public services such as health and welfare, transportation, and so on. Finally, at the level of local government (municipalities or, in Polish, *gminy*), there existed some protoforms of local government mainly responsible for garbage collection, maintenance of public housing, and other services. Although they had some autonomy, its extent was not clearly delineated or guaranteed. Deconcentration reforms in communist Poland amounted to transfer of authority within the same integrated administrative system, although they were accompanied by a de facto spontaneous devolution of some power. Lower levels remained responsible and subjugated to central government.

The existence of protolocal units under communism facilitated the local government reform implementation by the first noncommunist parliament. Before the collapse of communism, there began to emerge "alternative" local elites organized around Solidarity. Without them, it would have been virtually impossible to break the grip of the communist party over local affairs. These alternative elites organized an anticommunist opposition in the May 1990 free local government elections, and defeated those elites associated with the communist regime. In retrospect, local government, which obtained some independence in 1984, turned out to be a training ground for many local activists. Some of them, not associated with communist elites, were elected to new local self-governments. Their considerable experience in local politics often had a positive impact on the implementation of reforms.[6]

In the political realm some of the seeds of reform were sown well before the collapse of the communist regime. This was not so in the realm of financial relations within the general government. In fact, the legacy of communist rule in public finance amounted to an outright disaster. The system of public finance, devoid of any incentives to fiscal responsibility, remained purposefully murky under the administrative economic regime. In its pure Stalinist version, there was some semblance to the centrally imposed *Gulag*-style discipline. Money stayed passive, that is, it did not suffice to have budget allocations. Rather, the incentive became to gain favors of a monopolistic contractor. This situation persisted until 1989. Administrative reforms during the 1980s, although designed to restore central controls, eventually led to erosion of central government's power to dictate to regional and local authorities. As many analysts have noted, the traditional system was replaced by an unconstrained bargaining regime. It also spilled over to fiscal relations between central government and regional or local authorities.

The topsy-turvy public finance system and lax attitudes toward financial management, both inherited from the communist past, were among major obstacles that local government reformers had to overcome. The belief that everything is subject to negotiation and that obtaining access to resources depends only on bargaining power is difficult to eradicate, unless new rules are quickly introduced and fully enforced. Proliferation of various "extra-budgetary funds" and haggling over allocations produced people who at best might have learned how to negotiate, but they were ignorant of sound financial management.

Methods for distributing public services (including choice of technology, coverage, administrative practices, public finance instruments, and legal arrangements) were not compatible with the requirements of modern economy and democracy. Excessive involvement of the state in these services left many legacies that constrained newly established local self-governments. Inefficient and centralized enterprises, obscure legal status of state-owned properties, a distorted budget revenue structure based on SOEs, and enormous stocks of public housing are merely examples of problems that the local governments established in 1990 had to face. These legacies could not be eradicated at once, and thus the need for a transition.

Conditions immediately preceding the collapse of communism favored a rapid move to decentralize. The first "Solidarity" government acted quickly to establish local self-governments, through the Local Self-Government Act adopted by parliament on 22 March 1990. This legislation provided for transfer of responsibilities to relatively autonomous political units outside the direct control of central government, and it marked a break with earlier reforms. As a radical departure from the communist past, the Local Self-Government Act laid the legal foundation of a genuine devolution of power, accompanied by transfer of property rights from the central to the subnational government layer.

According to this law, *gminy* are an autonomous tier of government. It provides that local governments have legal status, with their autonomy protected by the courts; that local governments are responsible for "all public matters of local significance that are not reserved by law for other units"; that they are to be held accountable to their constituents through free elections (with provisions for recall); that local governments are autonomous for budget formulation and implementation, but the Ministry of Finance shall provide general subsidies (block grants) allocated on the basis of "objective criteria"; that local budget execution is to be audited by regional accounting offices; and, that *gminy* may form associations to provide services or for purposes of representation. Last but not least, the act called for a clear delineation of property rights—the so-called communalization of some state-owned assets.

The initial push toward decentralization, as embodied in the Local Self-Government Act, placed Polish subnational government on the right track to exploit benefits of decentralization. Responsibilities assigned to local governments coincided with provisions of the *European Charter of Local Self-Government* (Council of Europe, 1985). They included spatial organization, land use and environmental protection, local transport systems, water supply and sanitation, energy and heat, health services, social assistance, housing, kindergarten and primary education, and public order and fire protection, reflecting areas in which local governments as a rule tend to have comparative advantage in delivery, but not necessarily in financing (e.g., education, health).

Communalization, that is, transfer of property rights to local self-government, was a distinctive feature of transition from communism at the local level in Poland. In contrast to communist reforms, this was not a mere reshuffling of assets within the same "nonowner." The logic behind this move was similar to privatization in a sense that it complemented the devolution of power from central government. The decision whether assets transferred should be privatized, leased, contracted out, or managed by a public corporation was left to the discretion of the local government.

The subnational level of government under communism had often controlled various communal enterprises, either because of spontaneous or *de jure* actions. Communist local officials often benefited from revenues generated by "state-owned" assets, but legally they were not owners. By clarifying the legal base and making local self-governments directly accountable for managing assets previously under central government control, communalization marked a radical departure from the past.

The decision to transfer property rights within the general government contributed positively to the pace of transition in Poland. First, it changed the list of administrative priorities of the central government by compelling its agencies to take stock of state-owned property—quite an enormous task when most capital assets were state-owned and bookkeeping had been shoddy. Local self-governments were prime movers behind the "small privatization" drive in late 1990 and early 1991, a fact which is too often overlooked in analyses of Poland's transformation.[7]

Second, it accelerated privatization by making local governments responsible for managing property within their jurisdictions. Thanks to communalization, privatization could proceed much faster. Rapid privatization of retail trade and other local services represented a bright spot in the performance of local self-governments. It is worth noting that, in the public perception, aggressive privatization of local government assets was the major area where an initial "breakthrough" occurred.[8]

Third, communalization highlighted the issue of inter-*gmina* cooperation, indispensable to assure efficient management of activities previously controlled by voivodships, including public utilities, transport systems, and road-construction enterprises. Since most *gminy* were simply too small to assume control over many services previously supplied by a voivodship, it compelled them to cooperate and thereby contributed to strengthening of local self-government. The explosion of various functional associations of local government through 1991 testified to the increased weight of change from the bottom up. Although more time is needed for efficiency gains to materialize, the seeds of local entrepreneurship and accountability had been sown.

The push toward democratization and decentralization, provided by the Local Self-Government Act, was not supported fully, however, by the actions of the central government for implementation of the devolution policy as mandated by the law. During the first two years of the transformation-cum-stabilization program, decentralization of general government, understood as strengthening local self-government, lagged behind. As a result, benefits of decentralization were not fully tapped.

For potential macro- and microeconomic efficiency, as well as for the political gains of the public sector decentralization to be realized,[9] several general conditions should be met: first, devolution should be integrated with the transition program and the supply of institutions, norms, procedures, and the like, facilitating the operation of local governments; second, public goods that may be more efficiently provided at the local level should be identified and responsibilities assigned accordingly to local government; third, decentralization policy should clearly specify the rules concerning organizational and fiscal relations between various levels of general government; fourth, the legal arrangements should provide for accountability of local governments to their constituencies; and, finally, decentralization of general government should contribute to the consolidation of democracy. Analysis of the extent that reform measures implemented in Poland met those conditions would go beyond the scope of this chapter. We focus on three issues: the supply of institutions affecting the operation of local governments; accountability; and consolidation of democracy.

"INSTITUTIONAL" ENVIRONMENT OF LOCAL SELF-GOVERNMENTS

The decision to devolve power, as embodied in the 1990 Local Self-Government Act, created demand for assistance in setting up the new tier of general government as well as for laws and procedures facilitating the efficient transfer of responsibilities. It is the duty of the central government to provide a level playing field, administrative procedures, and other services that would enhance the capacity of local governments to operate wisely and effectively. Failures of devolution in many Third World countries can be attributable to the lack of a supporting institutional environment.[10]

International experience also suggests significant payoffs if a strong national actor is assigned a role of "principal agent" during the transition period, responsible for developing and implementing a decentralization strategy. The central government should establish a regulatory environment and design a financial system for expenditure and fiscal responsibilities, both at the central and subnational levels, that would support decentralization in providing public services effectively and efficiently. Thus, an interesting issue is how Poland fared in this respect.

At the initial stage for implementation of the Local Self-Government Act, the institutional setting of local governments, at both central and subnational levels, remained inadequate. It was weak and dominated by a central government administration that had limited interest in the decentralization of power. The institutional capacities of various agencies charged with local government reform were limited, and they lacked political clout. No single institutional actor capable of addressing the full range of issues (e.g., in such areas as education, health, transportation, public housing) regarding devolution of power to the subnational layer of general government had been established. In consequence, *gminy* fretted under the uncertain weight of central government.[11]

The institutions charged with local government reform at the national level were often deprived of authoritative information on current and proposed national policies, laws, regulations, and so forth. They obtained "inputs" indispensable to draft budgets past the dates set by legislation. They were deprived access to information about policies and performance of local governments. As a result, local governments did not obtain adequate technical assistance in developing approaches and programs to strengthen their capacity for dealing with increased responsibilities. They obtained little help on such issues as, for example, organizing bidding for sale of communal properties, undertaking competitive procurement and contracting, and drafting budgets. While it is impossible to assess quantitatively these losses, there is no doubt that the lack of a supporting institutional structure had a negative impact on local government activities.

The initial institutional weaknesses of local governments and uncertainties inherent in the implementation of the self-government reform were only marginally addressed in the Local Self-Government Act. It assigned supervisory functions over local government activities to the chairman of the Council of Ministers (prime minister) and, with regard to local finances, to the network of regional accounting offices.[12]

The act outlined in detail the duties and responsibilities of both *gminy* and voivodships with respect to Voivodship Assemblies of Local Self-Governments. The assembly of each voivodship brought together representatives of all *gminy* in its jurisdiction. The act also provided a legal framework for relationships between the subnational and central levels of government. Policy formulation and implementation at the national level was assigned to the local government reform office, operating from the Council of Ministers. At the regional and local levels this coordination was expected to be provided by Voivodship Assemblies of Local Governments and the Council of Ministers' local government reform office representatives in each of the 49 voivodships.[13] Local Self-Government Assemblies, representing local governments within a voivodship, were to be involved in management of relations between voivodship administration and local governments. The Voivodship Assemblies were not subordinated to the voivod (head of the voivodship). Rather, the voivodship merely represented the geographical boundary of each Voivodship Assembly.

Although voivodships depict the geographical boundary of each Voivodship Assembly, the latter with representatives of local government councils elected by council members from each *gmina* by secret ballot are legally independent of voivods. Voivodship Assemblies do not have regulatory powers, yet their scope of activity is significant. They provide a forum for discussing concerns of local governments and mediating conflicts between *gminy*. Each Voivodship Assembly has an Appeals Court empowered to decide upon matters related to local government responsibilities. Their notable function is to look after interests of local governments vis-à-vis the central government administration represented at a local level by the voivodship and its *rejon* offices and provide a check on voivods' interventions into *gmina* affairs. Voivodship Assemblies have a limited controlling function over voivods' activities to the extent that they are authorized by law to assess activities of "the civil service in the voivodship, including the passing of opinions on candidates for voivods" (Article 77.1.7 of the Local Self-Government Act). The latter are appointed by the prime minister. The law also stipulates that the voivod and the assembly meet at least twice a year.

In response to political expediencies, various actors surfaced in the local government setting whose existence had not been anticipated in the Local Self-Government Act, thus adding to legal confusion. These included the National Self-Government Assembly, composed of representatives from the 49 Voivodship Assemblies of Local Self-Government.

The National Local Self-Government Assembly emerged spontaneously as a nationwide lobbying organization of local governments. Because of its national scope, the commission representing the National Assembly became a major negotiating counterpart of the Finance Ministry. Various national laws regarding local self-government referred to consultations with a "Poland-wide representation of local self-governments." The National Assembly was not mentioned by its proper name, although its commission members were involved in drafting proposals on local financial arrangements.[14] Involvement of the National Assembly in central decision-making enhanced its standing vis-à-vis voivodship assemblies.[15]

The period following local elections also witnessed an emergence of organizations addressing various needs of local self-government. Associations of local governments operate at numerous levels and their major purpose is to provide fora to discuss issues common to some local governments (e.g., the Association of Local Governments of Small Towns) and to act as lobbying organizations. The Foundation for Local Democracy (partly funded by various Western public and private agencies) organized a network of training centers for local officials.[16] While these organizations have played an important role in implementing local reforms, they clearly could not fill all the major gaps in the institutional supply, which only the central government could have provided.

Judging from the number of actors involved in local government issues, it would seem that their interests were well represented at the central level. Although their pressures kept the issue of local government reform alive, they have not been successful in organizing strong institutional support. First and foremost, although all major political parties expressed support for local government reform, the reform movement was ineffectual and had no parliamentary lobby. As senator, Jerzy Regulski, a major architect of Poland's local government reform, bitterly observed: "Issues pertaining to local government are still marginal in our country."[17] Despite the prodevolution rhetoric, successive "postcommunist" governments were unwilling to devolve substantial power to *gminy*. Local government advocates, disillusioned with slow progress, formed a political party called the Congress of the Self-Governing Republic in May 1991 which, however, did not obtain sufficient electoral support to enter parliament. In consequence, the "voice" of prodevolution advocates remained marginal. Without central government commitment to significant devolution, little progress could be made in strengthening autonomous subnational governments.

Second, the Polish local government landscape lacked a strong national institution that would act as a "principal agent" responsible for the reform of general government. Experience in many Latin American countries shows that such an institution is especially important at initial stages of reassignment of responsibilities by level of government.

Third, institutional capacity and resources available to actors whose purpose was to implement local government reform measures were rather limited. All were understaffed and poorly equipped to deal with complex issues of transition to the "model" set in the Local Self-Government Act and other pertinent laws. Their capacity to evaluate actions focusing on local government was clearly inadequate to cope with the multiple demands of decentralization within the general government. This weak capacity explains to some extent why so little progress was made throughout 1991 in approval of local government legislation for 1992.[18]

Fourth, to make things worse, the allocation of administrative resources was not really conducive to promoting decentralization. The *primus inter pares* was the Finance Ministry, an actor with no apparent vested interest in enhancing local self-government responsibilities and autonomy. It not only had the power of the purse but was also entrusted with responsibilities for defining procedures related to intergovernmental fiscal transfers and setting the general framework of local policy. The Ministry of Finance, a dominant actor in terms of resources, had a department dealing with local government issues that remained devoid of professional and financial resources necessary to address adequately the broad range of issues related to reform. The national office for supporting local government reform (assigned to the Council of Ministers) was understaffed, its accountability diluted, and its future uncertain. The staff was too limited to provide any counterbalance to other government ministries, whose actions might bear on the situation of local government. It could passively react to other ministries' determinations, yet remained unable to aggressively address the broad range of decentralization issues (e.g., human resource development, infrastructure).

Designers of the reform were aware of obstacles that local governments would face at the beginning of their existence. They did not anticipate, however, the power struggle that would surface ". . . between a central level accustomed to full control (strongly supported by existing legislation and extensive bureaucracy) and newly elected local government officials equipped with only fragile and incomplete legislation."[19] They underestimated the strength of centralizing tendencies, rooted in the existing structures of governance.

As a consequence, Poland may have missed a unique opportunity to design a local government system that would be relatively free from the usually devastating impact of partisan politics on intergovernmental affairs. The (a) preoccupation with change from a supply-constrained to a demand-constrained economy, (b) implementation of the stabilization program, and (c) emergence of political divisions within the Solidarity ruling elite, followed by a deep fragmentation of the Polish political party system, did not create an environment favorable to focusing on local government. Experience from countries undertaking radical institutional reforms suggests the high importance of political leadership that would provide reformers with a shield against current partisan political pressures. The short period of euphoria and institutional vacuum that followed dissolution of the communist regime offered such an opportunity of "technocratic insulation." This opportunity could not be fully exploited for setting the institutional environment that would enable society to capitalize on benefits inherent in devolution. Once central democratic institutions were established, the process of local government reform became the captive of "normal" democratic politics and was largely ignored by the central government.

REFORM AND CONSOLIDATION OF DEMOCRACY

The criterion of democratic consolidation calls for creating an institutional environment, enabling genuine participation of citizens in making decisions relevant to community development. This should also include participation in the formation of local autonomy. At the initial stage of radical transformation, the "rules of the game" not only frequently change but they must be implemented from above. Only the central government can provide a level playing field. Poland was no exception: communities had "no say in the formation of this partial autonomy for local governments since most of the crucial rules that regulate their functioning were centrally legislated."[20] Although this represented a source of frustration to many local activists, the situation could not be avoided.

Various public opinion polls suggest that local government reform has fallen short of creating an environment enabling participation of inhabitants in decisions directly affecting their everyday lives. According to a national public opinion poll conducted in the spring of 1992, some 84.5 percent of respondents gave a negative answer to a question concerning their influence on community development. The local officials-inhabitants interface also leaves much to be desired, as council members rarely meet with their constituents: according to the same survey, around 70 percent of respondents never saw their local council members.[21] This alleged "fiasco of territorial self-government" has been blamed on unique circumstances surrounding the 1990 local elections and subsequent political fragmentation. These local elections were rather a plebiscite on "communists vs. noncommunists" (albeit to a lesser extent than the earlier national quasi-democratic elections in June 1989), and candidates' professionalism was of secondary importance. The perception of a lack of participatory democracy stems from too high expectations triggered by local election campaigns, ignorance of democratic procedures among the general public, and, to a large extent, the central government's failure to supply institutions, legal procedures, training, and so forth, supporting the activities of local government in Poland.[22]

Yet, these public opinion polls do not seem to render full justice to local self-government reform. The crux of the matter is that it will take time before some negative legacies of communism disappear. As an astute observer of postcommunist societies noted: "the demise of the communist regimes did not mean the demise of their communist political cultures—all the habits, mental attitudes, symbols, and values that had permeated social life for decades."[23] The absence of discipline, tolerance, and trust has clearly frustrated efforts to establish local democracy, yet its establishment provides the best venue to eradicate legacies of communist political culture and create a vibrant civil society.

ACCOUNTABILITY AND AUTONOMY OF LOCAL GOVERNMENTS

The assignment of responsibility by level of government should be clear, and both local communities and their elected officials should have a say in the formation of crucial rules regulating the functioning of local governments. The Local Self-Government Act and other relevant laws assigned to the subnational level a wide array of responsibilities which were to be transferred gradually over time. It also spelled out procedures to make elected officials liable for their actions. Procedures included both democratic elections and the rules of impeachment for individual council members as well as entire local councils.[24]

The concept of accountability, as discussed in the literature, has many shades: in its narrow interpretation, it simply states that elected bodies should be held responsible by their constituents for actions through free elections, transparent budgets, audits, and so on. This interpretation brings to the fore three questions: To be accountable for what? Can they be accountable for developments beyond their control? And to whom? Although various legislative acts seek to answer these questions, accountability implies responsibility for economic efficiency in fulfilling assigned responsibilities which can hardly be captured by law. Such an assessment must take into account the degree to which existing arrangements allow those held accountable to control factors crucial to fulfilling their responsibilities. Stated differently, the judgment requires checking for a consistency between financial resources available and their expenditure responsibilities and, on the other hand, between responsibilities assigned and autonomy in their implementation.

The potential for local governments to be held accountable for economic efficiency is high, while for equity and stabilization policies it is quite limited.[25] Polish local self-governments are not exceptions to this general rule. One of the economic arguments in support of decentralization for the public sector is that local governments may ration demand and produce many services more efficiently. However, for this potential to be realized, local governments must have the technical capacity to design service systems, generate and evaluate alternatives, and implement in a cost-effective manner investment and maintenance programs. The capacity of local government efficiently to provide services depends on the size of its jurisdiction and population.

In Poland many *gminy* are too small to provide efficiently the public services that are required of them. The average population of a Polish *gmina* is 16,000 (excluding voivodship capitals, the average drops to 10,900), and about 81 percent have fewer than 20,000 inhabitants. The latter's share in the total population of Poland is around 38 percent. Recognizing the existence of "economies of scale," the Local Self-Government Act encourages *gminy* to establish associations that would provide particular services. Throughout 1991, around 100 such associations were registered with the Office of Local Government Reform, and reportedly the interest in establishing associations has significantly increased.

Size, which can be addressed by forming an association, is not the only problem affecting local services and obscuring accountability of local self-governments. The problem that Polish *gminy* faced was that the central government continued to intervene administratively in local government affairs. It capped property taxation rates, imposed local civil service wage policy, set rates for some local user charges, and intervened in land-use policy and management.[26] These interventions were rationalized in terms of "newness" of the local self-government process and the need to make local self-government policy consistent with other national policies. In consequence, they blurred assignment responsibilities and undermined local government accountability. They also ran against the letter and spirit of the Local Self-Government Act.

Local self-governments operated under duress. Their accountability became negatively affected by ambiguities in public finance, inherited from the communist past and exacerbated by problems associated with the transition. During 1990-1991, the public financial system relied heavily on taxation of SOEs (state-owned enterprises). Transition to a modern national tax system began in 1992 with introduction of a comprehensive personal income tax; it will continue in 1993, when the value added tax is expected to be introduced, once again changing the composition of revenues of the public sector. Therefore, estimating the yield of future national taxes to be shared with local governments involves guesswork. While these uncertainties created by the transition cannot be avoided, they tend to reduce the degree to which local governments can be held accountable and to lower their standing in the public perception.

In the 1990-1991 period, the situation of local self-governments was aggravated by delays in information on proposed arrangements concerning local shares in national taxes. Because of limited institutional capacity of agencies responsible for designing the local financial system, new regulations were issued late in the budget year. Local governments were frequently unable to draw up a preliminary budget by the deadline set in the law. As a result, availability of resources was subject to great uncertainty, which impeded expenditure planning. This state of flux made it impossible for *gminy* to become involved in long-term municipal development planning, and limited the extent to which they could be held accountable for the quality of locally provided services.

In addition, the intergovernment fiscal transfer arrangements during 1990-1991 were not conducive to improvement of economic efficiency of services provided locally. Intergovernment fiscal transfers incorporated equalization block grants to compensate for disparities between *gmina* revenue generation and expenditure requirements. The equalization component accounted for around 50 percent of total block grants in 1991. Although the size of an equalization grant for a *gmina* was determined according to a formula,[27] the actual transfers in 1991 bore no significant relationship to per capita local source revenues.

Under these circumstances, it should come as no surprise that existing financing mechanisms did not provide incentives to promote local entrepreneurship in resource mobilization and in improved allocation efficiency for local service provision. Local governments inherited antiquated revenue-raising instruments, and they had limited discretion to take advantage of the existing local tax base, to set tax rates, and to set tariffs. They were excessively dependent on unpredictable fiscal transfers from the central government and shared national taxes, which altogether accounted for around half of local budget revenues during 1991. A fundamental problem was that both the tax rates (given nationally defined local tax bases) and user-fee rates were largely outside of local control. As a result, local government financial management was perceived as highly conditioned by the central government, and this contributed to perpetuating paternalistic state arrangements reminiscent of the communist past.

CONCLUSION

Our general conclusion is that despite adopting a legal framework creating a base for decentralization, central bureaucratic structures stifled local initiatives, and central policymakers failed to develop the institutional vision needed to tap fully the benefits of decentralization. From the outset, local government reform lacked a broader vision of the role of local government within the general governmental structure and in the context of the transition to a market-based democracy. Measures implemented suffered from conceptual weaknesses. The opportunity to set up local government with substantial autonomy and accountability, created by a transitory institutional vacuum that followed the collapse of communism in East-Central Europe during November and December of 1989, was at least partially, and inadvertently, lost.

On the other hand, however, the local government reform movement retained surprising vitality, and, considering the absence of active interest by successive postcommunist cabinets (with the exception of the Suchocka government), quite substantial progress was made. The overall assessment is that local governments performed better in their areas of responsibility than one might have anticipated, given the rather ambiguous environment in which they functioned, and they have had a positive impact on the pace of dismantling communism in Poland.

NOTES

1. A. Israel, "The Changing Role of the State," *Working Paper WPS-495* (Washington, D.C.: The World Bank, August 1990), p. 3.
2. See D. K. Rosati, "The Politics of Democratic Reform in Central and Eastern Europe," *Occasional Paper No. 7* (London: Centre for Economic Policy Research, 1992).
3. The analysis does not cover developments during 1992 which witnessed a revival of official interest in local government. The Suchocka cabinet, sworn in during July of 1992, has placed decentralization high on its agenda. There are multiple signs suggesting that a comprehensive effort to reform general government is under way.
4. Voivodships are regional entities of the central government. They had their own sources of revenue through 1990.
5. The share of total general government revenues in the GDP fell from 44 percent in 1985 to 28 percent in 1989, and then increased to 36.4 percent in 1990.
6. A local official noted: "The core group in the council and executive board of our *gmina* consists of people who were associated with local self-government since 1984." Quoted in "Dwa lata samorządności," *Gazeta wyborcza,* 27 May 1992.
7. *Rzeczpospolita,* 5 June 1991.
8. J. Bukowski and P. Świaniewicz, "Krytyczna ocena działalności władz lokalnych," *Wspólnota* 3, no. 13/28 (1992).
9. In countries dismantling authoritarian/totalitarian regimes, devolution of power to the local level provides a microfoundation crucial to the survival of democracy at a national level. Welfare gains obtained through decentralization relate to lower costs of providing local services, their better rationing, and better identification

of preferences for their provision. Because local government expenditure accounts for a significant share of GDP (in Poland around 4 percent), gains in economic efficiency are potentially quite substantial.

10. For an account of factors eroding decentralization, see G. Cheema and D. Rondinelli, *Decentralization and Development* (Beverly Hills, Ca.: Sage Publications, 1983).

11. The Suchocka government has initiated measures to fill this institutional gap, notably through setting up in 1992 the Office for Public Administration Reform in the Council of Ministers. The head of this office has the rank of minister.

12. The draft of a new Act on Local Finances, submitted by the Council of Ministers to parliament in September 1991, contained a separate chapter (number 5) specifying functions of regional accounting offices (covering one or several adjacent voivodships) which were to come into existence during 1992. In the Act on Local Finances, legislated by parliament, Chapter 5 was deleted and there is no reference to the date when regional accounting offices are to be opened. One possible reason for the delay is the strain that the introduction of the personal income tax in 1992 was expected to exert on already thin administrative resources of the Finance Ministry. Once these offices are established, their major task will be to supervise and monitor financial management in about 2,500 local governments. In the meantime, the minister of finance has been charged with financial supervisory functions.

13. The voivodship is a regional entity of the central government. The district offices for local government reform were to be closed by the end of 1991.

14. The Local Self-Government Act, which sets out the legal framework for local government, recognizes Voivodship Assemblies but contains no provision concerning the National Assembly. No other legislative act pertinent to local government does so either.

15. Nonetheless, its position as a representative of all local governments has been challenged by some voivodship assemblies. For instance, the Legnica Voivodship Assembly has refused to join the National Assembly because it has no legal status in Polish law.

16. For an assessment of these training programs, see J. Greenwood and G. Lambie, "Local Leadership Training in Europe: Western Europe and Poland Compared"; paper presented at the annual meeting of the APSA in Chicago, 3-6 September 1992.

17. *Gazeta samorządowa,* no. 20 (1991); quoted in J. Kubik, "Culture, Administrative Reform, and Local Politics: Overlooked Dimensions of the Post-Communist Transformation," *The Anthropology of East Europe Review* 10, no. 2 (1991).

18. For instance, the proposed Local Government Finance Act, accepted by the Council of Ministers and submitted to parliament in late September 1991, made it almost impossible for local governments to meet deadlines for presenting the

1992 draft budget. It had no supplement that would evaluate the impact of proposed measures against the background of the current system, although more than two months had passed since local governments submitted data on budget implementation in 1991.

19. J. Regulska, "Local Government Reform in Central and Eastern Europe"; paper presented at the annual meeting of the APSA in Chicago, 3-6 September 1992.
20. Kubik, "Culture, Administrative Reform, and Local Politics," p. 19.
21. About 6 percent of town and 12 percent of village inhabitants stated they had met frequently with their local representatives, according to Bukowski and Świanie-wicz, "Krytyczna ocena działalności władz lokalnych."
22. P. Adamowicz and L. Mazewski, "Demokracja lokalna w Polsce," *Biuletyn Zespołu do Spraw Opracowania Koncepcji Zmian w Organizacji Terytorialnej Państwa,* no. 10 (1991).
23. V. Tismaneanu, *Reinventing Politics: Eastern Europe from Stalin to Havel* (New York: Free Press, 1992), p. 243.
24. There was at least one attempt to recall a whole local government through referendum, because of "low quality of services provided by the [Józefów] *gmina* administration." E. Sękowska, "'My' i 'Oni' w Józefowie," *Gazeta wyborcza,* 27 May 1992.
25. World Bank, *Poland: Decentralization and Reform of the State* (Washington, D.C.: World Bank Country Study, 1992), pp. 7-9.
26. Rates are set on taxes which legally constitute local governments' own-source revenue. Land-use planning provides many examples of blurred accountability. Although the Local Self-Government Act gives full autonomy to *gminy* for land-use planning, a private owner willing to subdivide land for housing must obtain final permission from the *rejon,* not from a *gmina!*
27. For the procedure developed to determine the size of equalization grants, see Article 11 in "Ustawa z dnia 14 grudnia 1990 r. o dochodach gmin i zasadach ich subwencjonowania w 1991 oraz o zmianie ustawy o samorządzie terytorialnym," *Dziennik ustaw,* no. 89 (1990), p. 1209.

5

Constitutional Reform

A. E. Dick Howard*

The collapse of communism in Central and Eastern Europe has brought the peoples of that region the opportunity, long denied them, to chart their own future. The challenges and obstacles are many—weak economies, inexperience with democracy, and the excesses of nationality and ethnicity among them. The search for the "new world order" of which many spoke so bravely in the closing weeks of 1989 is a far harder road than many observers understood at the time.

One index of progress toward a stable future is the writing of new constitutions. In the modern age, a written constitution is a common device for recording a society's priorities, declaring its aspirations, creating its frame of government, articulating basic rights, and, unless the constitution is simply an empty promise, pointing a people toward constitutionalism and the rule of law.

One who surveys the efforts of Central and Eastern Europeans to write new constitutions is sure to be struck by the region's uneven progress toward this goal. Some countries, Bulgaria and Romania, for example, have indeed adopted new constitutions, but one must pause, especially as regards Romania, before declaring full-blown constitutional government to be the result. The Czechs and Slovaks agreed, in January 1991, on a bill of rights for their Federal Republic,

---

* The author wishes to thank Mme. Janina Zakrzewska, justice of the Constitutional Tribunal, for her responses to a series of queries about constitutional developments in Poland.

but the effort to hammer out a constitutional structure for the federation failed, and the Czech and Slovak parliament ultimately acquiesced in a decision to see the two republics become sovereign entities as of 1 January 1993.

Constitution-writing in postcommunist Central and Eastern Europe illustrates the practical and political problems that drafters of constitutions can encounter. One problem inheres in existing institutions and structures. For example, in Czechoslovakia the 1968 constitution created two houses— the House of Peoples and the House of Nations. In effect, however, there were three chambers, as on important bills there had to be concurrence of a majority of the deputies from each of the two republics in the House of Nations. This arrangement may not have mattered much as long as the communist party held sway, but after 1989, during the efforts to write a new constitution, Slovak opposition party members were able to exercise a veto in the House of Nations.[1]

Politics and personalities are factors in the writing of new constitutions. Ambitious politicians, such as leaders in Slovakia, and strong personalities, such as Poland's Lech Wałęsa, often define the banks and currents of the constitutional river. Another factor is the lack of recent democratic experience in Central and Eastern Europe. Czechoslovakia had a viable democracy between the two world wars, but that was over half a century ago. Some countries in the region have never had a full-blown democratic experience. Constitutions may tend therefore to have an abstract quality (especially in the bills of rights), untested by experience.

CONSTITUTION-WRITING IN POLAND

Poland has discovered just how difficult it can be to bring a new constitution into being. Inspired by the example of the cherished constitution of 3 May 1791, Poles had hoped to adopt a new basic law by the date of the first constitution's bicentenary. In a sense, the Poles had a head start over other countries in the region, as the transition to democracy in Poland began before cracks appeared in the neighboring countries.[2]

Poland's communist leaders, beset by mounting pressure, agreed in the spring of 1989 to Roundtable talks with the opposition led by Solidarity. A compromise arrangement gave the communists and their allies 65 percent of the seats in the Sejm; 35 percent of the seats would be filled in free elections. Further, the communists agreed to the revival of the Polish Senate (which they had abolished on taking power after World War II); all 100 members of the Senate were to be chosen in free elections.

Events were to move faster than the communists had hoped, however. The 1989 elections represented a crushing blow to the communists. Candidates fielded by Solidarity won every Sejm seat for which they were eligible and 99 of 100 seats in the Senate. In August 1989, Tadeusz Mazowiecki, a close associate of Wałęsa, formed Poland's first noncommunist government since the end of World War II.[3]

Constitutional reform began in December 1989 with the adoption of amendments to the existing constitution. One amendment eliminated the constitution's declaration of the communist party's leading role in Polish society. Another amendment assured equality for different forms of the ownership of property. The former amendment provided the basis for democracy in Poland; the latter sought to pave the way for private property and a market economy.[4]

These amendments were meant to be but the first step toward a new constitutional order. In early 1990 the *Sejm* appointed a special committee charged with drafting a new constitution. The Senate, not to be ignored, appointed its own constitutional committee, which began working on its own draft.

Politics, personality, and party interests soon surfaced in the drafting process. Solidarity, more of a movement than a party, split into factions reflecting, in general terms, the orientation to the workers found in Gdańsk and the interests of intellectuals and others in Warsaw. Solidarity leaders in Warsaw began to view the emerging constitution as a means of curbing excessive dominance by Wałęsa over the parliament.[5]

Much of the struggle over a new constitution has centered on deciding which powers, and how much power, should be given to the president and to parliament, respectively. The political bargain that resulted from the 1989 Roundtable talks was fraught with ambiguity, not all of it unintended. In that compromise Solidarity had, of course, achieved an important step toward free elections as well as its own place as a legitimate political actor. In return, however, in addition to conceding the communists 65 percent of the seats in the Sejm, the opposition agreed to the creation of a presidency whose principal aim, in the eyes of the communists, was to preserve much of the basis of communist authority.

The impetus for further change after the 1989 Roundtable lay, of course, with Solidarity. The communists would look to the presidency not to induce change but rather to block or at least to channel it. The opposition bargained, therefore, to offset presidential powers with those of parliament. Indeed, those who took part in the 1989 negotiations have conceded that they countenanced a degree of confusion in the Roundtable agreement's provisions on presidential powers, the better to curb the president's ability to control future events. In so doing, however, the opposition did not anticipate how quickly communist control would collapse, and soon they were to find themselves heir to an untidy political structure. The potential for conflict became more obvious when the 1991 elections created a parliament, all of whose members had been freely elected and which thus enjoyed political legitimacy on a par with that of the president.[6]

In July 1992 Hanna Suchocka became prime minister, heading a multiparty government. Against the backdrop of constant quarreling between the executive and legislative branches, the new government sought better relations with President Wałęsa. They signaled, for example, that they were willing to give the president the final say in the selection of several important ministries (defense, foreign affairs, and internal affairs), hitherto a festering issue.

The spirit of cooperation and compromise bore fruit. On 1 August 1992, the Sejm approved an interim constitution—the Little Constitution—which, rather than representing a victory for either the advocates of parliamentary power or those of the president, confirmed Poland's mixed presidential-parliamentary system of government. The required two-thirds vote was made possible by the votes of deputies from the seven parties of the government coalition and Solidarity, joined by deputies of the Polish Peasant Party and most of the postcommunist Democratic Left Alliance. The vote was 241 in favor, 110 against.[7]

In September the Senate acted on the proposed interim constitution. The Senate's constitutional committee recommended that the Senate reject the document as sent over from the Sejm, reasoning that it was too restrictive of the powers of both the Senate and the president. The full Senate decided, by a margin of only one vote, to approve the Little Constitution but only after adding a number of amendments aimed at protecting the Senate's prerogatives. For example, a Senate amendment provided that extending a state of emergency would require the concurrence of both houses, not just that of the Sejm.[8]

The next step was the proposed constitution's return to the Sejm for that body to decide whether or not to accept the Senate's amendments. Acting on the advice of a select committee, the Sejm rejected most of the Senate's substantive amendments, including that dealing with states of emergency and another that would have required the Sejm to muster a two-thirds majority to override Senate amendments to bills.[9]

A procedural hurdle to the Little Constitution's final adoption surfaced when the Senate's presidium and a group of 70 deputies (mostly representing opposition parties) appealed to the Constitutional Tribunal against last-minute changes that the Sejm had made in its rules of procedure as a basis for passing the proposed constitution.[10] In November, however, the Tribunal upheld the Sejm's procedures. An hour later, President Wałęsa put his signature to the interim constitution.[11]

THE LITTLE CONSTITUTION

The Little Constitution takes its name from the provisional constitution adopted in a single day by the Sejm of a newly independent Poland in February 1919. Following the October 1991 elections, Lech Wałęsa had submitted a draft of his own "little constitution," thus giving the name currency during the postcommunist debate over a constitution.

The Little Constitution, as adopted in 1992, is not a complete constitution. It lacks, in particular, articles on the judiciary and on human rights. The Little Constitution does, however, create the institutions of the political and governmental process. In so doing, the document does not represent a dramatic departure from the system that was in place at the time the interim constitution was enacted. It recognizes significant roles for the president, the parliament, and the government while trying to clear up some of the ambiguities of the *status quo ante*.[12]

The Little Constitution may be an attempt to make things clearer, but it is far from simple. Consider, for example, the procedures for forming a new government. The Little Constitution delineates five steps which may occur, each coming into play if the one before it fails:[13]

1. The president names a prime minister and, on the motion of the prime minister, appoints a cabinet. The government which thus comes into being can exercise power, but within 14 days the government must win a vote of confidence (which requires an absolute majority) in the Sejm.
2. If the government appointed by the president fails to get a vote of confidence, the next step is in the hands of the Sejm, which may elect its own candidate for prime minister (requiring, again, an absolute majority).
3. If the Sejm cannot muster a majority for its own government, the president can ask for another vote on his candidate. On this round, success requires only a simple, rather than absolute, majority.
4. If the president's nominee fails to get a simple majority in the Sejm, that body can make another attempt of its own, this time a simple majority being required.

5. If none of these steps yields a government, the president has two choices: he can dissolve parliament, or he can appoint a government empowered to rule for six months. During that period, the Sejm must build a majority either for the president's government or for its own alternative. If the Sejm fails to do this, parliament is automatically dissolved and new elections are held.

The Little Constitution pays particular attention to the question of special powers—the power of the government to issue decrees having the force of law. The notion of special powers had been advanced as early as 1989, when the first postcommunist government was developing its program of "shock therapy" designed to put Poland on the road to a market economy. The Little Constitution authorizes the Sejm to vest the government with the power to issue decrees. In granting such powers, the Sejm must decide which areas of legislation will be the subject of special powers and how long the government's power will be in effect. Important areas may not be the subject of special powers; these include personal freedoms, political rights, the budget, social security and labor benefits (an obvious concession to social democratic traditions), international agreements, and changes in the constitution.[14] It is likely that, to the extent special powers are used, they will be directed at such issues as economic reform and privatization.

In most respects, the president's place in Poland's political and governmental arrangements remains much as it was before the adoption of the Little Constitution. The president continues to be elected by the people for a five-year term. Moreover, the powers of the office, with subtle changes, are essentially those conferred upon the president in 1989. These include the right (shared with others) to propose legislation, the power to veto legislation (subject to the Sejm's power to override by a two-thirds vote), the right to ask the Constitutional Tribunal's ruling on the constitutionality of legislation, the power to respond to an external threat by declaring martial law and ordering military mobilization, the power (subject to limitations) to impose a state of emergency in response to a danger to domestic security or a natural catastrophe, and status as commander in chief of the armed forces.[15] Perhaps the most important shift is the Little Constitution's conferring an explicit primacy in foreign and defense policy upon the president.[16]

Reactions to the Little Constitution have varied. Some articles in the Polish press denounced the document as creating a "Sejmocracy," while others complained that it gives the president too much power.[17] Bronisław Geremek, the floor leader of the Democratic Union, summed up the Little Constitution as being an "imperfect act of compromise" but saw it as an improvement over the way things had been.[18] One way to read the Little Constitution is to see it as reflecting the ongoing debate over Lech Wałęsa, his program as president, and his aspirations for himself and his office. Indeed, the constitution's provisional status underscores its having an immediate, rather than long-term, purpose. Unlike the Philadelphia framers in 1787, those who hammered out the compromises inherent in the Little Constitution were not acting for the ages. The drafters in Warsaw seemed content, for the present, to work out a *modus vivendi* under which the Sejm can work with Wałęsa, granting him an activist role but putting safeguards in place. As one parliamentarian remarked, "This bill's greatest advantage is that it can be passed at all."[19] Meantime, drafting proceeds on a full-blown constitution (a constitutional commission held its inaugural meeting on 18 November 1992).[20]

ENFORCING CONSTITUTIONAL NORMS AND THE RULE OF LAW

The idea of a rule of law requires that there be means by which to control the state's use of power, lest use become abuse. During the 1980s, while the communists were still in power in Poland, several devices were put in place to control state institutions. These included the Supreme Administrative Court (created in 1980), the State Tribunal (1982), the Constitutional Tribunal (1985), and the Ombudsman (1987).[21]

In creating these institutions, the communists hoped to create the appearance of democratic safeguards. Appearance was what counted, as it would be naive to suppose that the managers of the one-party system, steeped in doctrines of Marxism and Leninism, sought to bring authentic checks and balances into play. As communism waned, however, façade gave way to reality as the new institutions gradually took on some measure of control over the state's actions.

The emergence of the office of ombudsman furnishes an apt example. The remarkable Ewa Lętowska brought the force of her mind and personality to this office, making it into a useful and respected instrument to which citizens seeking remedies for wrongs done them could turn. During her tenure as ombudsman, Lętowska looked beyond individual cases to systematic problems. In airing a citizen's complaint, she sought to create precedents that would further the rule of law in Poland.[22]

Constitutionalism can be a reality only if there are realistic expectations that the norms and principles laid down in the constitution itself will be respected. Fashioning the means of enforcing the constitution is one of the central challenges to those who draft constitutions in Central and Eastern

Europe. It is in this regard that the emergence of constitutional courts takes on such significance.

Before World War II, few European countries had constitutional courts. The idea of judicial review—the power of a court to strike down legislation as being unconstitutional—was largely unknown. Unlike the United States, where judicial review was entrenched early in American constitutional development, Europe had clung to the notion of parliamentary supremacy. In such a system, judges are essentially civil servants, interpreting parliament's will, but subservient to it.[23]

Post-World War II Europe has seen the rise of the constitutional court, the West German court being the most important model for other countries. Specialized courts that exist to interpret and enforce the constitution (unlike the United States Supreme Court, which is a court of more general jurisdiction), constitutional courts in Western Europe have created an important body of case law on such fundamental issues as abortion. Constitutional draftsmen in Central and Eastern Europe have typically followed the Western model, creating constitutional courts for the new democracies. Some of these constitutional courts, for example, that of Hungary, have been surprisingly active and independent—an important check on elected officials who, even though they may claim a popular mandate, are not immune to the temptations and mistakes (however well intentioned) that come with power.[24]

Simply creating a constitutional court does not, however, guarantee its effectiveness. Important questions must be resolved about the tribunal's jurisdiction and powers. Who may bring a suit in the court? What subject matter may the court review? What will be the effect of a ruling? These and other questions bear directly on the extent to which a constitutional court can do meaningful work.

Poland's Constitutional Tribunal Act, as enacted in 1985, places significant limits on the tribunal's ability to undertake authentic judicial review.[25] There is, to begin with, no right conferred upon individual citizens to take a case to the tribunal; access to the court is given only to certain state agencies (including ministries and parliamentary committees) and to organizations such as trade unions. Second, some legal acts may not be reviewed. For example, the tribunal may not review international agreements; thus, even though Poland has signed the European Convention on Human Rights, the tribunal has no authority to decide whether actions of the Polish state in fact conform with that covenant.

From the standpoint of constitutional adjudication, the most important limitation on the powers of the Constitutional Tribunal is that which limits the effect of a ruling. The tribunal's decisions regarding the constitutionality of administrative regulations have binding effect. But the same is not true when the tribunal reviews statutes enacted by the Polish parliament. If the tribunal finds an act of parliament to be in conflict with the constitution, that decision does not become final or binding; it simply obliges parliament to reconsider the statute. Authentic judicial review gives a court the power to limit even the legislative branch. That the powers given Poland's Constitutional Tribunal fall short of this mark is suggested by the comment of Professor Leszek Garlicki of the University of Warsaw: "The tribunal is designed not to supervise parliament, but to help parliament maintain its position as the country's supreme legislator."[26] This purpose is further manifest in the enabling act's provisions on selection and tenure of judges of the Constitutional Tribunal. The judges are elected by, responsible to, and removable by parliament; this arrangement is not what most observers would call an assurance of judicial independence.

RIGHTS AND THEIR INTERPRETATION

In November 1992, President Wałęsa submitted a proposed Charter of Rights and Freedoms to the Sejm. The draft includes civil rights and liberties, political rights, and a minimum guarantee of social security. Citizens claiming that their rights and liberties have been violated would be able to seek relief in the courts. Moreover, the Constitutional Tribunal would have jurisdiction to rule on laws and other legal acts alleged to conflict with the constitution.[27]

The draft charter is an ambitious document. Among the rights that would be protected are such familiar civil liberties as conscience, religion, and expression. Political rights include the right to organize political parties. Social security is the aim of such rights as a guarantee of basic health care. Of particular interest to those concerned with the transformation of Poland's economy are protections for property and inheritance and the right to undertake economic activities and to choose one's profession and place of employment.

This enumeration of rights raises important questions both of interpretation and of enforcement. The most traditional rights are those which place limits on government's power, for example, rights of free expression or free exercise of religion. These are negative rights; that is, they tell government what the limits of its power are, what it may *not* do. Social and economic rights (such as the right to old-age benefits), by contrast, are affirmative rights; they lay claims upon government. Affirmative rights are in the nature of entitlements; they tell government what it *must* or *should* do.

The inclusion of affirmative rights in a constitution makes it read somewhat like a political party's platform—a promise of the good life. Social rights entail, however, the allocation of economic resources, the carving up of the economic pie. This is a job for which legislatures, charged with raising revenue and adopting budgets, are best fitted. Remedies for the enforcement of negative rights are familiar where judicial review exists (for example, the issuing of injunctions or the awarding of damages). Judges have a more difficult time fashioning appropriate and workable remedies to enforce affirmative rights. It may therefore be better to view such rights as being essentially aspirational in nature. Thus read, they would be statements of principle, or directives for legislation and state policy, rather than provisions meant to be judicially enforceable.

Even the traditional, or negative, rights raise questions of interpretation and enforcement. It is possible to view such rights as flowing from notions of natural law, that is, as existing independently of civil society, or as being based on positive law. A review of draft constitutions in Central and Eastern Europe suggests that drafters are torn between these two traditions. Accepting the positivist tradition is likely to produce greater deference to legislative incursions on rights and a less generous judicial reading of those rights. Reading constitutional drafts in Central and Eastern European countries, one often discovers that a basic right such as freedom of expression is protected, but that constitutional protection will not exist for speech that undermines "public morality" or conflicts with the "public order" or defames the nation. Exceptions as broad and vague as these can operate to swallow up the general rule, making enforcement of the underlying right an unsure thing even where judicial review exists.

Might Polish judges have this problem in interpreting and enforcing a bill of rights? A Polish law makes it illegal to "publicly libel, laugh at, or belittle the Polish nation . . . or its chief authorities." For saying rude and vulgar things about President Wałęsa at a bus stop in a small town, Stanisław Bartosiński received a one-year sentence, suspended as long as he does not break the law again for three years, and a fine of about $230, more than the average Pole makes in a month. Some Poles have defended the law (which dates back to 1932) under which Bartosiński was convicted; others argue that it conflicts with democratic notions of free speech.[28] Such laws, in any event, are not unusual in Central and Eastern Europe. As long as there are laws that seek to protect the honor of the "nation" or of its leaders, judges charged with deciding how far rights of free expression extend will have their work cut out for them.

A charter of rights and freedoms such as that proposed by Wałęsa presents other tensions and ambiguities to be worked out. For example, the draft, like other constitutions in the region, reflects a tension between two goals: movement toward a market economy and retention of a social safety net. How to balance these goals requires both empirical and philosophical judgments. Just how far one can or should constitutionalize such balancing of values is a vexing question in the older democracies of the West. Lawmakers and judges in Central and Eastern Europe will find it no easier.

FROM A CONSTITUTION TO CONSTITUTIONALISM

Americans sometimes speak of there having been a "constitutional moment"—the era that produced the federal Constitution and Bill of Rights. Reinforced by such metaphors as Catherine Drinker Bowen's *Miracle at Philadelphia,* this notion of the constitutional moment obscures the fact that the founding period of American constitutionalism was one of trial and error. The state constitutions drafted beginning in 1776 were often quite flawed documents, and the Articles of Confederation (1781) soon proved inadequate to the purposes of the emerging nation.

By the same token, the countries of Central and Eastern Europe seem to have embarked on a process of trial and error in the making of new constitutions. Hungary seems to do well enough for the present with a provisional constitution. Poland now has its Little Constitution, with further action to be taken on the judiciary and on a charter of rights and freedoms.

The writing of a constitution, whether by parts or in one leap, is but a first step toward constitutionalism. Constitutional democracy requires not only certain institutions, but also a conducive social, economic, and political setting.[29]

For constitutionalism to flourish, there must be reasonable security against external aggression and civil conflict. However badly the people of Bosnia may seek after a decent civil society, they cannot have it so long as Serbian aggression renders it impossible. Some peoples—the Czechs and Slovaks, for example—have settled their differences peacefully, but the specter of rampant nationalism and revisionist history casts a shadow over much of Eastern Europe and the republics of the former Soviet Union.

Prosperity and economic growth enhance the prospects for constitutionalism. Despite the dislocations of shock therapy, Poland's economic prospects look brighter than they did in the late eighties. A healthy economy is no guarantor of constitutionalism, but it certainly bolsters its chances.

Constitutionalism requires the building of basic institutions such as an independent judiciary, an independent bar, a free press and media, and free political parties, among others. Judges must practice the independence required to stand up even against measures that, while unconstitutional, may be popular. Lawyers must see themselves as advocates for their clients' interests, not simply servants of the state's will. Reporters must be willing to lay aside prejudice and interest in order to enhance public understanding of critical issues. Political parties must acquire the know-how to contest elections and the patience, if defeated, to accept the electorate's decision while girding to fight another day.

Institutions aside, constitutional government requires the nurturing of a legal culture—the respect for the rule of law. Under communist rule, law and lawyers were often instruments of the dominant party's rule. This bred a popular mistrust of the law—a skepticism that will not quickly be laid aside.

Deeper still, constitutionalism calls for the inculcation of civic virtues— the habits of mind that bring citizens to prize their individual rights and liberties but also care about the common good. Civic education, the fostering of these values, calls not only for good schooling of a country's children but also for widespread commitment of the adult population to those habits of mind that make for a tolerant, concerned, humane society.

In his bill for the More General Diffusion of Knowledge (1777), Thomas Jefferson called for "rendering the people the safe, as they are the ultimate, guardians of their own liberty."[30] Three years before Jefferson penned his bill, Poland formed its National Commission on Education, the first of its kind in Europe. It is fair to think that the work of that commission in nurturing civic values among Poles was one factor in the survival of the Polish nation during those long years between the final partition and the reemergence of a Polish state after World War I. Poles who remember, and act upon, the legacy of the 1774 commission and the 1791 constitution are well on their way to securing, for themselves and their posterity, the blessings of freedom, democracy, and constitutional government.

NOTES

1. See Katarina Mathernova, "Czecho? Slovakia: Constitutional Disappointments," *American University Journal of International Law & Policy* 7 (1992): 471.
2. For a splendid article on Poland's constitutional heritage, see Mark F. Brzeziński, "Constitutional Heritage and Renewal: The Case of Poland," *Virginia Law Review* 77 (1991): 49.
3. On the Roundtable talks and the 1989 elections, see Timothy Garton Ash, *The Magic Lantern* (New York: Random House, 1990), pp. 25-46.

4. Andrzej Rapaczyński, "Constitutional Politics in Poland: A Report on the Constitutional Committee of the Polish Parliament," *University of Chicago Law Review* 58 (1991): 595 and 601.

5. Ibid., 601-04.

6. Louisa Vinton, "Poland's 'Little Constitution' Clarifies Wałęsa's Powers," *RFE/RL Research Report* 1, no. 35 (4 September 1992): 19-20.

7. Ibid., 20.

8. "Senate Approves Small Constitution, Passes Amendments to Popiwek Law," *BBC Summary of World Broadcasts,* Part 2: Eastern Europe (16 September 1992), p. EE/1487/B/1.

9. *Rzeczpospolita,* 17-18 October 1992, p. 1.

10. *Gazeta wyborcza,* 17 November 1992, p. 3.

11. *Rzeczpospolita,* 18 November 1992, p. 1.

12. See Vinton, "Poland's 'Little Constitution' Clarifies Wałęsa's Powers."

13. Articles 58-63.

14. Article 23.

15. Chapter 3.

16. Articles 33-36.

17. See Michał Wichowski, "Small Constitution: A Louder Voice for Government," *The Warsaw Voice,* 19 August 1992 and "Too Much Power for President in New Constitution, Daily Says," *PAP News Wire,* 3 August 1992.

18. Quoted in Vinton, "Poland's 'Little Constitution' Clarifies Wałęsa's Powers," p. 25.

19. Janina Paradowska, "No Rejoicing as New Constitution Was Voted In," *Polityka,* no. 32 (8 August 1992).

20. *Rzeczpospolita,* 19 November 1992, p. 2.

21. Anna Sabbat-Świdlicka, "Toward the Rule of Law: Poland," *RFE/RL Research Report* 1, no. 27 (3 July 1992): 25.

22. I base these observations on conversations with Ms. Lętowska in Warsaw and on the comments of other Poles who admire her work.

23. See Louis Favoreu, "American and European Models of Constitutional Justice," in David S. Clark, ed., *Comparative and Private International Law* (Berlin: Duncker & Humblot, 1990), pp. 105, 109.

24. See Herman Schwartz, "The New East European Constitutional Courts," in A. E. Dick Howard, ed., *Constitution-making in Eastern Europe* (Washington, D.C.: Woodrow Wilson Center Press, 1993), p. 163.

25. For an analysis of the constitutional tribunal and limitations on its authority, see Mark F. Brzeziński, "Constitutional Tribunal: Guardian of the Legal System," *The Warsaw Voice,* 19 January 1992.

26. Ibid.

27. *Rzeczpospolita,* 13 November 1992, p. 1.

28. Linnet Myers, "Polish Farmer's Rude Remark Stirs Furor over 'Word Police,'" *Chicago Tribune,* 9 September 1992, p. 1.

29. See generally A. E. Dick Howard, *The Road to Constitutionalism* (Charlottesville, Va.: University of Virginia Press, 1992).

30. Thomas Jefferson, *Notes on the State of Virginia,* ed. William Peden (Chapel Hill, N.C.: University of North Carolina Press, 1954), p. 148.

6

Interaction between Political and Economic Freedom

Edward P. Lazear*

The countries of East-Central Europe have recently taken major steps forward to obtain political freedom of the sort which they had not experienced during the preceding 40 years. The question now becomes whether political freedom will be followed by the kind of economic freedom that most economists associate with growth.

There is no automatic connection between economic growth and political democracy. While some studies have shown that democracy and economic progress are positively correlated, there are some important recent exceptions. Most obvious are the cases of South Korea and Chile. Rather than attempting to analyze the big picture and to say at the macro level whether political freedom and economic freedom go hand in hand, this writer will instead consider more specific goals. By focusing on each of the detailed policies, it is possible to determine whether political forces affect the ability to adopt the economic policies that are important for economic growth.

The theme of this essay is that there are countervailing forces. Democracy has the advantage that the best solutions get the opportunity to work their way to the top. In a totalitarian state, the views of one particular group are played out almost irrespective of their consequences. If things go badly, it can take a very long time to change the course of government, and it may

* The author expresses his thanks to Senator Andrzej Machalski (president, Confederation of Polish Employers) for his comments on a draft of this paper.

require a violent revolution to do so. A democracy, on the other hand, allows changes to be made in a much more continuous fashion. If some policies are clearly inappropriate, the public can replace current leaders with those who will adopt the better strategies.

There are two difficulties with democracy. First, the electorate must know what is best for the country. Second, it must act in the country's interests, rather than in the special interests of particular groups. Just as a totalitarian regime allows special groups to govern, a democracy may also allow particular groups to capture the government and use it for their own purposes. Still, the presumption is that democracy has a better chance of resisting this kind of political pressure.

Let us start, then, by going through the list of general reform strategies that most Western and East-Central European economists accept as necessary ingredients for creating a successful and growing economy.

THE LIBERALIZATION OF PRICES TO MARKET LEVELS

It is generally agreed that to prevent distortions in the economy, it is necessary to allow prices to move to their market equilibrium levels. Sometimes this implies a decrease in prices. In other cases, it implies an increase in prices. While virtually everyone agrees that prices should be freed, bringing them to market levels is another issue.

Even in the United States, which has probably the fewest price controls of any major economy in the world, there are still examples of government intervention and of prices which create distortions in markets. The best example takes the form of agricultural price supports. The American government has engaged in a policy of keeping the prices of some goods high, so as to protect farmers and increase their incomes. The agricultural lobby in the United States has been a very important force, far more important than its numbers would indicate. Agriculture has been and remains a relatively small part of the U.S. economy, and yet it has always wielded a significant amount of political power.

The situation in East-Central Europe is actually the reverse. Historically, the communist governments had kept agricultural prices low rather than high, and forces continue to exert pressures which push in that direction, even though communist regimes have been replaced for the most part. A good example comes from Russia. When Boris Yeltsin instituted price reforms on 1 January 1992, he decided that certain commodities were too important to allow market prices to prevail. Thus, he allowed the price of butter to rise, but regulated the price of milk, keeping it down well below market levels. As a result, dairy farmers, who had the option of producing butter or milk, turned all of their milk into butter, and there was a tremendous surplus of butter and a dramatic shortage of milk. Yeltsin, who was reacting initially to political cries to keep milk prices down, eventually had to yield to another form of political pressure, which protested the absence of milk on the market. Later in the year, he freed up milk prices and milk supplies were restored to Moscow shelves.[1]

While economic arguments have prevailed on the prices of most consumer goods, they have not prevailed in two very important areas—namely, energy prices and housing prices. Throughout most of East-Central Europe, energy prices remain below market levels.[2] The prices of coal and oil in Russia, for example, do not reflect the prices at which those commodities are exported. As a result, there is a tremendous amount of pressure to appropriate goods from the local economy and to export them to the rest of the world. The so-called Russian mafia has captured a large proportion of energy resources, and has made tremendous profits arbitrating this difference between domestic prices and international prices. The obvious solution is to allow domestic prices to rise to market levels, and to subsidize through direct income transfers those individuals who are forced to buy energy at the new and higher prices. But such methods have been opposed by purchasers of energy who fear that their inability to make a profit now on the goods which they produce will only get worse as energy prices rise. The political pressure, not only in Russia but also throughout East-Central Europe, to avoid raising energy prices has been tremendous and has prevailed.[3]

One advantage to having a democracy is that the forces that benefit from having low energy prices can be offset to some extent by those forces that benefit from higher energy prices. For example, in the United States, the private oil industry would not like to see energy prices kept at low levels. The industry has been effective in preventing users of energy from exerting political power to keep energy prices below market levels.

Housing presents the other important example where prices deviate from the market. Again, for primarily political reasons, housing has been deemed too important a good to allow market forces to operate. As a result, rents have been kept well below market levels, and a gray or black market has developed in housing. Individuals are able to acquire apartments at low prices from the state and then sublet them to other individuals who are able to pay much higher prices. Incidentally, this phenomenon is not restricted to the former command economies of East-Central Europe. New York City, which has rent control, and Santa Monica, California, which also instituted a rent control program, find the same activity occurring. In New York, "key fees" are commonly paid to superintendents and other housing authorities who have the ability to award apartments at below market prices to individuals who can bribe their way into these residences.

But political forces keep these prices low. There are many individuals who have much to gain from keeping prices below their market levels. In the case of housing, current residents of Poland receive transfers when prices are kept below market levels. The same is true not only for housing but for any other good. If market prices are kept below market levels, then managers who have the right to allocate these scarce resources can capture a large part of the return. As a result, those individuals will use their political muscle to prevent prices from moving to the appropriate numbers.[4]

THE GROWTH OF PRIVATE CAPITAL

One of the clichés of market reform is that privatization is an important part of moving an economy from a command structure to a market structure. It is probably in this area that political and economic forces interact most closely.

It is important to point out that private property does not necessarily imply massive privatization. There are a number of ways to have a large proportion of the economy operating with private property. The most obvious is massive privatization of state property. But in some countries, state capital is simply not worth a great deal and will be replaced in a moderate amount of time by new private capital. The issue then becomes permitting private capital to rise and to compete successfully with state capital, and therein lies a major political problem.[5]

The state generally has a tendency to want to protect its own capital. In the United States for example, the U.S. Postal Service maintains a monopoly over first-class mail. No individual private company is permitted to compete with first-class mail, although others have succeeded in producing products that are substitutes, albeit imperfect substitutes, for first-class mail. Like other companies, state-owned companies simply do not like competition from rivals. The difference is that the state has the power to prevent rivals from competing with its companies. As a result, one of the major benefits to getting the state out of many industries is that the state will then permit competition to take place, and competition is necessary for economic growth.

One example from Russia currently comes to mind. In the process of privatization, managers in some of the coal mines in that country are concerned about equipment manufacturers. The process of privatization would divest the equipment plant from the coal mine company. After this is done, many of these factories may sell out to become other kinds of factories or even tourist hotels, as is the case with one factory located in central St. Petersburg. Coal mine managers argue that the equipment produced by those factories is essential and that the factories should not be permitted to become independent. They ignore the fact that the value of such factories is much greater in other uses. Indeed, the coal mine would profit by selling off the division and using the money to buy the equipment elsewhere. Alternatively the mine might choose to go out of the mining business altogether. It is wasteful to maintain this equipment factory, which is located on very high-priced land. However, when the state owns the property, the state tends to use it in inefficient ways, reacting to political pressure rather than economic pressure. Instead of looking at the highest value of the land, politicians listen to those voices that scream the loudest. Often, those voices belong to individuals who are hurt the most, rather than to those who benefit the most.

Another major problem with maintaining private capital in state hands is that economic and political forces tend to be confounded. Since the state owns the capital, one way to get back at the state is to affect the industries owned by the government. An example from Romania is telling.

Several years ago, the Romanian government prohibited sailors from bringing in goods from abroad and selling them at market prices without paying any tax on these sales. The sailors objected, claiming that their jobs were hard and they had a right to receive a return for their efforts. They went on strike against the shipping company. The strike was effective, in large part because the company was owned by the state and because there were no competing ones around.

A similar situation rarely occurs in Western economies. For example, in the United States, the federal government may adopt policies that this writer finds objectionable. His reaction is not to go on strike against Stanford, for two reasons. First, the government does not care a great deal about what happens at Stanford, since it is a private university and the government does not receive revenue from Stanford. Second, and related, Stanford has very little influence on what the government does. Even if a personal strike is very effective in bringing Stanford to its knees, there is no way for Stanford to exert pressure on the federal government to correct the situation. Thus, privatization of state capital will tend to separate economic and political actions that are confounded when the government owns major industries.

Another point, and the one that is most frequently cited, is that private capital creates better incentives for production than state-owned capital. The argument is generally correct as a direct result of political considerations, but it is not necessary to make the case. If state-owned capital were concerned primarily about profit maximization in the way that private capital is, then there would be no difference between firms owned by the state and those owned by private industry. Unfortunately, the premise is invalid. When the state owns the capital, it uses its firms to pursue political as well as economic goals. Such considerations as high levels of employment, low consumer prices, and other social goals are pursued through the enterprise. While such activities are noble in intent, they have adverse consequences because they only serve to raise costs in the industries affected, and bring about their eventual demise.

INDIVIDUAL OWNERSHIP OR CONTROL
OF AGRICULTURAL LAND

A number of countries have demonstrated the value of having agricultural land in private hands. Poland and China are among the best examples. Polish agriculture, while perhaps far from perfect, is a leading model for East-Central Europe and has succeeded in producing relatively abundant supplies of food for its people. The same is true in China. But often political forces are important in bringing about the transfer of ownership of agricultural land from the state to individuals. And here is an area where democracy and totalitarian states differ in their ability to transfer resources from one group to another.

China provides an interesting example. Local Chinese bureaucrats have a tremendous amount of power. The country is very large, communication is somewhat backward, and transportation is poor, relative to the standards of the West. As a result, Beijing could not exert tremendous influence on the localities. When the central government decided to free up land and put some of the proceeds from the land into the hands of individual farmers, they recognized that obtaining the support of local bureaucrats would be absolutely essential. Rather than allocating the land directly to the peasants, they allowed the local bureaucrats to do so. They knew implicitly that the local bureaucrats would keep a large proportion of the land for themselves, but they viewed this essentially as a bribe that was worth paying. Local bureaucrats could not keep all the land for themselves, because the local populations simply would not tolerate it, even in the somewhat constrained and totalitarian structure of China. But the local bureaucrats were able to keep a large enough fraction of the land to make them support the land redistribution scheme and push for its rapid implementation. The results in China are a testimony to such possibilities.

The same kind of bribes can be paid implicitly in a democracy, although the process is more complicated and somewhat slower. An examination of the issue of restitution in Czechoslovakia is a case in point. The Czechoslovak legislature was tied up for months trying to decide how much of state capital should be given back to the pre-1948 owners. These questions are essentially political, in large part redistributive rather than efficiency-promoting. But in the democratic structure of the then-new Czechoslovakia, arguments on both sides prevailed. The compromise that resulted satisfied no one and was somewhat inefficient. The value of democracy is that the institutions provide a check on transfers which could otherwise go to one group, irrespective of their fairness and efficiency considerations.

DEMONOPOLIZATION

As is well understood, monopoly implies restricted output and higher prices. In order to have an efficient and growing economy, it is necessary that industries face competition internally and internationally. As mentioned earlier, the state is reluctant to give up its monopoly position easily. However, when capital is in private hands, those private forces will use the political structure to the extent possible to maintain their monopoly positions. Such is the case in the United States when industries, such as trucking, attempt to maintain a cartel position through regulatory agencies like the Interstate Commerce Commission.

The key point here is that getting the state out of industry is no guarantee that political forces will not come to bear. However, it is this writer's view that a democratic structure, because of the trade-offs on both sides and the ability for all individuals to exert political muscle, is more likely to provide for competition than is a structure dominated by one particular group. It is simply easier to capture one party or one leader than it is to capture an entire population which has the power to replace leaders with others. Of course, incumbency is a powerful force, and current managers, whether state or private, will use their influence to affect the way in which property is held in the future.

ESTABLISHMENT OF WELL-DEFINED PROPERTY RIGHTS

Perhaps the area in which democracies have the most important advantage over totalitarian systems is in the establishment of property rights. Such well-defined rights are essential for the encouragement of domestic and foreign investment. It is necessary that investors feel secure, so they will be willing to put money into an economy. The only incentive to invest money is the assurance that they will be able to take it out and receive at least the market return on the investment. A democracy provides for a much more stable set of property rights than totalitarian regimes. In an authoritarian regime, rules can change very easily with the identity of the person in power.

Even now, one sees the same insecurity in Russia that was the case in the past, in part created by a very strong executive and a relatively impotent legislative branch. Boris Yeltsin has made economic policy by decree independent of the support which he has in the Supreme Soviet. While that may be an effective strategy in the short run, it creates great uncertainty and potential disaster for the long run. If, in the next several years the Supreme Soviet is able to increase its influence, many of the economic decrees instituted by Yeltsin in 1992 may be quickly overturned by the parliament.

The same is not true when parliament has passed such laws in the first place. The composition of a legislative body is much more stable than the composition of the executive branch simply because the numbers are so much greater, and voting patterns do not change that dramatically over time. That is the idea which lies behind a constitution. A constitution is a document which can of course be changed, although only with great difficulty and with the acquiescence of the legislative branch. When a constitution is replaced by a totalitarian government, change can be very rapid and instability can be great.

AN EFFICIENT AND FAIR TAX SYSTEM

The wrong tax system can choke an economy. It can be used to confiscate property by imposing such high taxes that it is essentially not worthwhile to own the property in the first place. It can also be used to stifle investment, to reduce labor effort, and to prevent farmers from investing efficiently in their land. The tax system is among one of the more politically charged structures of any society.

Totalitarian governments have used implicit tax structures for the most part, and have concealed the taxes from their public. Thus, in a command economy, the revenues from goods and services accrue to the state which then pays out wages. The difference between revenue and wages is tax revenue, earned by the government. In a command structure, therefore, it is possible to raise taxes by raising prices, or to raise taxes by lowering wages, neither of which is thought of as an explicit tax hike. In a market economy, taxes are explicit. And in a democracy, in particular, fights over which individuals will pay taxes tend to lead to compromise in the tax structure. Compromise is not always good, because compromise is often a euphemism for loopholes which allow certain interest groups to gain from detailed provisions written into the tax code. A political structure operating under democracy may very well lead to a less efficient tax code than one chosen by a benevolent dictator. The problem, of course, with an authoritarian regime is assuring that the dictator remains benevolent and knowledgeable.

FREE INTERNATIONAL TRADE

While many countries in East-Central Europe, Poland being the leading example, have taken a number of steps toward freeing up trade, the issue of free trade remains politically tense. International competition and related political issues are rarely discussed in a logical manner. Because so many interests are involved, politics rather than economics almost always prevail. Even in the United States, where the environment is quite open to free trade as compared with other countries, protectionist barriers are frequently constructed. It is not clear, however, that democracy is more vulnerable to political forces than is a totalitarian government.

To the extent that state ownership of industry goes along with totalitarian control, the state is likely to protect its own industry. Further, even if private ownership is associated with authoritarian control, it may be easier for that interest group to capture an individual than it is to capture an entire legislative body. Over a prolonged period, private interests have a much more difficult time capturing legislative bodies in general. When a legislature protects special interests to too great an extent, its members can be removed by political forces.

It is interesting how protection has worked, both in the United States and in East-Central Europe. In the former, the thrust of protectionism goes back to the mercantile debate of an earlier time. The discussion among protectionists is in terms of protecting and creating jobs, rather than producing goods and services. Consumers may benefit greatly from having free trade, but the discussion is usually cast in terms of the workers that will be hurt by it.

In East-Central Europe, the discussion has a somewhat different tone. Perhaps as a holdover from communist doctrine, political opposition to free trade is based on the fear that natural resources will be exported to the rest of the world. While the emerging economies are anxious to supply the West with consumer goods produced in their countries, they are reluctant to see natural resources being depleted. This somewhat misguided view is based on the assumption that exchange rates and prices will not adjust to clear markets in an appropriate way. Still, with the exception of a few countries, of which Poland is perhaps one, international trade remains restricted.[6]

MONETARY STABILITY

A stable money supply with low rates of inflation is a goal for almost any growing economy. This requires tight control over the money supply, which in turn requires that the government not run significant deficits. But political pressure in the current environment is tremendous, and it is almost impossible for the government to avoid running deficits. This is particularly true under a democratic structure, where the incumbent must fear the short-run interests of the public. But in fact, the argument can be turned around. The public, which has to suffer with the long-term consequences of actions taken by current administrators, may actually be more farsighted than the politician himself. In a democratic structure, actions which promote the country's long-term interests may be more likely to be undertaken than in a structure where authority is autocratic. A dictator may be able to extract more rent from a community than the public would tolerate under democracy.

The problem here relates in large part to the inability to tax explicitly. If tax revenue cannot be raised, then the government must be financed through a deficit. A deficit can be financed only by borrowing explicitly or by taxing implicitly through inflation. For most emerging economies, explicit borrowing by floating government bonds is unrealistic on a large scale, so the only option has been inflation.[7]

WAGE-SETTING BY INDIVIDUAL ENTERPRISES

There are few variables in which the public has more interest than wages. Constrained wages in the face of increasing prices can give rise to social unrest and topple a standing government. In fact, in Poland, the government of Prime Minister Tadeusz Mazowiecki suffered in part because wages were frozen while prices were rising.

The state has been reluctant to grant wage-setting authority to individual enterprises, because those enterprises have no obvious incentive to keep wages down. The essential problem is that managers' compensation and job security are not based on the performance of the enterprise but rather on the political environment in which the manager works. To a significant extent, managers retain their jobs by keeping good will among the work force. Additionally, since wage increases must be paid for by the government, a wage increase is implicitly a tax decrease. The solution to these problems is to rationalize managerial compensation and to privatize industry. Whether democracies or totalitarian governments are more likely to create rational compensation schemes remains a question.

ESTABLISHMENT OF A GENEROUS YET LIMITED UNEMPLOYMENT SYSTEM AND A FAIR AND EFFICIENT STATE PENSION PLAN

In order to cope with a society that is going through transition, unemployment compensation must be provided. No country has attempted to get through the reform without setting up such a system. However, the specifics are crucial. A compensation system that is too tight will end up harming the population, will create social unrest, and will prevent firms from being permitted to dismiss workers. Without reasonably generous benefits, a manager will be unable politically to lay off a worker because the consequences that the worker will face are too severe.

Yet there must be limits to the benefits, because a system that is too generous will induce people to join the ranks of the unemployed and avoid a return to work. Such is the case in the five eastern provinces of Germany. There, unemployment compensation has been so generous, as it has approached western Germany's levels, that workers may actually profit more by being unemployed than employed. Thus, an unemployment compensation system must place end limitations on the amount of time during which benefits can be received.

One of the weaknesses of a democracy is that when unemployment rates are high, it is very difficult for a democratically elected legislature to resist pressure to increase unemployment benefits. To the extent that the policy encourages unemployment, it can stifle recovery and actually end up making the situation worse.

In most command economies, state pension benefits were quite generous, with replacement ratios as high as or higher than those of Western economies. Gradually, these high replacement ratios should be phased out and replaced by private saving and private pension plans. In the short run, however, it is socially undesirable and simply unfair to abandon pension recipients who have made their plans with the expectation that high replacement ratios would continue.

Again, the appropriate democracy can prevent a tyrannical majority from oppressing, in this case, an elderly minority. While the majority always has the incentive to renege on its promise to the elderly, a strong constitution or other implicit institutions can prevent this from happening. Thus, self-serving myopia suggests that the young generation should simply abandon its promise to provide social security benefits to older workers. This has never happened on a major scale in the United States, and it is unlikely to happen in other democracies.

The same cannot be said for totalitarian structures. Again, consider the case of Russia. The Yeltsin government has imposed significant hardship on elderly pensioners. The Russian executive branch has not resisted the temptation to allow real benefits of the elderly to diminish. The elderly are currently a weak political force without much recourse. Not yet a true democracy, the Russian legislature has only limited power, especially on economic matters. The foregoing attempted to outline a number of issues on which economics and politics conflict. While this chapter in no way provides a full understanding of the points, it may suggest some interesting areas in which further discussion can be pursued.

NOTES

1. Edward P. Lazear, *Prices and Wages in Transition Economies* (Stanford, Ca.: Hoover Institution Press, 1992).
2. Recent evidence (questionnaires cited in ibid.) documents the prevalence of constrained energy and housing prices throughout Eastern and Central Europe.
3. Kevin M. Murphy, Andrei Shleifer, and Robert Vishny in "Transition to Market Economy: Pitfalls of Partial Planning Reform" (Department of Economics, University of Chicago, 1991; unpublished paper), point out the problems associated with freeing some prices while constraining others.
4. Andrei Shleifer and Robert Vishny, "Reversing the Soviet Economic Collapse" (Department of Economics, University of Chicago, August 1991; unpublished paper).
5. See Mieczysław Kuziński, *Foreign Investor's Guide to Poland 1990* (New York: Ernst and Young, 1990) for discussion of the growth of private capital in Poland.
6. See Susan M. Collins and Dani Rodrik, *Eastern Europe and the Soviet Union in the World Economy* (Washington, D.C.: Institute for International Economics, 1992).
7. Jim Leitzel, "Soviet Economic Reform: Is Economics Helpful?" (Stanford, Ca.: Hoover Institution, 1991); unpublished paper, argues that currency in the former Soviet Union is convertible despite appearances.

7

Privatization Strategy and Its Political Context

*Łucja Świątkowski Cannon**

Privatization of state-owned enterprises is a key to the transformation from centrally planned to market economies. In the West, the debate on this issue centered on the techniques of privatization in the absence of market institutions, mass scale of the enterprise, and a scarcity of domestic and foreign investors. In Poland, the question of an alternative to central planning and state property is intensely political. It involves a major shift in political and economic power, contributing to other issues such as political democracy, liberalization, and decentralization. Thus, the issue of privatization raises fundamental questions about the nature of the state.

Poles have a certain vision of democracy and a free market that was defined over many years of struggle against communist rule. Methods of privatization, imported from the West, not only turned out to be impractical and unsuitable to local conditions but also produced undesirable political results. Thus, the strategy for transformation in Poland turned into a struggle among different economic groups over methods and the pace of privatization. This struggle has brought the rate of privatizations to a crawl.

The principal lines in this political battle emerged between those who claimed they wanted to copy the economic structure of mature Western societies and those who wanted to overturn the economic structure of the discredited commu-

* The author wishes to thank Dr. Tomasz Gruszecki, former acting minister of ownership tranformations, for his critique of an earlier version of this chapter.

nist state. The first group used the methods of privatization that emphasized the role of the owner of capital, in the Polish case, the state. The second group blamed representatives of the state—high officials in the bureaucracy and industrial managers—for the current disastrous state of the Polish economy and emphasized the decentralization of decision-making power to other groups that might do better in managing the Polish economy.

BACKGROUND

Consensus on the need for privatization was first reached in Poland after the 1980-1981 crisis, when the economy had virtually collapsed. Its level of inefficiency precluded further growth, whereas the central plan and state ownership lost all credibility.

Throughout the 1980s, the opposition had tried to provide an answer regarding the kind of economic system that is right for Poland. An answer emanating from the grass roots was in many ways the opposite of the communist system, which had been based on centralization, authoritarianism, and state interference in the economy. Polish society desired reforms that included far-reaching decentralization of government power, participation in decision-making at the local level, populist capitalism, and limited government. These values were behind reforms during the 1980s.

In 1981, Solidarity initiated an alternative to the old system by forcing adoption of the legislative Act on State-Owned Enterprises and the Act on Employee Self-Management. They tried to bring democracy to the industrial enterprise and subjected the power of state managers to oversight by employee councils. Instead of taking orders from the central state administration, authority in a state-owned enterprise was shared by the founding organ (usually the ministry), a chief executive officer, and the employee self-management council. Such councils assumed some of the prerogatives held by boards of directors in private companies: they reviewed the performance of the chief executive officer, usually a communist appointee, and approved his major decisions.

Solidarity regarded that self-management could solve the two main problems of the central planning system: "concentration of economic authority in the hands of the state bureaucracy and its arbitrary definition of national interest, including economic goals."[1] Communists regarded self-management as a compromise, imposed by the opposition, and suspended it with the invocation of martial law. Self-management councils were resurrected later to serve as a substitute for Solidarity, and many of its activists found a home there.

In the late 1980s, the communist government made a number of its own proposals for reforming the economy. First, it concentrated on reorganization of state property to make it more efficient. One important concept pertained to a stock exchange, instead of central bureaucracy, as arbiter of capital investments. It was proposed that all state-owned enterprises (SOEs) be transformed into joint stock companies, owned by the State Treasury and other institutional shareholders, such as holding companies, banks, or local self-governments. These entities could then issue bonds, with the future prospect of a quasi-capital market. However, such a move would still preserve state property and not necessarily result in efficiency gains.

The second proposed alternative clearly involved private property but in the form of "spontaneous privatization" resulting from relaxation of rules for relations between private enterprises and SOEs. Such private companies were usually created by SOE chief executive officers, who transferred uncompensated or undervalued assets to themselves or their relatives and made unauthorized and self-serving concessions to foreign companies. This did not increase the effectiveness of the economy but represented a form of "legalized parasitism." Colloquially, the development was called *nomenklatura* capitalism. Such experience created a certain amount of distrust of privatization in general.

EARLY PRIVATIZATION CONCEPTS

By the late 1980s, the political opposition came to a consensus that SOE privatization would be absolutely essential for improvement of the economy. Greater efficiency would be achieved through decentralization of decision-making, limiting the power of the state, depoliticization of the economy, and a populist form of capitalism. These objectives would provide political and economic self-determination for ordinary citizens, who would become the main beneficiaries of such reforms. Such goals seemed to be tacitly accepted by the communist government, when initial contacts were established with Solidarity in 1988. The regime was interested in offering Solidarity wide responsibility for management of the economy, eventually codified in the Roundtable agreements.

One of the influential proposals on how to privatize the economy through decentralization, a limited government role, and populist capitalism originated with Janusz Lewandowski and Jan Szomburg.[2] They considered as most desirable the dispersal of property ownership. Because of capital scarcity, the sale of state property was thought not to be feasible. Instead, the two men proposed free distribution of shares, so that every Polish household would receive some property rights.

The main goal was to establish foundations for unrestricted evolution of an ownership structure, with the use of a capital market as regulator of subsequent change. Aside from providing free distribution of property rights, this method would also free companies from administrative control and subject them to control by shareholders and, at the same time, satisfy the self-management aspirations of employees. It would also contribute to elimination of inflationary threats by temporarily restricting share trading (sale), paralleled by the creation of conditions required for the proper operation of the capital market and its barometer—the stock exchange.[3]

The Roundtable discussions emphasized development of self-managed state enterprises. Solidarity employee self-management activists began thinking about how to transform these councils into a capitalist form under new free market conditions. It was envisaged that employees would purchase a significant share of their factories and that the employee councils would be transformed into representations of employees on boards of directors. The majority of shares would be sold to foreign and domestic investors or remain under state control.[4]

Group ownership was rejected as too socialist, although shareholding by individual employees was regarded as a real alternative to state ownership. It would no doubt be a step forward, toward liberation of economic life from administrative control and the *nomenklatura*. The main problem was that it created a system of exclusive yet nontransferable property rights, directly tied to employment, which would not contribute to establishing a capital market. Furthermore, subsidized employee ownership would exacerbate inequities between employees of profitable enterprises and employees of unprofitable enterprises and government agencies. There were also fears that employee ownership might discourage foreign investors.

As soon as Solidarity became legalized, many of its old members had to decide whether to continue as self-management activists or to rejoin the Solidarity trade union. Most of the 1980 veterans decided to stay in self-management councils, where they had made a considerable commitment to study management and law. Most of the younger and more impatient workers, who were joining Solidarity for the first time, opted for the union. They were interested mainly in pressing for higher wages. For the veteran self-management activists, the main issues were participation in management and organized individual employee ownership. This created three separate issues: the role of employee councils in SOEs transformed into joint stock companies, the right to buy shares through a trust or foundation, and representation in the privatized enterprises.

After establishment of a government under Prime Minister Tadeusz Mazowiecki in August 1989, a team of Polish and American experts outlined a program for stabilization, liberalization, and privatization. Although quite similar to the one eventually adopted, it had some important differences. One such key recommendation was that on the starting date of the reform program, 1 January 1990, all SOEs employing over 250 persons would be transformed into joint stock companies and 20 percent of their shares would be given free to the employees. At the same time, only such shares would carry votes, not the 80 percent of State Treasury shares.

"The transfer of shares carrying the right to vote in supervisory board elections to the employees of these enterprises identifies private owners who, until the sale of the remaining 80 percent of the shares, are—through the supervisory council—the sole decision-makers on the affairs of the enterprise."[5] This team also rejected, except as a last resort, introduction of a special category of securities with restricted circulation, such as nontransferable employee shares.

PRIVATIZATION LAW OF 1990

On 1 January 1990, the economic "shock therapy" reform program, which consisted of stabilization, liberalization, and privatization of the Polish economy, was launched. The foreign investment law was modified to make it easier for such companies and individuals to invest in Poland by forming joint ventures and buying enterprises directly or through the stock market. At the same time, talks commenced on renegotiation of the $40 billion hard-currency debt. No contradiction was perceived between a failure to repay this debt and high hopes for new foreign investment in Poland.

Starting immediately, the Finance Ministry introduced a program of so-called small privatization. It involved efforts to make all small service and manufacturing establishments private. That was to be accomplished mainly through encouragement of new private enterprises which initially were expected to be small. The second approach would transfer ownership of small enterprises, such as shops, bus companies, land, and real estate, to the local municipalities (free local government elections were held in May 1990). Their sale to private Polish investors followed.

On 13 July 1990, the Law on Privatization of the SOEs[6] established general rules for organizing joint stock companies, wholly owned by the State Treasury, or legal liquidation of enterprises. This legislation did not incorporate any of the proposals by reformers. It presented a narrow vision of privatization which centralized all decisions in the hands of a new Ministry of Ownership Transformations. Experimental privatization already initiated by employee councils and other groups had to be abandoned in order to await decisions from the central ministry.

Legal ambiguities of ownership in the centrally planned economy were resolved by transformation of all SOEs into joint stock companies, whose shares were to be owned by the State Treasury. The treasury itself would become the clear legal owner of state property, and the function of management would be clearly separated from government economic policy or tax policy.

The employee councils would be abolished. Instead, employees could elect one-third of the board of directors for a joint stock company. In essence, these companies were renationalized, vesting all authority in the privatization ministry, and secondarily, in management.

After financial and legal analysis and debt restructuring, the enterprise would be offered for sale through public offer of shares on the soon-to-be-organized stock market to both domestic and foreign investors or through sale to foreign investors. The goal was to make it possible for passive foreign individual investors to invest money in the Polish economy through the stock exchange. Employees had a right to buy up to 20 percent of shares at half price, but no more than the average annual earnings of state employees.

Privatization through liquidation could be implemented by the founding organ (usually the ministry) or an employee council. It applied to companies that were either in good financial condition or on the verge of bankruptcy. The enterprise could be sold as a going concern or its assets disposed of at auction. On initiative of the employee council, the company could also be leased to a group of employees.

The Ministry of Privatization presented its own plans for open sale of shares as "people's capitalism," where all Polish citizens could freely buy stock. This was an unconvincing argument because, behind the appearance of equality of access, there existed great inequality. It was known that Polish society was poor and only higher level communists and black marketeers possessed large savings which could be used to buy shares. In addition, the stabilization program during the first few months lowered the standard of living by a further 30 percent. At the same time, it was argued that effects of the stabilization program weakened the condition of SOEs and reduced their price for foreign buyers.

This narrow vision of privatization was based on grounds of economic efficiency and property rights theory which holds that the concentration of ownership and management provides the highest incentives for good performance of the enterprise because the manager bears the full personal risk of decisions. As the number of proprietors increases, a common property problem emerges which adversely affects performance of the enterprise. Only private proprietary firms and joint stock companies are free from adverse effects of nonexclusive property rights because of competition. This theory claims that common property owned by employees as a group, or through an Employee Stock Ownership Plan (ESOP), will lead to a much lower level of industrial performance.[7]

On the basis of this analysis, it was decided that the goal of Polish privatization should be establishment of a modern capitalist class which would have enough stake in privatized enterprises to act as owners. Based on this theory, without comparing it with the experience of developed countries, the Privatization Ministry fought off challenges from the employee management movement and proponents of free share distribution.

The ministry's strategy introduced unfamiliar Western financial concepts and institutions. As a result of the communist experience, however, Polish citizens distrusted large government-run institutions, such as the stock exchange, which they really did not understand. They understood employee councils which, in the public's perception, signified a decentralization of economic decision-making and local initiative. Employee council activists were veterans of Solidarity who made a major effort to increase their managerial potential, and they looked upon themselves as an alternative to incompetent managers. The question of participation in management represented their key demand, particularly in nonprivatized enterprises. The privatization law destroyed the motivation of employees to adapt themselves to market conditions at their own initiative and forced them into uncertainty and passivity.[8]

Most importantly, however, this decision effectively negated urgent aims of the reform to replace a majority of managers as well as government bureaucrats who had already demonstrated a lack of free market skills. The new Ministry of Ownership Transformations came into being, although other ministries retained their old staffs as a result of the Mazowiecki government policy. The decision to abolish employee councils, instead of making them boards of directors as originally planned, was most controversial. In enterprises, employees were supposed to elect the supervisory boards of joint stock companies that would name a chief executive officer. "In this way our programme proposed to kill two birds with one stone. On the one hand, state enterprises-turned-joint stock companies would immediately find owners with better defined property rights, while on the other, the process of getting rid of the communist *nomenklatura* appointees would be greatly accelerated."[9]

The idea of immediate transformation of SOEs into joint Treasury stock companies (commercialization) could be regarded as a meaningless change in titles. If managers were the same and boards of directors were dominated by representatives of the ministries and the state sector, it is doubtful that they would be more competent and less subject to political pressures than the government in guiding the process of restructuring or liquidation. This commercialization and the abolition of employee councils was justified by concerns about asset-stripping by employees. However, there was no concern about a much more likely danger: asset-stripping by the managers. Commercialization was not necessary to guard against either. The rule of law and conflict-of-interest laws would prevent asset-stripping more effectively than new boards of directors.[10]

In addition to transferring new powers to the state bureaucracy and managers, the Finance Ministry did not prosecute perpetrators of fraud who had profited under the *nomenklatura* capitalism system. As a matter of fact, some advisors to Mazowiecki openly argued for encouragement of *nomenklatura* capitalism.[11] Thus, the system of turning political influence into capital property continued unabated.

As a result of this continuity in personnel and activities of the governing class, the privatization law lost all legitimacy. Lech Wałęsa challenged the authority of the Mazowiecki government and announced his candidacy for the office of president. He called on the Finance Ministry to devise methods of privatization that would benefit ordinary citizens. Various self-management federations and clubs denounced the 1990 law as "propertisation" of the *nomenklatura*. They denounced the concentration of decisions in the hands of *nomenklatura* bureaucracy.[12] Thus, both the concentration of power in the hands of the state officials and the fact that these officials were regarded as illegitimate constituted the basis for rejection.

To have a chance at success, the underlying philosophy, aims, and methods of the program must be found politically acceptable. To achieve such acceptance, an intensive propaganda campaign should be carried out and support of key groups secured through consultation.[13] In a sense, such a campaign did take place during the 1990 presidential campaign but only as a negative reaction to the already passed Law on Privatization. Attacks on the ministry's arbitrary and bureaucratic methods, its centralization of authority, and provision of special privileges to *nomenklatura* and foreign investors underscored the illegitimacy of the privatization law.

The next major problem with the 1990 law was that it had been based on the limited British experience, disregarding that in Poland it would be applied on a vastly larger scale. There had been no experience with the stock market and no infrastructure or skills on which to base such an innovation. Thus the privatization strategy, based on time-consuming individual analyses hitherto unknown in Poland and conducted by expensive foreign consultants, was unsuitable to Polish conditions.

MASS PRIVATIZATION SCHEMES

The mass privatization plan originated at the beginning of July 1991, just as it became evident that the privatization law had not gained popular support. Furthermore, it was inadequate to accomplish privatization of 8,000 SOEs within a reasonable period of time. It had been devised on the basis of a combination of old communist proposals for holding companies with SOE shares distributed among state institutions, and the Lewandowski-Szomburg proposal for citizen vouchers, with one important exception: these holding companies would be managed by foreign consultants.

The essence of the plan centered on 20 quasi-private investment trusts which would essentially be closed mutual funds. These trusts would contract with foreign advisors to assist in establishment and distribution of dividends. All such financial institutions would take an active part in restructuring and management of enterprises.

These trusts would assume control over the 500 largest enterprises which would become immediately "commercialized," turned into joint stock companies, in order to abolish employee councils, as a means of making them more efficient. Shares in the trusts not given free to Polish citizens would be retained by the state, and the remainder distributed among pension funds, commercial banks, and other state institutions. It was hoped that such a strategy would sidestep the difficult, costly, and time-consuming process of enterprise valuation and recognize the scarcity of capital in private hands. This plan encompassed a strategy to quicken the pace of privatization.

Emphasis on speed was motivated explicitly by politics. Jeffrey Sachs and David Lipton, key advisors, detested employee councils, which they regarded as "pernicious." They were afraid that, unless workers were given some concessions, they might resist the privatization process. With mounting unemployment, employees might decide that it was not in their best interest. The plan was to privatize large firms as rapidly as possible, before the expected political backlash developed. Sachs and Lipton argued that such a pace might lead initially to an inappropriate distribution of ownership, resulting in a diffused ownership or one in the wrong hands. Capital markets would then encourage a reshuffling of ownership through takeovers, mergers, and buyouts, so that there resulted a proper matching of owners and firms.[14] This argument was generally not accepted. In addition, while the program was motivated by a desire for speed, two and a half years after its introduction, it was still being debated in the Sejm.

After the government had performed preliminary work on the scheme in the first half of 1991, the 400 large and profitable companies that would be included in the mass privatization scheme were selected. However, the parliamentary debate on this issue was put off in the fall because of opposition that criticized it as a "quick and dirty" approach to dispose of national assets in a hasty and uncontested manner. Others argued that only a new and fully democratic Sejm (the first free elections were held in October 1991) should have the authority to vote on such a fundamental issue.[15]

In early 1992, the government of Jan Olszewski decided to continue with the program. The next prime minister, Hanna Suchocka, presented the proposal to the Sejm in August 1992. It provides that 60 percent of shares in large SOEs will be allocated to about 20 National Investment Trusts. The trust can be either a "core investor" in a company, with 33 percent of the stock, or a "minority shareholder" with 27 percent. Ten percent of the shares will be given free to employees of each enterprise. The State Treasury will retain 12 percent. A newly created investment fund for retirees and public servants will receive 18 percent.

Managers of the National Investment Trusts will be chosen from international investment and consulting firms and supervised by a board of directors with a majority of Polish citizens. They will be compensated both in cash and stock, based on their performance. Their goal is to increase the value of companies under their management through restructuring, improved management, and access to Western capital and technology. Each receives a contract for ten years, after which these companies will be sold.[16]

Some 27 million adult Polish citizens are eligible to buy vouchers, for about 20 percent of an average salary; these vouchers can be traded or exchanged for shares in the National Investment Trusts. These can be also traded on the Warsaw Stock Exchange, starting in 1994. The original list of 400 large and well-managed SOEs dropped to 183, because the financial condition of the others had severely deteriorated due to the recession. However, a decision was taken to increase the number of participating companies to 600. Also, due to employee resistance against privatization, the consent of employees is no longer required to transform the SOEs into Treasury joint stock companies.[17]

Overall, the positive aspect of the program involves recognition that the scale of privatization is large and that a methodology has been devised to deal with it in an efficient manner. Its attractive quality is the equity of giving away shares to all citizens. It is also a belated attempt to recognize the problem of ineffective SOE management and provide Western guidance and resources on a mass scale.

On the negative side, mass privatization was presented at the beginning as an alternative to employee ownership and a means to eliminate the influence of employee councils. As a result, many employees strongly oppose this plan. Therefore, it is doubtful that Western managers can improve the performance of enterprises against the will of their employees. There are objections that the best Polish enterprises will be controlled by foreign consulting companies, employing numerous former *nomenklatura* officials and working closely with the central bureaucracy. The plan also created a new problem of effective monitoring over managers of these holding companies, since they are not owners themselves and would find ways to self-deal and perpetuate their existence.

There is also a threat that the program will deteriorate into quasi-privatization. A ten-year management contract period is mentioned but very vaguely. If the object of the program is restructuring and better management, a much shorter (five years is a more typical timetable) period would be sufficient. Otherwise, many problems associated with state-owned property would still apply, in an even more complicated form. At the same time, the effort made to set up these quasi-privatization schemes could not be spent on devising solutions to more immediate problems of privatization.

It is interesting that, aside from Poland, this kind of holding-company privatization has been attempted only in Romania. Czechoslovakia, Russia, and Ukraine adopted individual vouchers which can be freely traded and exchanged for a wider range of state property. That carries considerable risks, although it promises greater flexibility and a possibility of real privatization in the future.

SECTOR PRIVATIZATION

The sectoral approach to privatization involves a grouping of companies in the same industrial sector and assigning them to the same financial advisor who has to formulate and implement a privatization strategy for all of these companies. The advisor must analyze the entire sector to determine key competitive factors, consider the current structure of the relevant industry, look at likely changes, and examine alternative policy scenarios. After this preliminary work, a privatization strategy for each individual company is devised that fits within the expected future industry structure.[18]

This approach is regarded as superior to individual sell-offs, because the cost of foreign consultants is less expensive and the seller is in a better bargaining position. This constitutes the beginning of an industrial policy. It also provides better information to outside investors and sellers about the relative competitive position of enterprises. About 30 sector advisors were chosen.

Some enterprises were sold under this program. During 1992, however, this approach ran into problems. It was not clear what to do with unsold enterprises within the sector, while expensive financial analyses were quickly becoming obsolete. The sector privatization program was transformed in the October 1992 "pact on SOE" into an idea for sector contracts that would restructure entire industrial branches through state intervention.[19]

REPRIVATIZATION

The politically controversial issue of reprivatization required immediate attention from the beginning. The refusal to address it complicated implementation of other privatizations due to unclear legal ownership of property, particularly land. It was also the least expensive form of privatization, not requiring armies of consultants. On the other hand, it was legally complicated and aroused mixed political emotions in Polish society.[20]

Several proposals were submitted to the Sejm beginning in 1991, but none was accepted. In 1992, the new government of Jan Olszewski reassessed the economic and political situation and made reprivatization one of its priorities. A bill was submitted to the Sejm, although the government's political weakness and eventual fall in June 1992 allowed little time for implementation.

MANAGEMENT OF STATE-OWNED ENTERPRISES

The 1990 privatization law was as significant for what it omitted as for what it contained. The legislation ignored the fate of state-owned enterprises. That was because the government expected to have all 8,000 SOEs privatized within a three-year period. That meant that these enterprises languished while waiting for a decision by the Privatization Ministry. They became heavily indebted to banks, other enterprises, and state tax authorities.

The poor performance of these passive enterprises contributed to the deepening recession over the past two years. In addition, all companies in

Poland operate in an essentially hostile business environment, with bureaucratic red tape, strict regulations, and a lack of business infrastructure.

The Olszewski government first took up the problem of the 80 percent of Polish enterprises that are still state-owned and in need of an improved overseeing mechanism, and which will remain in state hands for the foreseeable future, and decided to separate property management from state administration. Legal preparations commenced for a bill on the State Treasury. In a key policy change, it was decided that a part of the proceeds of privatization should be used to finance restructuring of privatized enterprises rather than go to the State Treasury.[21]

The government of Hanna Suchocka, formed in July 1992, also made an effort to deal with the management of SOEs. Their condition had triggered widespread strikes and protests. In its October 1992 "Pact on SOE,"[22] the government again proposed to accelerate privatization and change the management rules for the remaining SOEs. In essence, it involves employees in restructuring and privatization of SOEs. Management would be rationalized by a new institution, the State Treasury. The pact proposes to combine functions of property manager and transaction agent in making decisions about sale or lease of SOEs.

If the SOE is in good financial condition, employees must decide within three months on a privatization strategy, such as

sale to domestic or foreign corporate investor,

sale of shares on the stock market,

management / employee buyout,

transfer of majority control to a bank or institution.

If the SOE is in poor financial condition, it can still privatize. However, it must sign a contract with the bank and restructure its debts. This restructuring can result in forgiveness of the debt or rescheduling or an exchange of the debt for shares in the enterprise. Management contracts are another way to improve performance with bonuses in stock for all involved. Small enterprises bought by employees would have to obtain an agreement from a bank in case of debts.

SOEs that did not choose their own privatization strategy would be transformed automatically into joint stock companies by the Privatization Ministry. The most important part of the pact is the proposal to change the mechanism of controlling wages in the state sector from the excess wage tax to negotiated settlements and abolition of the state dividend.

The "Pact on SOE" represents the most ambitious attempt to deal with the legal form of the state sector and establish a direction for the future, thus ending the uncertainty that deeply affected performance. In another positive development, giving a voice to employees in deciding the future of their enterprise has been universally praised. A new element of the proposal is a recommendation that the buyer should have a right to purchase land where the enterprise is located. Debt restructuring and better wage incentives are two issues that had been long overdue.

The most controversial aspect of the proposal pertains to the declaration that employee interests in privatization will be decided by trade unions. In 1990 the Ministry of Finance abolished employee self-management councils, which claimed to represent interests of employees under privatization, in enterprises entering the first phase of privatization, namely, transformation into a joint stock company. Subsequently, they lost influence in SOEs also. The direct result of this change is the increased influence of the trade unions, particularly those most militant in pressing workers' wage demands.[23]

There are several trade unions in Poland. The largest, best organized and financed, is the former communist union which is favored by the proposal. Solidarity had been largely a social movement and not structured as a formal trade union. Furthermore, the drive to gain more members may lead to competing pay demands which will generate more conflict in enterprises. There is also the fact of countrywide quarterly negotiations on pay, free from the excess wage tax. Thus, the elimination of employee councils removed the ownership-aspiring Solidarity activists from the political scene and brought forward irresponsible and radical trade unionists. Now the government is proposing to vest ownership rights in these radical trade unions, which have no ownership claims, to induce moderation in their wage demands.

The second important issue is the deteriorating condition of both state-owned and Treasury joint stock companies, thereby undermining the rationale for privatization. The strategy pursued so far has not resulted in any increased efficiency of Polish enterprises. The pact aims to restructure enterprise debts with a possibility of debt-for-equity swaps and a change in legal organization of enterprises, including greater incentives for management, and for better adaptation to a market economy. More thought is given to previous proposals for management contracts, where reward is based on the level of improvement in performance of the enterprise.[24] Debt restructuring must be combined with recapitalization of state banks. The government has proposed that banks be recapitalized with $1 billion in funds from the Polish currency stabilization fund.[25]

However, it is not clear that giving all authority over restructuring enterprises to the banks, which are dominated by former communists and which already represent a major obstacle to reform, will solve the problem. Banks also have no vested interest in improvement of SOE performance. They are already plagued by major financial scandals, and have created uncontrolled mechanisms for transfer abroad of Polish capital. Absence of a supervisory institution of the State Treasury places all responsibility for enterprises on banks, and ultimately the Ministry of Ownership Transformations, thus further centralizing important economic decisions in the government bureaucracy.[26] The banks themselves need restructuring and greater financial skills to take on the role of an active participant in transformation of the Polish economy.

RESULTS OF PRIVATIZATION POLICY

The results of privatization through the end of August 1992 were the following. About one-fourth (1,841 cases) of all SOEs were affected by privatization proceedings. About three-fourths of these (1,368) were privatized through the liquidation strategy. Most were on the verge of bankruptcy (757 cases) and their physical assets were sold, resulting in unemployment. A total of 611 enterprises were privatized through liquidation in good financial condition. These were mainly leased to employee-run companies. Such methods mostly applied to smaller companies, with up to 500 employees. Only 191 companies had more than 500 employees.

Another 290 enterprises were transformed into joint stock companies as a transition to privatization. They were mostly large, successful entities. Only 74 companies were privatized through the capital market and 44 of these through a public offer. These privatizations were highly individualized and slow. Of the 44, foreign capital participated in 21 as active investors. A total of 216 enterprises were turned into state-owned joint stock companies as preparation for privatization. Another 183 companies, almost all of them large, became part of the mass privatization project. There are 7,685 joint ventures with foreign capital in Poland, generally small- or medium-sized. The small privatization has been quite successful and resulted in 80 percent of shops and service establishments being sold to private owners.[27]

Liquidation emerged to be the most popular and practical method of privatization. For enterprises in good financial condition, this method usually involved a lease to a group of employees. Such companies have turned out to be rather successful. Liquidation of enterprises in bad financial condition is a worrisome trend, reflecting the difficulties of SOEs in a recessionary economy induced by the stabilization program.

Overall, privatization of smaller enterprises through auction, liquidation, or lease to groups of employees has been a great success and is complete to a large extent. Together with the creation of new small businesses and private agriculture, the private economic activity now constitutes over half of the gross domestic product.

There are severe problems with privatizations of large SOEs. In terms of their motivations, generally enterprises themselves ask to be privatized because that excludes them from the obligatory state dividend and the excess wage tax. The key issue involves agreement between management and the employee council. Disagreement about the course of action often arises when the council favors some kind of employee ownership. Despite earlier expectations regarding superiority of private enterprises, at the practical level no differences have been noted. Recession affected all equally. The direct result of privatization involved maximum pay raises. The main goal was avoidance of layoffs. Principal changes in organization contributed to strengthening of management and centralization of policy-making. Employees of privatized enterprises were less positive about privatization than those who planned to do it in the future, because they saw the privatization process as favoring management and hurting the employees. That was reinforced by the lack of improvement in enterprise functioning.[28]

The October report of the prime minister's Privatization Council describes the accumulated negative trends in the process:

1. lowered pace of privatization, irrespective of methods
2. increasing social resistance and worsening climate for privatization
3. increased levels of uncertainty in SOEs, leading to abandonment of privatization projects
4. continuing recession in the state sector, increasing numbers of SOEs threatened with bankruptcy, and decreasing numbers of those that fulfill minimum conditions for successful privatization
5. a virtual lack of interest by foreign and domestic capital
6. a lack of progress in legislative preparation of new privatization programs: reprivatization, mass privatization, privatization of banks and local self-government property.[29]

Furthermore, the style of carrying out privatization has been arbitrary, bureaucratic, and dominated by the centralized administration, leading to a gap between motivations of economic subjects and state authority.

CONCLUSION

Privatization strategy in Poland was based explicitly from the beginning on Western experience. Reformers wanted to transplant a proven method from developed Western countries, particularly Great Britain, and avoid compromise solutions that might not be successful. Yugoslavia with its system of employee self-management councils, though much different than in Poland, served as a negative example for Polish reformers. However, since privatization is a major political change and must take root in society, it should be based on a combination of historical, political, and value elements that are unique to each country. Modeling a privatization policy on that of other more developed countries is of limited value, because all countries are unique, even if they subscribe to a common capitalist system.

As a result of its historical and political experiences, particularly the scars of communism and the struggle by Solidarity as well as the prevalence of Roman Catholic social philosophy, Poland's society values decentralization, limited government, participation in decision-making at the societal and enterprise level, and populist capitalism, where an ordinary person has a stake in the economic system that allows some self-determination. These values also widely exist in developed Western countries. What is surprising is that Polish reformers did not share these mainstream values, did not respect society for its values, and chose largely those elements from Western experience that contradicted these values.

The privatization projects that were based on values prevalent in Polish society and which made an original contribution to privatization methods, such as privatization through liquidation, mainly by lease to employee groups, have been most successful. Those foreign methods which were grafted unchanged into Polish conditions turned out to be ineffective and conflict-generating. In the long term, only methods accepted by society turn out to be economically effective.

Furthermore, the Polish government's methods were not only centralized but also dependent on the same group of state officials and managers who already were regarded as illegitimate by Polish society. The Mazowiecki's government decision to overturn previous plans and to retain their services and increase their influence, accomplished through the policy of writing off their communist past and the elimination of Solidarity-dominated employee councils, seriously contributed to the illegitimacy of the privatization policy. Continuation of the communist practice of turning political influence into material assets, both by former communists and the postcommunist elite, undermines social confidence in government.

Another problem is the method by which privatization policy has been imposed. Western democratic societies are based on free discussion, political compromise, pluralism, piecemeal practicality, and change without chaos. Polish reformers operate on the belief that the state can solve all problems in a quick, revolutionary manner, overriding all resistance with force. The emphasis on rapid privatization has led to disorder as well as political and economic destabilization. Haste carries the danger of major mistakes. The lack of success in privatization policy ironically has led to calls for further acceleration. That has strengthened political pressure and led to a rejection of government policy.

This emphasis on speed also resulted in a complete neglect of those SOEs whose status was undefined. Some members of the Leszek Balcerowicz team openly boasted that they wanted to drive all SOEs out of business. The floundering of the state sector, which constituted 80 percent of the Polish economy, contributed to the recession of 1990-1992. The issue of creating appropriate incentive structures within SOEs to minimize their costs of production and to maximize their market value remains vital. Incentives right now are perverse.

The current Suchocka government has attempted to remedy this mistake in its "Pact on SOEs." The practical result of its strategy may be to give more power and authority to additional *nomenklatura* groups of former communists in the banks and trade unions, while restraining some wage demands. But these demands are an expression of the illegitimacy of the government privatization policy.

The proposed "pact on state-owned enterprises" of the Suchocka government does not seem to lay out a promising direction for the further evolution of privatization policy. It tries to engender a feeling of ownership among workers by involving trade unions in the privatization process. However, there are numerous and antagonistic trade unions, so finding an acceptable representative of employees will be difficult. Moreover, such representation might not be interested in acting in a conservative manner as owner, only in pressing wage demands.

The government has an accepted representative of employees in the employee councils which have strong ownership claims; but the government refuses to deal with them. Employee councils managed to survive the full onslaught of the military regime of General Jaruzelski during martial law and became influential in 1989. They were a motor of the government privatization policy, widely supported by workers. Their arbitrary elimination turned employees toward opposition to privatization and removed political support from government policy.

The effort to restructure enterprises, to adapt them better for a market economy, is commendable although again does not go far enough. Enterprises cannot function well with the same discredited managers in a business environment of high taxation, lack of access to investment credits, banks that do not perform their basic tasks, and political uncertainty about government policy which may change rapidly. There is significant evidence that mechanical privatizations of individual enterprises are inadequate.

Poland should concentrate on promoting development of the domestic private sector and an environment in which all enterprises can grow. One key issue is the clarification of property rights, especially ownership of land for those planning to invest. Property rights are doubtful, if an enterprise owner cannot own the land where his enterprise is located. Creation of a business infrastructure, such as financial institutions, insurance, and telecommunications, is vital to the performance of all enterprises in Poland. This has been neglected. The issue of creating appropriate incentive structures within SOEs to minimize their costs of production and to maximize their market value for privatization remains vital.

The discussion of privatization in Poland has turned full circle and is now back where it started, asking about the place of employees and management in the process, and how to privatize large numbers of SOEs. The answers given to these questions during 1989-1990 were wrong. The political decisions of the Mazowiecki government to eliminate representatives of employees (dominated by Solidarity) from the privatization process, not to eliminate discredited communist officials from the state bureaucracy and industrial management, and to privatize SOEs individually in a centralized, arbitrary manner, led to limited success for the privatization policy. The answers to these questions provided by the Suchocka government are better, although the animosity engendered by earlier mistakes might make it impossible to reach a successful compromise.

NOTES

1. Jerzy Hausner and Jerzy Indraszkiewicz, *Samorząd załogi: Sprzeczności i perspektywy rozwoju* (Warsaw: Państwowe Wydawnictwo Ekonomiczne, 1988), p. 137.
2. Janusz Lewandowski and Jan Szomburg, "Property Reform as a Basis for Social and Economic Reform," *Communist Economies,* no. 3 (1989), pp. 259-260.
3. Ibid., p. 264.

4. Łucja Świątkowski, "Workers-Shareholders Can Reform Polish Economy," *The Wall Street Journal,* 23 August 1989.

5. Janusz Beksiak, Tomasz Gruszecki, Aleksander Jędraszczyk, and Jan Winiecki, "Outline of a Programme for Stabilisation and Systemic Changes," *The Polish Transformation: Programme and Progress* (London: The Centre for Research into Communist Economies, 1990).

6. *Vademecum prywatyzacji* (Warsaw: Międzynarodowa Fundacja Rozwoju Rynku Kapitałowego i Przekształceń Własnościowych w Rzeczpospolitej Polskiej, 1991).

7. Jan Winiecki, *Privatization in Poland: A Comparative Perspective* (Tübingen: J.C.B. Mohr, 1992).

8. "Stanowisko Nr.15/90, Prezydium Warszawskiego Klubu Samorządu Pracowniczego . . . ," *VI Krajowe Forum Samorządu Załogi* (Warsaw: Zarząd Główny, 10-11 September 1990).

9. Janusz Beksiak, et al., "A Comparative Analysis of Our Programme . . . ," *The Polish Transformation.*

10. Lawrence Summers, "Comments," *Brookings Papers on Economic Activity* (Washington, D.C.: Brookings Institution, 1990), pp. 334-342.

11. Anthony Levitas and Piotr Strzałkowski, "What Does 'uwłaszczenie nomenklatury' Really Mean?" *Communist Economies,* no. 3 (1990).

12. "Stanowisko Gdańskiego Klubu Samorządu . . . ," *VI Krajowe Forum.*

13. Beksiak, et al., "A Comparative Analysis . . . ," *The Polish Transformation.*

14. David Lipton and Jeffrey Sachs, "Privatization in Eastern Europe: The Case of Poland," *Brookings Papers on Economic Activity* (Washington, D.C.: Brookings Institution, 1990), pp. 293-333.

15. "Privatisation by Sector Achieves Economies of Scale and Better Prices for the State in Poland," *Privatisation International* (September 1991), p. 3.

16. "Poland Gears Up for Mass Privatization," *PlanEcon Report,* 19 February 1992.

17. "Rozdanie Świadectw w 1994," *Rzeczpospolita,* 20 August 1992.

18. "Privatisation by Sector . . . ," *Privatisation International.*

19. Piotr Aleksandrowicz, "Niebezpieczne słabości," *Rzeczpospolita,* 8 October 1992.

20. Krzysztof Fronczak, "Rządowy program prywatyzacji: przeciw ogólnikom," *Życie gospodarcze,* 1 March 1992.

21. "Poland's New Salesman Sets Agenda," *Privatisation International* (January 1992), p. 3.

22. Government Program, "Założenia polityki społeczno-gospodarczej" (Warsaw: October 1992); mimeographed.

23. "Trudny nadzór," interview with Dr. Jerzy Drygalski, secretary of state in the Ministry of Ownership Transformations, *Życie gospodarcze, 6 December 1992.*

24. Ministry of Privatization insert, "Stages of Privatization through Restructuring," *The Insider,* no. 25 (22 January 1992).

25. "Poland wants new use for $1 bn fund," *PlanEcon Report,* no. 25 (9 December 1992).

26. Dariusz Grabowski and Janusz Szewczak, "Uwagi o 'pakcie o przedsiębior-stwie,'" *Tygodnik Solidarność* (9 October 1992).

27. Monthly Report of the Polish Ministry of Privatization (September 1992); mimeographed.

28. Wanda Karpińska-Mizielińska and Tadeusz Smuga, "Przebieg procesu przekształceń własnościowych," *Gospodarka Polski w procesie transformacji 1992 r.* (Warsaw: Instytut Rozwoju i Studiów Strategicznych, 1992).

29. Opinia Rady Przekształceń Własnościowych przy Prezesie Rady Ministrów (October 1992); mimeographed.

8

Product and Labor Markets

Benjamin H. Slay and Michał Rutkowski*

This chapter examines the extent to which market forces made an impact on Polish product and labor markets during 1990-1992. Developments in industry and, to a smaller extent, agriculture, are surveyed under the "product market" heading; special attention is paid to questions of branch and sectoral restructuring, as well as to changes in levels of concentration and monopoly. The "labor market" section focuses on the evolution of wage regulation and the collective-bargaining framework, changes in employment, income distribution, and the development of labor-market and social welfare policies.

PRODUCT MARKETS

Although the introduction of the "Balcerowicz Plan" (named after Deputy Prime Minister Leszek Balcerowicz) in January 1990 is often considered the beginning of Polish economic transformation, liberalization of the price system, foreign trade, regulation of state enterprises, and the private sector began in the 1980s, and acquired a certain momentum during 1988-1989 in particular. As a liberalization program, the Balcerowicz Plan represented an

* Benjamin Slay would like to acknowledge his gratitude to the Radio Free Europe/Radio Liberty Research Institute for providing the research materials on which this chapter is based, as well as the Social Science Research Council and the American Council of Learned Societies for research funding.

Table 8.1
Changes in Gross Industrial Production, 1990-1991
(percentages)

Branch	1990	1991
industry (overall)	-24.2	-13.5
fuels and power	-22.1	-22.4
metallurgy	-19.7	-28.4*
engineering	-22.0	-21.0*
chemicals	-24.6	-10.2
minerals	-21.5	-05.8
wood and paper	-24.9	-05.1
light industry	-33.8	-15.1*
food processing	-23.7	-00.8
other branches	-33.6	n.a.

Gross industrial sales, in constant prices; 1991 data are preliminary.

Note: * Approximations derived by using price indices that are unweighted averages of component subbranch price indices to deflate nominal branch growth rates.

Sources: *Rocznik statystyczny 1991*, pp. 275-276; *Biuletyn statystyczny 1992*, no. 2, pp. 56, 72-73.

intensification of reforms prepared during the late 1980s and in part introduced by the communist government of Mieczysław Rakowski. However, the stabilization element of the Balcerowicz Plan marked the real sea change in Polish economic policy. By dramatically tightening fiscal, monetary, and credit policies during the first half of that year, it became possible to wipe out shortage pressures on virtually all product markets, thus allowing liberalization to bear important fruits (e.g., złoty convertibility) that would not otherwise have been forthcoming.

While such qualitative assessments about the stabilization program's pathbreaking nature are fairly well accepted, interpretation of quantitative measures of post-1989 changes in Polish industry is fraught with difficulty. On the one hand, the official statistics depict steep production declines in virtually all industrial branches during the 1990-1991 period (see Table 8.1), accompanied by reductions in enterprise profits and investment spending. Enterprise profitability fell from 29 percent in 1990 to 6 percent for the following year. By the end of 1991, almost two-fifths of state enterprises were losing money, and about one firm in three had lost its financial creditworthiness. Investment spending declined by some 18 percent during 1990-1991 which, following large reductions in the investment share of GDP during the 1980s, left a large share of Poland's capital stock completely depreciated.

On the other hand, the official declines in industrial production probably overstate associated welfare loss. The well-known bias toward underreporting in official statistics implies that the actual extent of the drop in industrial production was almost certainly less than that depicted in Table 8.1. Also, declines in output levels resulted in part from the cessation of value-subtracting activities, which could actually increase welfare rather than reduce it. Declines in industrial production also helped reduce the scale of Poland's pollution problem, although this can hardly be described as a policy objective. It is also clear that industrial production during 1990-1991 declined more than agricultural production or services.[1] The implication is that this market-based restructuring corrected some of the intersectoral distortions from the communist era.

The situation with intraindustry restructuring is less clear, however. Given the traditional policy emphasis upon heavy industry and the energy-fuels complex, the introduction of market forces was widely expected to lead to decreases in the share of industrial production represented by these branches, and increases in the share of such branches as light industry and foodstuffs. However, according to official statistics, the pattern of intra-industrial restructuring between 1990 and mid-1992 had not been consistent with this hypothesis. As Table 8.2 shows, the share of light industry in total industrial output fell by 53 percent during this time, while fuels and power more than doubled. Although the share of food processing increased by some 14 percent, that of engineering (a branch that includes many higher-technology and consumer products) declined by some 30 percent. The implication is that the impact of market forces on intraindustrial restructuring during the first years of the transition was rather weak, if not perverse.

This conclusion can also be challenged on a number of grounds. First, since the private sector is represented much more strongly in light industry, food processing, and electrical machinery than in fuels and power,[2] a more accurate reporting of private-sector activities would have increased the share of the former branches at the expense of the latter. Second, even if the picture of industrial restructuring presented in Table 8.2 is relatively accurate, this does not prove that market forces failed to take hold during 1990-1991. The declines in light industry and engineering in part reflected reductions in

Table 8.2
Changes in the Branch Structure of
Gross Industrial Output, 1989-1991 (percentages)

Branch	1989	1990	1991	1992*
industry (overall)	100.0	100.0	100.0	100.0
fuels and power	11.2	15.9	20.6	24.5
metallurgy	10.1	12.7	8.6	8.2
engineering	25.3	24.2	20.4	17.8
chemicals	9.1	9.5	9.4	9.4
minerals	3.9	4.2	4.8	3.9
wood and paper	5.0	4.8	5.4	5.1
light industry	12.2	8.1	7.4	5.7
food processing	20.9	18.6	21.9	23.9
other branches	2.3	2.0	1.8	1.5

Shares of gross industrial sales, current prices.

Note: * Midyear figures.

Sources: *Rocznik statystyczny 1991*, p. 276; *Biuletyn statystyczny*, no. 2 (1992), pp. 72-73; "Statystyka Polski," supplement to *Rzeczpospolita*, 4 August 1992, p. V.

exports to the USSR and other former members of the Council for Mutual Economic Assistance (CMEA) during this time, as well as increasingly stiff competition from Western imports. Likewise, the increase in the share of fuels and power can in part be explained by the relative price- and income-inelasticity of demand for these products, so that sales and production in these branches held up better in the face of higher prices and lower real incomes during 1990-1991 than did other branches. Finally, it may also be that Poland in fact enjoys a comparative advantage in energy, fuel, and power products.

The demonopolizing tendencies that began to take hold in Polish industry during the late 1980s seemed to accelerate during 1990-1991. Within the state sector alone, the number of industrial firms increased by some 30 percent during 1987-1990, and concentration ratios for industrial branches generally fell as well. Moreover, the number of private industrial firms increased by some 40 percent during 1986-1990, so that by late 1992, the private sector was officially responsible for almost 30 percent of total industrial output. The import competition that followed the increase in złoty convertibility in 1990 introduced much stronger competitive pressures into Polish industrial markets, thanks in particular to the złoty's rapid appreciation during 1990-1991.[3] In addition to deconcentrating industrial structures, market entry by private producers and importers effectively eliminated the shortages and narrowed the scope of product-level monopoly.

On the other hand, the degree of marketization in Polish industry declined as one moved upstream in the production process toward the extractive and energy branches. Although most industrial prices had, by the end of 1990, reached equilibrium levels, the price correction was generally greatest for energy products. The price of coal (Poland's key fuel source) rose 600 percent in January 1990 alone, and jumped further after controls were removed on 1 July. Although the magnitude of these price increases reflected the extent of shortage pressures formerly present on these markets, they were also an indication of the monopoly power present in the energy-fuels complex. Indeed, price liberalization in 1990 allowed firms in the extractive sector to raise prices tenfold and record above-average (for industry) profit rates, despite reductions in subsidies and a decline in sales volume by over 25 percent. On the other hand, equilibrating these markets helped to rationalize energy and material usage.

As inflation began to subside after mid-1990, tougher subsidy and credit policies began to cause problems for many state enterprises, especially in heavy industry and the energy-fuels complex. The slowdown in domestic demand, the appreciation of the złoty, loss of CMEA markets, stiffer application of environmental regulations and fines, and stabilization in real wages—all this pushed many firms into insolvency. Although joint venture partners were found for some of these firms (e.g., steel and automobiles), for most the prospects of privatization deteriorated with their worsening financial condition. With fresh subsidies ruled out by sharpening budgetary tensions, many of these firms simply stopped paying their bills. This spread of enterprise arrears during 1991-1992 created very serious problems for the state budget and especially the banking system.

These problems were most severe for the inefficient, heavily polluting extractive sector, which had been largely untouched by the first and second stages of economic reform introduced in the 1980s. Some steps were taken during 1990-1992 to marketize the extractive sector. Coal mines formally became independent of administrative organs in 1990; the Polska Miedź copper monopoly was commercialized into a state-owned corporation; and monopolistic coal distribution chains were broken up.

In general, however, these branches responded unfavorably to marketization, especially during 1991-1992. As inflation slowed, costs rose dramatically due to higher real wages, the liquidation of the remaining subsidies, and dramatic increases in pollution charges. Although output in the energy-fuels sector continued to decline in 1991 (by another 8.3 percent), domestic and export demand fell more rapidly, increasing inventories and reducing profits. The coal industry recorded a 3.6 trillion złoty (approximately $260 million) loss in 1991, and losses on the order of 12.5 trillion złoty (almost $900 million) were forecast for 1992. Few of the now "independent" mines and foundries tried to restructure themselves, nor did many make headway in improving the labor-management tensions inherited from the communist era. In light of these developments, the fact that Poland's two strike waves during the second half of 1992 were centered in the coal industry should hardly have come as a surprise.

Polish agriculture was also strongly affected by programs for liberalization and stabilization. Difficulties with privatization have cast a long shadow over future prospects for some 1,500 state farms. Unlike industry, however, the private sector already dominates Polish agriculture, producing some 74 percent of gross agricultural output, and cultivating 76 percent of arable land in 1989. The problem instead lies in the excessively atomistic nature of agricultural landholdings. As of mid-1989, the average Polish farm was undercapitalized and contained only 7.3 hectares (17.8 acres) of land. Fewer than one- fifth of Polish farms in 1990 were larger than 10 hectares or approximately 22 acres; this percentage in Western Europe ranged from 52 percent (Germany) to 81 percent (Denmark). Some 28 percent of total Polish employment in 1990 was taken up by the agricultural labor force, more than double the figure for Czechoslovakia and more than quadruple European Community levels.

The agricultural policy introduced in 1990 was based on a "farmerization" strategy that relied on market forces to encourage a "rational concentration" of agricultural landholdings and production. For the vast majority of Polish farmers, however, the post-1989 transition to the market has brought little to cheer about. This is because agricultural policies during the 1980s were generally quite favorable: farmers were guaranteed income parity with urban households, and preferential credits were supplied to both private and state farms. The Rakowski government in August 1989 also lifted controls on food prices, while retaining controls on farm input prices. This helped farm incomes to increase by some 39 percent during 1988-1989, outpacing the overall rate of real income growth of 21.2 percent during that time.

The farmerization policies introduced in 1990 thus represented a drastic exercise in shock therapy. In addition to the terms-of-trade shock that followed the liberalization of input prices, farmers also had to face rising import competition and the cancellation of preferential credits. In real terms, farm interest rates rose significantly during 1990-1991; they may have been as high as 65 percent in 1991. In addition to being a particular hardship for rural families, these high interest rates prevented the financing of the recon-centration in landholdings and production anticipated by the proponents of marketization. All in all, according to the official statistics, farm income declined by an incredible 51.4 percent in 1990 alone, and by another 7 percent in 1991.

Agricultural policy during 1990-1992 not surprisingly became a battle-ground over farmers' attempts at restoring the benefits they enjoyed prior to the collapse of communism. While their attempts were not wholly unsuc-cessful, budgetary tensions precluded the rescue of small farmers[4] and complicated the privatization of Poland's 1,500 state farms. Polish agricul-ture in early 1993 thus seemed poised to return to its pre-1939 status as an underdeveloped, undercapitalized, and perpetually depressed flashpoint of political instability. Agriculture did score some important successes, how-ever. Exports of food and agricultural products in volume terms during 1990 were up 22.4 and 77.4 percent, respectively. The increases recorded in exports of food and agricultural products were most impressive.[5] And if Poland's associate membership in the European Community leads to in-creased integration with Western Europe, agriculture and food processing could be major beneficiaries of increased foreign investment.

THE LABOR MARKET

The Polish labor market prior to 1990 displayed the following characteristics:

1. A high degree of excess demand associated with substantial labor hoarding or disguised unemployment. Excess demand was caused by the soft-budget constraint of state enterprises and their attempts at insulating themselves from supply irregularities. In December 1989, there were 25 registered vacancies for every job seeker. At the same time, many of those formally employed were either idle or searching for scarce consumer goods. While estimates of labor hoarding are problematic, about one-fourth of the labor force in the late 1980s seemed to fall into this category.

2. Low levels of labor productivity. Although this issue is also plagued with measurement problems, it appears that for the mid-1980s productivity in Poland was about a third of that in a middle-income OECD country.

3. Large concentrations of employment in agriculture and industry. As a result of lower productivity growth (and policies promoting heavy industry), the share of total employment in agriculture and industry has remained very high in Poland (see Table 8.3).

4. High female participation rate. Economic growth in Poland has typically come from extensive use (i.e., quantitative increases) of inputs, including labor, and to a lesser extent from their more intensive (i.e., more efficient) use. This has meant a remarkably high level of labor-force participation by all age groups of the population. The labor-force participation rate for women was particularly high, whereas male participation rates were broadly comparable with the OECD rates.

5. Small wage differentials. Intersectoral wage differentials have been relatively small and stable over time. The structure of wages with respect to educational qualifications was also compressed, although to a lesser extent than is often believed. For instance, average earnings in 1989 for Polish men with a university education were around 21 percent higher than men having completed secondary education, and 61 percent higher than men with primary education or less. (For Austria, the comparable figures were 26 and 74 percent respectively.) As far as the overall earnings distribution is concerned, a substantial difference between Poland and the West appears to exist. Whereas the highest average earnings received by full-time employees in the ninth decile of the earnings distribution in Poland was 2.4 times higher than that of the first decile in 1989, the comparable figure for the United Kingdom in 1990 was 3.3 times higher.

6. Relatively low labor mobility. Although conventional wisdom posits that there was a large difference between labor mobility in the West and in Poland, data on turnover rates and internal migration offer only partial confirmation of this view. Mobility appears to be lower in Poland than in some Western countries, but not in all of them, and significantly higher than in Japan.

7. Ineffective containment of cost-push inflationary pressures. Historically, wages were determined according to administrative, highly centralized procedures. These procedures did evolve over time, however, and a tax-based incomes policy was introduced during the early

Table 8.3
Comparison of Employment Structure
(percentages)

Employee category	Poland	Austria	Holland	Japan	Germany	Sweden	USA
professional	16.0	7.3	13.8	4.8	10.6	18.7	12.2
administrative	6.0	16.6	18.9	18.3	19.4	9.9	12.2
sales and service	0.4	3.7	9.9	5.5	6.4	6.0	5.3
production	75.3	72.1	55.7	71.3	60.3	59.0	58.4
other	2.2	0.2	1.8	0.1	3.3	6.4	0.5
total	100.0	100.0	100.0	100.0	100.0	100.0	100.0
production workers in total nonagricultural employment	53.4	38.3	25.7	38.1	34.0	26.7	27.5
employment shares	100.0	100.0	100.0	100.0	100.0	100.0	100.0
— agriculture	27.8	7.8	4.6	7.2	3.7	5.0	2.8
— industry	28.2	28.9	19.7	24.6	33.5	22.7	19.9
— construction	7.9	8.5	6.5	9.4	6.7	6.0	6.5
— services	36.0	54.8	69.1	58.7	56.1	66.4	70.7

Sources: International Labor Organization, *Yearbook of Labor Statistics 1991* (Geneva, 1991); and *Yearbook of Labor Statistics, Retrospective Edition on Population Censuses, 1945-89* (Geneva, 1989).

For Poland and Sweden: censuses from 1988 and 1985, respectively. For Austria, the Netherlands, Japan, Germany, and United States: Labor Force Surveys from 1989, 1990, 1990, 1989, and 1990, respectively.

1980s. While various forms of this policy were applied, all involved prohibitive taxation of wage growth exceeding a certain percentage of actual or forecasted inflation rates. Due to numerous exemptions according to output growth and branch specificity, these policies were rather ineffective, and wage-push inflationary forces were generally not contained.

These problems took on special significance once the postcommunist transition began. The effects of the 100 percent wage indexation provision Solidarity forced upon the communist regime during the Roundtable negotiations in early 1989 meant large increases in nominal incomes, which grew by some 284 percent in 1989. The end of increasingly ineffectual communist rule was also marked by growing chaos in industrial relations, as organized and wildcat strike activity often undermined the authority of enterprise management, the central authorities, and official trade union structures. Wage-push pressures and then strike activities spun out of control during 1988 and 1989, as real incomes increased in those years by 13.8 and 6.5 percent, respectively.

In light of this legacy, the stabilization program introduced in 1990 did not liberalize wages commensurately with the degree of price liberalization introduced. Instead, the *popiwek* tax on excess wages became the basis of a tax-based incomes policy, giving the overall stabilization program a markedly heterodox character. The coefficients for nontaxable wage growth were set at 0.3 during January 1990, then 0.2 for February-April 1990, and 0.6 since that time, with the exception of a 0.1 coefficient in June and a 1.0 coefficient in the remainder of 1990.[6]

The *popiwek* was initially successful in slowing nominal wage growth, and real wages fell by some 22 percent over the course of 1990. On the other hand, the *popiwek*'s effectiveness as a stabilization tool declined dramatically after mid-1990. This was apparent in the higher coefficients adopted in mid-1990, in the increasing numbers of firms which were exempted from paying the *popiwek,* and in the rapid growth in *popiwek* arrears that began in 1991. Consequently, the large declines in real wages that occurred during the first half of 1990 were subsequently reversed: real wages increased by some 36 percent during June-December of 1990, and registered only a slight increase during 1991. The weakening of inflationary pressures in other parts of the economy, the merchandise trade deficit in 1991, and the growth of unemployment all contributed to a certain moderation of wage demands after 1990, which helped compensate for the *popiwek*'s growing ineffectiveness. On the other hand, despite the *popiwek*'s shortcomings, it would have been difficult to contain wage pressures during the transition, given the strong wage-push inflationary pressures and the decentralized collective-bargaining framework, especially during 1990. In any case, the *popiwek* has served as a lightning rod for popular and professional criticism of the stabilization program. In addition to being the focus of popular ire as a symbol of "low" wages, the *popiwek* hinders the rationalization of employment patterns by preventing enterprises from changing relative wages to better reflect labor productivity differentials. The *popiwek* also penalizes those firms with above-average productivity growth, and perpetuates the politicization of wage determination.

With the notable exception of the *popiwek,* however, the labor market had been largely freed of arbitrary government interference by the end of 1990. Legislation dating from the Roundtable agreement established a new labor code. This code attempted to create a more consensus-oriented collective-bargaining system, in which workers' rights to strike were guaranteed once other stages of the process had been exhausted. Wage setting in a formal sense was decentralized to the enterprise level, although it was understood that the importance of moderating nominal wage growth and the supra-enterprise structure of Solidarity and other trade unions would partially remove wage-setting from the purview of individual enterprises.

Still, despite this legislation and early cooperation between the Solidarity government and the Solidarity trade union, the development of Poland's post-1989 labor relations framework has been quite chaotic. Communist party influence within state enterprises was replaced by the growing role of workers' councils and trade union officials, including the large, former communist OPZZ trade union federation as well as Solidarity and its radical anti-Wałęsa offshoot, "Solidarity '80." The important role played by labor organizations in the management of some state enterprises led to what has become known as a "Bermuda triangle" syndrome, in which authority within state enterprises is divided among the enterprise director, workers' councils, and trade union officials. Since privatization of "their" enterprise is not necessarily consistent with any of these actors' self-interest, this unholy alliance constituted one of the more important sources of grass-roots opposition to privatization after 1989. Also, enterprise managers were often prevented from taking unpopular but necessary decisions by workers' councils and/or trade union officials.

Combined with continued state ownership of many enterprises, this lack of a clear delineation of responsibilities between labor and management prevented the establishment of an orderly collective-bargaining framework. Instead, tensions among different union groups as well as among unions, workers' councils, and management often exacerbated intraenterprise conflicts and produced wildcat strikes beyond the control of national or local union officials.

The inability of the Roundtable labor relations system to put a halt to this confusion led Prime Minister Hanna Suchocka in August 1992 to propose (under strike pressures) a "social pact" with workers in state enterprises that would restructure much of this system. Wage determination would be further centralized: permissible wage increases would be authorized by the Sejm on a quarterly basis, depending on the state budget. Workers would have the opportunity to play a greater role in privatizing "their" enterprises: labor representatives would be guaranteed seats on the board of directors in the privatized firms; individual workers would receive as gifts 10 to 15 percent of their firms' stock; and part of firms' after-tax profits would subsidize further stock purchases by employees.

While this system would seem to leave little room for flexibility at the plant level (which might exacerbate unemployment problems), it did offer the prospect of developing a social contract that would impose some order within the chaotic postcommunist system of labor relations. Whether Poland's dispirited workers will accept increases in ownership rights and participation in enterprise governance in lieu of higher real wages remained to be seen. The strikes during December 1992 in Silesia cast doubts on the feasibility of this approach.

Employment has declined markedly in Poland during the transition. From the beginning of 1990 to June 1992, the number of employed dropped by 1.7 million people. However, job losses have been relatively smaller than the fall in output, so that labor productivity has also declined. At first glance this looks surprising, because labor hoarding was widespread at the start of the transition. There are two important reasons why declines in output should not be expected to produce fully commensurate declines in employment.

First, labor productivity is generally procyclical. Although the extent of this procyclical character in Poland during 1990-1991 is impossible to ascertain, evidence from other countries indicates that, on average, output declines by about 1.25 percent when man-hours employed fall by 1 percent. If this coefficient for Poland were 1.25,[7] the 1 percent drop in output would have produced a 0.8 percent drop in employment.[8]

Second, although demand shocks reduce employment by reducing real incomes (the so-called macroeconomic or Keynes-Kalecki effect), declining real wages also encourage firms to substitute labor for capital and other inputs which tends at the microeconomic level to increase employment. While the declines in real wages and employment since 1990 imply that the macroeconomic effect has outweighed the microeconomic effect, the latter helps explain why employment has declined less than output since 1990.

The extent to which falling real wages can increase employment (or reduce the growth in unemployment) can be measured by the price (wage) elasticity of labor demand.[9] The demand for labor in Poland is thought to be relatively inelastic with respect to wage rates (around 0.15-0.2), largely because payments to labor are a small fraction of total costs (below 20 percent). Given the relationship between changes in output and real wages described above, this relative unresponsiveness of employment to changes in wage rates implies that an increase in the quantity of labor demanded, due to the micro effect, could not then have been more than 0.20-0.25 percent for a 1.0 percent drop in output. This implies that factors other than the substitution of labor for capital must have contributed to the relatively small decline in employment.

One such explanation can be found in the link between capacity utilization and the theory of the shortage economy. Prior to 1990, the attempted capacity utilization in the Polish economy was generally above its "tolerance limit," defined as that point at which the marginal social cost of increasing capacity utilization exceeds its marginal social benefit.[10] Excessive capacity utilization resulted in bottlenecks, forced substitution, the use of lower quality labor, and other distortions in employment practices. These distortions produced slack (underutilized resources) as well as intense shortage pressures, for labor as well as for other inputs.

The significance of this factor in reducing the employment-generating effects of declining real wages depends in part on the extent of previous capacity overutilization. The magnitude of these effects is extremely difficult to estimate, since very little is known about the slack created by shortage in an "overheated" economy characterized by excessive capacity utilization. Assuming very roughly that an n percent rate of shortage creates an n/4 percent "rate of slack,"[11] we need to know estimates of the rate of shortages. An extension of work by Kołodko and McMahon suggests results within the range 1.0 to 1.5 percent of the decrease in labor slack. This means that 0.05 to 0.075 percent of the increase in the quantity of labor demanded, corresponding to the 1.0 percent decline in output, can be explained by reductions in capacity utilization since 1990.

Vacancies in a shortage economy are an important component of labor demand. The number of vacancies advertised in Poland declined from 250,000 in December 1990 to 50,000 a year later; this allows us to account for 0.05 percent of the fall in employment which "should" have otherwise occurred.

These are rough estimates, of course; other factors not examined here could also have played an important role in the relatively small decline in employment, such as sectoral shifts.[12] Even if major structural shifts within the labor force toward light industry and the service sector have not taken place (and the initial data indicate that they have not—see Table 8.4), dramatic changes have occurred in the distribution of the labor force by ownership of enterprises. Poland experienced a significant increase in the private share of employment, even if the latter is seriously underrecorded by

Table 8.4
Sectoral Profile of Job Losses in Poland
(percentages)

Sector	Percentage change from previous year	
	1990	1991 (third quarter)
agriculture	-2.4	-27.3
industry	-5.8	-6.0
construction	-5.8	-5.9
services	-2.5	-8.6
total	-3.7	-7.7
public sector (in figures)	-9.3 (-1,126,700)	
private sector (in figures)	9.8 (498,200)	

Source: Central Statistical Office, Warsaw.

official statistics. The rise of employment in privately owned enterprises was, however, insufficient to absorb labor produced by employment losses in the public sector. Job losses in the public sector were twice as large in magnitude as officially reported job gains in the private sector (see Table 8.4).

Poland has witnessed a dramatic rise in open unemployment, from zero at the start of the stabilization program in 1990 to 13.8 percent in September 1992.[13] Rapid increases in the official unemployment statistics during 1990-1992 were also matched by the government's inability to forecast this growth. While it was anticipated that some 400,000 workers would be unemployed at the end of 1990, about 1,125,000 Poles were classified as unemployed at year's end, producing an unemployment rate of 6.1 percent. On the other hand, the unemployment rate seemed to be stabilizing at 14-15 percent by the end of 1992, below the 17 percent forecast by the Central Planning Office's "optimistic" scenario for that year, and well below the 19 percent in its "pessimistic" scenario.

The unanticipated severity of the recession during 1990-1991 over-whelmed efforts at developing active labor market policies, and sharpening budget tensions forced reductions in the scope and magnitude of unemployment compensation. Initial legislation passed in December 1989 had been in many respects quite generous: unemployment benefits were paid out of the newly established Labor Fund to anyone out of work, even to those who had not previously been in the official labor force.

Those employed previously received for a three-month period compensation equal to 70 percent of the wages earned at their previous place of employment. Although benefits declined to 50 percent during the next six months, and to 40 percent after that, there was no cutoff date for benefits. (On the other hand, given the high rates of inflation, the real value of these benefits linked to past wage rates diminished quickly.) Those receiving unemployment compensation were also eligible for state-funded health care and other social programs, and the time spent officially registered as unemployed counted toward a retirement pension.

These provisions proved too lavish for Poland's constricting budgetary resources, and restrictions were introduced in September 1990, December 1991, and February 1992. Budgetary pressures also forced the transfer of funds to unemployment compensation that had been earmarked for other labor-market programs; some 80 percent of the total public funds spent on labor-market activities went to unemployment benefits. Job retraining programs were one such casualty: during 1990-1991, only some 2,000 workers were able to participate in such programs.

In addition to budgetary pressures, increased restrictions on unemployment benefits reflected the belief that the system had been subject to widespread abuse. According to various estimates, the number of workers classified as unemployed during 1990-1992 who were employed in the second economy ranged from 30 to 80 percent of those registered with the unemployment offices. On the other hand, tightening eligibility criteria had the effect of depriving many of those on the unemployment rolls of benefits they had previously received. By April 1992, some 27 percent of those officially registered as unemployed had lost their eligibility, and discouraged workers (who had dropped out of or never officially entered the labor force) would add to this figure. According to one estimate, as many as 1.5 million unemployed workers (about 8 percent of the labor force) could "make the transition" from unemployment compensation to subsistence via other welfare programs by the end of 1992. Since a large share of this group presumably would be leaving the official labor force, this gives some estimate (probably a conservative one) of the discouraged-worker problem.

How serious is the unemployment problem in Poland? According to one source, frictional unemployment (i.e., people between jobs, moving from one part of the country to another, etc.) accounted for up to 600,000 among those registered as unemployed in March 1992. Taking the official statistics at face value, this would imply that, as of June 1992, between 1.6 and 1.7 million workers would have been the victims of cyclical or structural unemployment. Assuming that 30 percent of this number was employed in the underground economy, some 1.1 million workers (about 6.4 percent of the labor force) would then be involuntarily unemployed. By Western standards, this rate would be considerable, but not unprecedented.

There is evidence that unemployment contributed to the growth of poverty. One study found that income levels in 90 percent of the households "touched" by unemployment were below the social minimum, while some 52 percent lived in severe poverty, near biological subsistence. Moreover, the rising numbers of unemployed individuals no longer qualifying for unemployment benefits will also find their access to other social services, such as public health care, reduced.

Official statistics also depict a wide regional variance in unemployment rates. As of June 1992, these ranged from 5 to 8 percent in the counties where Warsaw, Wrocław, Kraków, and Katowice are located, while in those centered around Koszalin, Elbląg, Słupsk, and Olsztyn, as well as in the Suwałki region, the rate exceeded 20 percent. Other hard-hit areas included the Wałbrzych coal-mining region, the center of Poland's textile industry at Łódź, and some of the rural southeastern areas of former Galicja. Large metropolitan centers with diversified economies and relatively strong ties to international trade and finance seemed to be doing rather well, while the areas most devastated by unemployment had none of these advantages. The geographic proximity of many of the high-unemployment areas—Elbląg, Olsztyn, Suwałki—to the former Soviet Union may also have been a contributing factor, in the aftermath of the reductions in traditional Polish exports to the USSR during 1990-1991. This certainly was a factor in the Łódź textile industry collapse and the rise in unemployment there.

As is the case across East-Central Europe, unemployment in Poland is higher for women than for men. At the end of March 1992, women accounted for some 52.4 percent of the unemployed, although they only comprised 45.7 percent of the labor force at the end of 1990. Workers with only a basic technical or secondary-school education were hardest hit by unemployment: these groups comprised 37.7 and 31.2 percent of the total number of unemployed, respectively, at the end of March 1992. Young workers were also hard hit: almost two-thirds of the unemployed at the end of 1991 were under 35. (Data about unemployment rates in different categories of unemployed in November 1991 are presented in Table 8.5.)

Table 8.5
Unemployment Rates (November 1991)

Category		Unemployment Rate (percentage)
gender:	females	12.8
	males	10.6
age:	under 25	26.4
	25-54	10.7
	above 54	3.7
education:	primary	9.8
	vocational	13.3
	secondary	11.7
	higher	4.2

Source: Central Statistical Office, Warsaw.

The costs of this problem include lost output, represented by the unemployed and the burden upon the state budget. According to one source, if all 2.2 million Poles registered as unemployed in March 1992 had instead been working in the official economy, they could have added as much as 150 trillion złoty (approximately $11 billion, or 15 percent of national income in 1991) worth of goods and services to the official economy. Thanks to expanded early-retirement benefits (an antiunemployment measure), a disproportionately large number of workers (1.1 million) left the labor force during 1990-1991 which both reduced potential, and probably actual, output and increased the burden on the state pension fund. Finally, in budgetary terms, some 10 trillion złoty were devoted to unemployment compensation during 1991, and another 10 trillion went to fund the expanded early- retirement program. These are considerable sums, accounting for roughly half the budget deficit in that year.

On the other hand, there were numerous indications that unemployment was not nearly as serious a problem as it seemed. Only 24 percent of those classified as unemployed in March 1992 had lost their jobs as a result of group layoffs, in which poor economic conditions at the workplace were the unambiguous cause of unemployment. While the share of group layoffs (relative to total unemployment) rose throughout 1990-1992, the 24 percent figure suggests that the majority of people who lost their jobs during this time did so for individual (rather than macroeconomic) reasons. A Central

Statistical Office survey of 2,500 employment offices during early 1992 found that only about one case of unemployment in six was completely genuine. Labor shortages continued to exist in numerous areas, not only in such high-technology fields as computer programming, but also for unskilled labor in some of the large metropolitan areas with low unemployment rates. Strikes over higher pay and better working conditions, rather than job-security issues, continued to affect many industrial sectors (e.g., the strikes by coal and copper miners in mid-1992).

Introduction of unemployment compensation represented only one institutional aspect of social policy reform attempted during 1990-1991. Another was the official acknowledgment of poverty, which led to the passage of the Social Assistance Law in November 1989. Since poverty had not been officially acknowledged in People's Poland, assistance (largely in kind) had been awarded mainly on the basis of extenuating circumstances (e.g., to the infirm, elderly, or individuals with chronic health problems). Total expenditure on social assistance therefore rose rapidly after 1989, from under 2 percent of expenditure on social benefits in 1990 to 7.7 percent in 1991.

A dramatic change in budget priorities also occurred during this time, as funds were reallocated away from product, enterprise, and sectoral subsidies toward direct transfer payments to the population. Real expenditures on social services (e.g., education, health care, etc.) declined some 22.8 percent during 1990-1991. Reductions in education (26.3 percent), culture (50.3 percent), and sports and tourism (58.1 percent) were particularly large. Transfer payments increased by some 17 percent in real terms during this time, with particularly large increases noted in health care payments (42.3 percent) and retirement pensions (30.9 percent). These trends had the effect of increasing the share of transfer payments in personal incomes from 16 to 22 percent, while the share of labor income fell from 40 to 31 percent. Cuts in social services in turn helped reduce public consumption by some 15 percent during 1990-1991. (By contrast, private consumption fell by approximately 8 percent.)

These changes had important implications for income distribution. While real incomes declined across worker, peasant, and pensioner households during 1990-1991, the reductions were hardly even. Pensioners' incomes fell by "only" 5 percent (thanks largely to a 15 percent increase in 1991); while real incomes in worker and peasant households declined by a whopping 25 and 45 percent, respectively. Within worker households, workers in the "budgetary sphere" (i.e., public services and state administration) were especially hard hit following the 1991 suspension of their indexation to wages in the so-called productive sphere.

CONCLUSIONS

The liberalization of product markets and the accompanying stabilization program have exposed Polish enterprises (public and private) to greater competition from domestic firms and imports. The share of many product markets held by private producers has increased significantly, and many state firms have been able to increase exports to Western markets. On the other hand, reductions in enterprise profitability and the crisis in the state budget and banking system linked to these policies raise difficult questions about the costs of these successes. The lack of progress in rapidly privatizing large firms left the industrial landscape dominated by hundreds of insolvent state-owned dinosaurs, a problem for which no solution has been found. And the introduction of market forces in agriculture has demonstrated the poor preparation of many private farms for the new era. So while market forces have since 1990 made a significant impact upon product markets, they have not provided a magical cure for Poland's economic problems.

Summary judgments about Poland's labor-market transformation during 1990-1992 are difficult to make, but they cannot ignore the fact that major barriers to rapid adjustment of the labor force have been removed. In particular, the removal of most non-*popiwek* wage regulations would seem to have been the most favorable development. However, a modern labor market cannot operate without well-defined collective bargaining institutions, and the chaos and fragmentation in this area, which were so apparent in the strike wave during the summer of 1992, the negotiations on the "pact on state enterprises," and the Silesian strikes in December 1992 would perhaps be the largest negative aspect. Judgments about declines in real wages, the rise in unemployment, rapid increases in private-sector employment, or the fate of workplace democracy are highly normative, since they involve trading off qualities that are hard to compare (i.e., more efficiency for less job security) or measuring gains made by some groups at the expense of others.

In addition to reducing the chaos in labor relations, the introduction of labor-market policies capable of addressing persistent, long-run unemployment is perhaps the greatest challenge facing policymakers in the labor field. In 1992 more than 95 percent of Labor Fund expenditures were allocated for unemployment benefits, leaving virtually no resources to fund active labor-market policies. Continuing this policy indefinitely could be disastrous. Obtaining increased budgetary support for active labor market policies that would remain separate from funding sources for unemployment benefits would seem to be a major priority. So would the introduction of regional restructuring plans. Differentials between unemployment rates and job openings in different areas call for appropriately differentiated labor policies (e.g., different eligibility criteria for unemployment benefits in different areas). There are also a number of small policy changes which should have already been introduced and which could have eased the situation in the labor market. The development of more flexible work-time arrangements would seem to hold promise in addressing the issue of unemployment among women.

However the labor-market transformation is evaluated, this assessment would have to contrast well with the post-1989 reorientation of social policy. On the one hand, the shift away from product- and especially enterprise-specific subsidies was a gain, since it significantly reduced the scope for central paternalism vis-à-vis enterprises. However, the combination of expanded funding for transfer programs and reductions in tax revenues, linked to the recession and the growth of the less-taxed private sector, has decimated the delivery of public goods. Moreover, the beneficiaries of the shift to transfer payments are not necessarily groups most at risk during the transition. Likewise, many of the product-specific subsidies that have been retained do not provide special help for those at risk. The continuation of subsidies for central heating and water benefit middle-class urban apartment dwellers at the expense of residents of rural areas and those without housing; free university educations subsidize relatively well prepared students from predominantly middle- and upper-class backgrounds. Effective reform of the so-called budgetary sphere would seem to be an urgent priority.

Along with the difficulties that have appeared in the attempts at transforming Poland's financial system, problems in the creation of the social safety net have perhaps been the greatest failure to date. Still, in less than two years an entirely new legislative framework has been put into place in Poland, a process which took decades in many OECD countries. Ultimately, however, success in creating Western-type labor-market and social safety-net institutions depends on the overall development of market capitalism.

NOTES

1. In constant prices, gross industrial production during 1990-1991 declined 33.2 percent; retail sales fell by 11.3 percent (a very rough proxy for service sector activities); and gross agricultural production dropped by only 3.1 percent. *Maty rocznik statystyczny 1992*, pp. 347, 351, 355.

2. While private firms in 1990 accounted for 98.5 percent of the production units in the engineering sector, 99.5 percent of the units in light industry, and 97.3 percent

of the units in food processing, they accounted for less than .01 percent of the production units in the energy and fuels sector. *Rocznik statystyczny przemysłu 1991,* p. 2.

3. According to PlanEcon, the złoty appreciated against the dollar by "a staggering 136 percent in real effective terms" between January 1990 and April 1991. The złoty's real effective appreciation between January 1990 and April 1992 was 128 percent, despite two devaluations and the adoption of a crawling-peg regime in October 1991. "East European Currency Exchange Rates," *PlanEcon Report* (28 April 1992), pp. 1-2.

4. Some four-fifths of Poland's 2.1 million private farms are ten hectares or less in size, and are thought to be too small and inefficient to compete in a market environment. Andrzej Mozolski, "Zabawa w długi," *Polityka* (16 May 1992).

5. Exports of food and agricultural products in volume terms during 1990 increased 22.4 and 77.4 percent, respectively. Exports of agricultural products in 1991 were up 25.5 percent in volume terms, while food exports increased 3 percent in value terms. *Rocznik statystyczny 1991: Handel zagraniczny,* p. 11; and Tomasz Telma, "Polish Foreign Trade," *PlanEcon Report* (19 June 1992), p. 19.

6. A 0.2 coefficient meant that firms could only raise wages by 20 złoty for every 100-złoty increase in the general price level. Larger wage increases were subjected to prohibitive taxation at rates initially set at 300 to 500 percent.

7. Differences between the labor input measured by man-hours and the number of employees are assumed to be relatively unimportant.

8. Coefficient for East-Central Europe could be even higher than 1.25 due to labor hoarding at the start of the transition, since labor hoarding tends to reinforce procyclical productivity behavior. Two economists have shown that firms which hoard large quantities of labor have lower marginal costs than those that do not; hence, the wedge between price and marginal cost is larger, and productivity is more procyclical. J. J. Rotemberg and Larry H. Summers, "Inflexible Prices . . . ," *The Quarterly Journal of Economics* 105, no. 4 (1990): 851 - 874.

9. The elasticity of labor demand with respect to wage rates is defined as the percentage change in the quantity of labor demanded, divided by the percentage change in wage rates. If this number is less than 1.0 (in absolute value), labor demand is said to be relatively inelastic, meaning that changes in wage rates produce relatively small changes in employment.

10. See János Kornai, *Economics of Shortage* (New York and Amsterdam: North Holland Press, 1980), Chapters 10 and 12, and especially pp. 281-282.

11. This relationship is based on microobservations about behavior of raw materials' stocks in state enterprises.

12. Poland's increased integration with the international economy could be expected to produce a reallocation of employment from nontradables to tradables, since

many firms have been forced to find new sales outlets on Western markets. Since labor intensity in East-Central Europe is higher in the tradables sector than in nontradables, wage-driven sectoral shifts toward tradables could offset the standard Keynes-Kalecki macro effect and thus explain the relatively small decline in employment. However, the data do not seem to confirm this hypothesis in Poland. See Michał Rutkowski, "Is the Labor Market Adjustment in Poland Surprising?" *Labour* 3, no. 5 (1991): 79-103; and E. R. Borensztein and J. D. Ostry, "Structural and Macroeconomic Determinants of the Output Decline in Poland: 1990-1991," IMF Working Paper (October 1992).

13. The remainder of this section draws heavily on Polish press sources, especially "Bezrobocie po polsku," *Sztandar młodych,* 29-31 May 1992; Irena Dryll, "Bezrobocie: Fikcja czy dramat?" *Życie gospodarcze,* 3 February 1991, pp. 1, 4, and "Spadek statystyczny, czy faktyczny?" *Życie gospodarcze,* 7 June 1992; Stanisława Golinowska, "Polityka społecznych cięć," *Życie gospodarcze,* 7 June 1992; Krzysztof Kraus, "Bezrobocie-co dalej?" *Trybuna,* 25 June 1992; Marzena Próchnicka, "Jak się zarejestrować i dostać zasiłek?" *Sztandar młodych,* 31 May 1992; Andrzej Radek and Jacek Welter, "Dwa lata zamętu," *Polityka,* 30 May 1992; and Krystyna Sonntag, "Życie codzienne w transformacji," *Życie gospodarcze,* 30 August 1992, p. 2.

9

The Role of Monetary Policy in Market Economies

*Thomas J. Sargent**

This chapter discusses monetary policy during the transition to democracy in Poland. Despite the fact that the author is not an expert on that country, he undertook the assignment because he agrees with Milton Friedman that the lessons of monetary theory and history apply to all countries and times. Thus, Milton Friedman has typically advocated the same set of simple rules for conducting monetary and fiscal policies, no matter what country or continent he was advising. Friedman's advice to monetary authorities is based on an understanding of the technicalities of monetary policy operations and what those operations could and could not be expected to accomplish.[1]

MONETARY POLICY OPERATIONS

The objective of monetary policy is to manage the portfolio of debts owed by the central government. Popular discussions impute great power for producing good or bad economic effects to the government officials who administer monetary policy. In truth, monetary policy is much less powerful than is often depicted, because its administrators are constrained by economic forces beyond their control. Most important, the monetary policy authorities do not control the

---

* The author wishes to thank Mme. Hanna Gronkiewicz-Waltz (president, National Bank of Poland) for her comments on this chapter.

size of the portfolio of government debts that they must manage: that is determined by the fiscal authorities (i.e., those who set taxes and expenditures).

In many Western governments, the responsibility for determining the total size of the government debt is nominally separated from responsibility for determining the financial composition of that debt.[2] Whether it takes the form of no interest-bearing debt (currency and bank reserves) or interest-bearing debt at any time is the cumulative result of past federal government deficits, which are determined jointly by the legislature and the executive. Given the total debt, responsibility for determining its composition is assigned to the central bank. That institution continuously conducts open-market operations, equal-value trades of one form of government debt for another. By executing these trades, the central bank alters the composition of the debt owned by the government's creditors while leaving the total value of that outstanding debt unchanged at a point in time. "Monetary policy" or "open-market policy" or "debt management" are three phrases used to describe the responsibilities of the central bank. "Fiscal policy" is the phrase used to describe the activities of the executive and legislature that generate the stream of government deficits that have to be financed.

Although the United States and other Western countries have decentralized authority for making fiscal and monetary policy across distinct and nominally independent institutions, it would be possible and perhaps even desirable to distribute responsibility in different ways. Indeed, the nominal independence of monetary from fiscal institutions is fictitious because the arithmetic of the government's budget constraint requires interdependence. The goal of United States economic policy institutions is to leave that interdependence implicit and, therefore, to leave the procedures for coordinating monetary and fiscal policy to be worked out haphazardly through the interactions of the succession of person-alities that happen to occupy economic policy-making positions. Milton Fried-man's long-standing proposal that monetary policy be executed according to a simple rule that increases the monetary base a constant percentage (close to zero) each year ought to be interpreted as one device for removing this haphazardness and for making explicit and predictable the terms according to which monetary and fiscal policies are to be coordinated.

This chapter describes limitations, possibilities, and suitable goals for monetary policy within the existing pattern of institutional responsibilities. A discussion of limitations and possibilities is necessary as a prolegomenon to any discussion of proper goals for monetary policy. Limitations on what monetary policy can accomplish are determined by the arithmetic of the government budget constraint and by the behavior of the parties who demand the U.S. government debt that the central bank markets.

FRIEDMAN'S PRESIDENTIAL ADDRESS REVISITED

The starting point for describing the limitations and possibilities of monetary policies is Milton Friedman's celebrated 1968 article.[3] His theme is that we should not expect too much from monetary policy. He warned that monetary policy could not be counted on to accomplish some of the goals that were then being advocated for it, such as controlling the paths of unemployment, output, and interest rates. Friedman argued that the structure of the economy is such that monetary policy can have no permanent effects on the levels of unemployment, GNP, or real interest rates. He did maintain that monetary policy can be used to control the time path taken by the price level.

In the light of the 25 years of research on macroeconomics that has occurred since the above article, this author would like to reexamine, re-present, and lengthen Friedman's list of limitations and possibilities for monetary policy. Subsequent research has reinforced the cautionary notes Friedman sounded. The following discussion will center on seven propositions governing the role of monetary policy.

MONETARY POLICY AND UNEMPLOYMENT

Proposition 1.
Monetary policy cannot be used to influence unemployment.

Friedman's 1968 article contained an early version of the natural unemployment rate hypothesis, formulated independently by Friedman and Edmund S. Phelps.[4] Friedman and Phelps sought to interpret the Phillips curve, the inverse correlation between inflation and unemployment traced out by United States and United Kingdom data in the first two decades following World War II. Paul Samuelson and Robert Solow had earlier interpreted that correlation as a stable relationship confronting the macroeconomic policy authorities with a trade-off between inflation and unemployment.[5] According to this interpretation, by running larger government deficits and incurring higher rates of currency expansion, the policy authorities can engineer a reduction in the average unemployment rate. In the late 1960s many macroeconomists recommended that the government accept this trade-off and run a high-inflation, low-unemployment policy.

Friedman and Phelps described a theory that explained the inverse correlation between inflation and unemployment in the postwar data but that also implied that the correlation would not endure in the face of an attempt permanently to exploit it. Friedman and Phelps reasoned that at a given level of their expectations about future rates of inflation, labor suppliers' behavior would cause unemployment to vary inversely with the current rate of inflation. However, if workers' expected rate of inflation were to increase, Friedman and Phelps reasoned that the terms of the apparent trade-off between inflation and unemployment would worsen. Indeed, it would worsen so much that no decrease in unemployment would accompany an increase in actual inflation that was just matched by a corresponding increase in people's expected rate of inflation. This theory, constructed by analyzing the factors underlying workers' decisions to supply labor, implies that there is no permanently exploitable trade-off between inflation and unemployment. Unemployment is interpreted as responding only to the part of inflation that is surprising or unexpected, a part that cannot be permanently set to a value other than zero. This theory is known as the natural unemployment rate theory.

Friedman used the foregoing, together with a theory that people's expected rate of inflation was formed as a moving average of actual rates of inflation (the so-called adaptive expectations theory), to conclude that monetary policy cannot be used permanently to influence the unemployment rate. With adaptive expectations, people eventually eliminate any discrepancy between actual and expected sustained rates of inflation, and monetary policy's effects on the unemployment rate are entirely mediated through that discrepancy.

Whereas Friedman's formulation denied the possibility of any permanent effects, it left open extensive possibilities for dynamically intricate temporary effects of monetary policy on the unemployment rate.[6] These effects could be achieved by subtly manipulating private agents' errors in forecasting future rates of inflation. However, subsequent research has strengthened Friedman's argument by eliminating or greatly weakening even these temporary effects. This modification has resulted from replacing Friedman's hypothesis of adaptive expectations (the weakest part of his theory in relation to economic motivation) with the hypothesis of rational expectations.[7]

One can motivate the idea of rational expectations by noting that in Friedman and Phelps's model the people made worse forecasts of future inflation than did the government, which owns the economists' model. The model showed how to make better forecasts of inflation than those made by the simple moving-average schemes attributed to people by Friedman and Phelps. The idea of rational expectations is to remove this asymmetry between the forecasting ability of the person who owns the model and the agents who live in the model by positing that the agents in the model forecast at least as well as the outsider (the government) who owns the model.

Attributing rational expectations to private agents substantially strengthens the limitations on the ability of monetary policy to influence the unemployment rate. There is no systematic monetary policy capable of influencing the unemployment rate, even temporarily. Monetary policy affects the unemployment rate only by inducing surprises, and there is no systematic (i.e., predictable) way to manipulate those surprises. As for the likely distribution of unemployment rates, monetary policy can do no better than to use a constant growth rate rule, such as the one Friedman recommends.

MONETARY POLICY AND INTEREST RATES

Proposition 2.
Monetary policy cannot be used to influence real interest rates.

As a corollary of the natural-rate hypothesis, it follows that monetary policy cannot be used to influence real rates of interest. A version of this principle was stated in Friedman's 1968 article, and subsequent research has strengthened his statement by replacing his assumption of adaptive expectations with the assumption of rational expectations.

That real interest rates are beyond the influence of monetary policy follows from two features of the economic environment. The first feature, embodied in Irving Fisher's famous theory, is that at given tax rates, real interest rates are determined once the levels of aggregate employment and national product are determined.[8] Thus, given a time path for national product, real interest rates are determined by the marginal productivity of capital along that path. The second feature is the natural-rate hypothesis, which makes the expected path of employment and national product independent of the choice of a monetary policy rule. According to Friedman's principle, the monetary policy authority could exert no permanent influence on real interest rates because it could not permanently influence the unexpected component of inflation. Under the adaptive expectations system, assumed by Friedman, the monetary policy authorities still had the power to influence real interest rates temporarily by inducing sequences of errors in private agents' forecasts of inflation.

Again, research subsequent to Friedman's has strengthened his result by replacing the assumption of adaptive expectations with that of rational expectations, a replacement that withdraws from monetary policy authority the superior wisdom and forecasting advantage that would permit it to manipulate private agents' forecast errors.[9]

MONETARY POLICY AND INFLATION

Proposition 3.
Monetary policy can be used to influence the time path of the price level (assuming that the monetary authority's powers are augmented by sufficient powers to levy taxes).

Proposition 3 embodies the main possibility left open to monetary authority in Friedman's analysis, with this writer's parenthetical qualification. The latter was implicit in Friedman's treatment, and subsequent research has emphasized its importance.

The ability of monetary authority to influence the price level rests on two aspects of the economic structure: (1) the demand schedule for government-issued currency (currency and bank reserves, so-called high-powered money) and (2) the intertemporal sequence of government budget constraints. The amount of government currency demanded varies proportionately with the price level, a doubling of the price level leading to a doubling of the amount of money demanded. This proportionality reflects the idea that the economic demand is for a "real" quantity of money, the nominal amount deflated by the price level. The real amount of money demanded also depends partly on the levels of real output and real interest rates (which propositions 1 and 2 state are outside the influence of monetary authority) and on the path of future price levels expected by private agents.

A demand schedule for money with these features implies that by making the supply of government-issued currency follow a path with a steady and low growth rate, the price level will also follow a fairly steady path with a growth rate comparable to that of the path of the currency stock. This is a version of the quantity theory of money. According to this theory, subject to exceptions caused by disturbances in the demand for currency, monetary policy can choose a stable and low-inflation likely time path for the price level by executing an open-market strategy that sets a path of government-issued currency along which currency is growing slowly and steadily. But is it *feasible* for monetary policy to select such a path for the stock of currency? This question brings us to the second condition required to validate proposition 3, the part alluded to in the parenthetical qualifier.

The government has an intertemporal sequence of budget constraints. In each period, the real value of government expenditures plus interest payments on government debts plus retirements of outstanding debts must exactly equal the sum of three components: tax collections, proceeds from issues of new interest-bearing government debt, and the change in government-issued currency divided by the price level. The last term on the receipts side, sometimes called seigniorage, is under control of the central bank. Government expenditures and tax collections are formally under the joint control of the legislature and the president. (Legally, the parenthetical qualifier behind proposition 3 is usually not met in most Western countries. However, for proposition 3 to hold, we shall see that it must be met at least implicitly and informally.)

The preceding argument states that the monetary policy authority would be able to control the path of the price level, if it could permanently control the path of the rate of growth of currency. But it follows from the government budget constraint that if the rate of growth of currency is controlled with an eye toward stabilizing the price level path, then other elements of the government budget constraint must be adjusted to assure that it is always satisfied. To take the simplest case, suppose that monetary policy is executed according to Friedman's k percent growth rule, with k equal to zero so that no growth in currency is ever permitted by the monetary authority. For this to be feasible, fiscal authorities must manage their affairs so that government expenditures plus interest payments equal tax collections plus the net proceeds from new issues of interest-bearing debt.[10]

One way to accomplish this is to freeze the level of outstanding interest-bearing government debt and to set government expenditures plus interest payments equal to tax collections, period by period. This is a balanced-budget rule for fiscal policy, with the gross-of-interest government deficit for each period being equal to zero. This rule is one of many that set the net-of-interest government surplus equal in present value to the outstanding stock of interest-bearing government debt. In general, supporting the no-seigniorage zero percent growth rule monetary policy requires a fiscal policy satisfying the condition that the present value of the government's net-of-interest surplus always equals the current stock of interest-bearing government debt. This fiscal rule instructs the government to behave like a firm (one without a printing press) and to balance any current deficits with the credible prospect of future surpluses sufficient to service debt created by those deficits.

For the monetary authority permanently to influence the price level path, a mechanism must be in place for coordinating monetary and fiscal policies that gives the monetary authority the power permanently to withhold a flow of seigniorage from the fiscal authority.[11] To support a no-seigniorage monetary policy, the government budget must be balanced in the present-value sense just described.

To emphasize the importance of the qualifier in proposition 3, it is useful to focus on the assumptions used to rationalize neutrality-of-money experiments in textbook models representing the quantity theory of money.[12] These experiments imagine that the monetary authority engineers a once-and-for-all decrease in the stock of currency by open-market sales of government interest-bearing bonds to the public. This operation increases the stream of interest payments that the government must pay to its creditors. To finance these payments, the textbook experiments assume that the open-market sale of bonds is accompanied by an increase in the stream of taxes just sufficient to service the higher interest payments resulting from the sale. This experiment illustrates the way tax adjustments are required to support the monetary policies that control the price level.

Under current institutional arrangements in the United States, monetary authority does not have the power assumed in the qualifier to proposition 3. It is an open question whether it can acquire that power by engaging in a "game of chicken" with the fiscal authorities, as described by Neil Wallace.[13] In any event, under United States institutional arrangements the following proposition, which can be viewed as a corollary to proposition 3, is actually pertinent.

MONETARY POLICY AND INFLATION AGAIN

Proposition 4.
Monetary policy cannot permanently prevent inflation (given a fiscal policy implying a stream of net-of-interest government deficits).

Proposition 4 follows from the same premises underlying proposition 3. Assuming that fiscal policy is managed to create a permanent stream of net-of-interest deficits, it follows arithmetically that monetary policy must supply a permanent stream of seigniorage sufficient to make up the shortfall in the budget. This is an aspect of the "unpleasant monetarist arithmetic," explored by Sargent and Wallace.

The economic forces underlying propositions 3 and 4 also produce a fifth proposition that characterizes the ability of monetary policy to influence the value at which United States currency exchanges for the currencies issued by foreign governments.

MONETARY POLICY AND FOREIGN EXCHANGE

Proposition 5.
Monetary policy is incapable of determining the rate of exchange of domestic currency for foreign currencies (unless supported by an appropriate fiscal policy).

This principle follows from adding to propositions 3 and 4 the logic of purchasing-power parity: the rate of exchange of a domestic for a foreign currency equals the ratio of the foreign price level to the domestic price level. For example, given a constant British price level, a 25 percent rise in the United States price level is predicted by purchasing-power parity to be associated with a 25 percent depreciation in the value of the dollar in exchange for the pound. Purchasing-power parity is a particular application of the law of one price. Although there can be substantial transitory deviations from the value of exchange rates predicted by the principle of purchasing-power parity, sizable and sustained divergent movements in price levels across different countries' exchange rates tend to adhere to the paths predicted by the principle.

Combining the logic of purchasing-power parity with that of propositions 3 and 4 immediately produces proposition 5. By propositions 3 and 4, monetary authority cannot permanently set the domestic price level along a noninflationary path unless it is supported by an appropriate fiscal policy. Given time paths for foreign price levels (determined by the operation of principles 3 and 4 in foreign countries), it follows that domestic monetary policy cannot affect the time path of foreign exchange rates unless it is supported by the same fiscal policies consistent with the required domestic price level paths.

Proposition 5 leaves open the possibility of operating a monetary regime keyed to stabilizing a foreign exchange rate. The international gold standard is one example of a regime under which principle 5 is respected by all participating countries and the foreign exchanges are stabilized. A gold standard regime is a set of rules for running monetary and fiscal policies designed to stabilize rates of exchange of foreign for domestic currencies among all participating countries. Under a gold standard, each participating government borrows only by issuing promises redeemable in gold. Government debt in the form of currency assumes the form of a note for a given amount of gold payable to the bearer on demand. Under this system a British pound is an immediate claim on x units of gold, whereas a United States dollar is an immediate claim on y units of gold. The exchange rate between pounds and dollars must be x/y.

To adhere to a gold standard, a government must back its debts with gold or other assets that are themselves as good as gold. In practice as well as in theory, it is unnecessary to hold stocks of gold equal in value to the entire stock of a government's liabilities. Instead, it is sufficient to back debts by sufficient prospects of future government surpluses. By accepting a gold standard rule, a government in effect agrees to operate its fiscal policy by a present-value budget balance rule. Under this rule government deficits can occur, but they are necessarily temporary and are accompanied by prospects for future surpluses sufficient to service whatever debt is generated by the deficit.

Thus, a gold standard is as much a fiscal regime as it is a monetary regime. Indeed, during the high tide of the gold standard in the late nineteenth century, most of the central banks of Europe faced rules imposing a low ceiling on the amount of government loans they could purchase. The central banks were permitted to issue bank notes on the security of gold, foreign exchange, and safe evidences of short-term commercial indebtedness. Such rules well capture the spirit and structure of the gold standard as a fiscal institution supported by monetary arrangements that deny the fiscal authority access to the printing press as a source of finance.

THE "LENDER OF LAST RESORT"

During the period of the gold standard, the role of lender of last resort began to be assigned to the central bank. A tradition developed to guide the central bank's behavior during periods of unusual stringency in credit markets. The central bank was supposed to lend as freely as possible (albeit at a high interest rate) to forestall what threatened to be contagious defaults on commercial banks' liabilities, in the form of either suspension of convertibility into central bank notes or outright bankruptcy.[14]

Feasible practical limits on the range of such operations were imposed, first, by the commitment of the central bank to keep its notes convertible into gold at par and, second, by the limited capital of the central bank. In acting as a lender of last resort during bad times, the central bank was conducting open-market operations by paying out good assets (central bank notes) in exchange for bad assets (commercial loans originally owned by the banks in jeopardy). Such operations would impair the central bank's capital and, if conducted without limit, would destroy the central bank's ability to honor its commitment to convert its notes into gold on demand. Under some constellations of threat to the commercial banks, the central bank simply could not act as a lender of last resort and also honor its commitment to manage its portfolio according to the rules of the gold standard.

The lender of last resort ultimately acts as an insurer of banks' liabilities. The absence of deposit insurance, requiring a central bank to act as a lender of last resort, amounts to setting up an underfunded insurance scheme. For a lender-of-last-resort scheme to be feasible and also consistent with gold standard commitments, it must be properly funded. Alternative ways of funding such a scheme are either explicitly to charge sufficiently high and sufficiently risk-indexed fees for deposit insurance or to commit the general taxing authority of the government as a funding source. In the Great Depression, central banks failed to be lenders of last resort because they lacked such funding.

These considerations indicate how, under a gold standard regime, the provision of a lender of last resort to the banking system is a matter for fiscal policy. Though somewhat less obvious, it remains a matter of fiscal policy under the fiat standard, with which we live today, that is not anchored by the commitment to convert government debt into any bundle of physical assets. Under a fiat standard a central bank's commitment to pursue price level stability limits the amount of seigniorage it can supply to the fiscal authority, thereby requiring discipline on the part of the fiscal authority. In a fiat system, commitment to price level stability constrains the actions of the monetary authority just as it does under the gold standard. If the central bank is not bound by a commitment to price level stability, it acquires some ability to act as a lender of last resort. By giving up the constraints imposed on its actions by price stability, the central bank in effect acquires a set of taxing powers (it controls an inflation tax) that enables it to reallocate resources between borrowers and lenders. These taxing powers are strongest when loan contracts are denominated in nominal terms and when loans have long terms to maturity.[15]

The preceding discussion can be summed up in the following proposition, which can be interpreted as another corollary to proposition 3.

Proposition 6.
Monetary policy cannot insure bank deposits by acting as a lender of last resort, while simultaneously managing the central bank's portfolio in a way designed to assure price stability.

Note that proposition 6 does not deny the ability of monetary policy, in some circumstances, to play an important role in bailing out threatened banks. However, without support in resources from the fiscal authority, monetary policy will at times have to sacrifice price stability to prevent failures of commercial banks. This is the meaning of the old adage that "the role of monetary policy is to convert bad loans into good ones."

SIMPLE RULES

A feature of the rules for conducting monetary and fiscal policies that Milton Friedman has advocated is that they are *simple*. When he first proposed those simple rules, they were widely judged by macroeconomists to be inferior to complicated state-contingent or "look-at-everything" rules. The "rational expectations revolution" showed that simple rules could often be no worse than those complicated rules, thereby providing at least a weak defense of simple rules like Friedman's.

Recently there has been an explosion of work on "bounded rationality" and learning in game theory and macroeconomics. While this work is still in its infancy, some patterns are emerging that promise to strengthen the case for simple rules.

When people do not have all of the information needed for "rational expectations," they engage in a continuous process of learning about the environment. As a general principle, people can learn about the policy environment *faster* the simpler it is. It usually turns out to be easier to learn about the workings of simple rules than more complicated ones. This principle is tentatively summarized in terms of the following:

Proposition 7.
Simpler rules for the conduct of monetary policy are easier for traders to learn about and, therefore, lead to more stable and predictable outcomes.[16]

CONCLUSION

The first two propositions describe limits placed on monetary authorities by an economic system in general and by the way monetary policy impinges on the opportunities (budget constraints) available to private economic agents in particular. The next four propositions describe limits placed on the potential accomplishments of monetary policy by the arithmetic of the government's own budget constraint. These propositions provide concrete meaning to an old maxim in central-banking circles: with a tight fiscal policy that hands the monetary authority a small portfolio of government debt to manage, it is easy to run a noninflationary monetary policy; however, under a deficit-spending policy, it is impossible to run a noninflationary monetary policy. These propositions are as relevant for Poland as they are for the United States.[17]

NOTES

1. This chapter borrows extensively from Thomas J. Sargent, "Monetary Policy Under American Institutions," in Annelise Anderson and Dennis Bark, eds., *Thinking About America* (Stanford, Calif.: Hoover Institution Press, 1988), pp. 311-322.

2. On coordination problems facing monetary and fiscal authorities, see the following by Thomas J. Sargent: "Reaganomics and Credibility," Chapter 2 in *Rational Expectations and Inflation* (New York: Harper and Row, 1985); "Interpreting the Reagan Deficits," Federal Reserve Bank of San Francisco, *Review* (Fall 1986); *Dynamic Macroeconomic Theory* (Cambridge, Mass.: Harvard University Press, 1987). See also Thomas J. Sargent and Neil Wallace, "Some Unpleasant Monetarist Arithmetic," Central Bank of Minneapolis, *Quarterly Review* (Fall 1981).

3. Milton Friedman, *A Program for Monetary Stability* (New York: Fordham University Press, 1960), and his "The Role of Monetary Policy," *American Economic Review* 58, no. 1 (March 1968): 1-17.

4. Edmund S. Phelps, "Phillips Curves, Inflation Expectations, and Optimal Employment Over Time," *Economica* 34, no. 3 (August 1967).

5. Paul A. Samuelson and Robert M. Solow, "Analytical Aspects of Anti-inflation Policy," *American Economic Review* 50, no. 2 (May 1960): 177-94.

6. These effects are analyzed formally in Phelps, "Phillips Curves."

7. John F. Muth, "Rational Expectations and the Theory of Price Movements," *Econometrica* 29, no. 3 (1961): 315-35.

8. Irving Fisher, *The Theory of Interest* (New York: Macmillan, 1930).

9. Thomas J. Sargent, "Rational Expectations, the Real Rate of Interest, and the Natural Rate of Unemployment," *Brookings Papers on Economic Activity* 2 (1973): 429-72 (correction in ibid., vol. 3 [1973]).

10. For formal analyses, see Sargent and Wallace, "Some Unpleasant Monetarist Arithmetic," and Sargent, *Dynamic Macroeconomic Theory.*

11. In "Some Unpleasant Monetarist Arithmetic," Sargent and Wallace describe what will happen if the monetary authority tries to control the price level when no such mechanism is in place.

12. Sargent, *Dynamic Macroeconomic Theory,* Chapter 5.

13. For a description of Wallace's "game of chicken," see Sargent, "Reaganomics and Credibility," and Sargent, "Interpreting the Reagan Deficits," both cited above in Note 2.

14. Walter Bagehot, *Lombard Street: A Description of the Money Market* (London: Smith, Elder & Co., 1873).

15. For further analysis, see David Beers, Thomas Sargent, and Neil Wallace, "Speculations About the Speculation Against the Hong Kong Dollar," Central Bank of Minneapolis, *Quarterly Review* (Fall 1983).

16. This proposition should be regarded as less secure and proven than the previous ones.

17. American fiscal authorities of recent years have given United States monetary authorities a large portfolio of debts to manage.

10

Emerging Patterns of Foreign Trade

*Bartłomiej Kamiński**

Transformation of the Polish economic system, made possible by the collapse of communism and the demise of "international" institutions created by the USSR to control its client states, triggered an abrupt breakdown of trade patterns established in the 1949-1989 period. During the initial two years of the transformation-cum-stabilization program, launched by the first noncommunist government on 1 January 1990, the reorientation of Polish trade was swift and dramatic. Imports from the Soviet Union and other CMEA (Council for Mutual Economic Assistance)[1] countries fell, and trade with the West spectacularly expanded. The EC (European Community) replaced the CMEA as Poland's major trading partner. (See Table 10.1.)

This chapter addresses the issue in its title by taking a broad look at the evolution of the trade regime and export performance over the last decade. The focus is on Poland's exports to the West. Trade within CMEA had been shielded from changes and remained subject to administrative rules

* The author wishes to acknowledge helpful comments from Ronald Duncan, Grzegorz Kołodko, Andrzej Olechowski, Jacek Tomorowicz, and Alexander Yates. The views expressed here are his own. They should be in no way attributed to the organizations with which he is affiliated.

Table 10.1
Directions of Poland's Exports and Imports, 1985-1991
(in percentages)

Exports to	1985	1989	1990	1991
— European Community	23.2	32.1	47.2	59.2
— CMEA (Europe)	48.8	34.8	21.4	12.1
— Others	28.0	33.1	31.4	28.7
Imports from				
— European Community	20.5	33.8	45.6	53.3
— CMEA	53.6	32.2	22.3	9.8
— Others	25.9	34.0	32.1	36.9

Source: *Zmiany struktury i efektywność gospodarowania w latach 1989-1991* (Warsaw: Centralny Urząd Planowania, June 1992), p. 46.

until the end of the 1980s. The first section deals with evolution of the foreign trade regime since the early 1980s. Gradual dismantling of the state monopoly of foreign trade in the 1980s did not produce significant improvement in export performance, although it contributed significantly to export expansion once the administrative economic system was dismantled through 1990. The next section examines the anatomy of export supply response during the 1990-1991 period to the transformation program. It shows that export expansion to the West was driven, not by raw materials and food products, but by manufactures. An intriguing question concerning the impact of CMEA's collapse, especially that of the Soviet Union, on Polish exports to the West is addressed in the next section. The analysis indicates that a considerable redirection of trade from CMEA to the EC occurred between 1985 and 1991. The process accelerated in the 1990-1991 period. The last section briefly sketches Poland's prospects for fully integrating with the world economy. The demise of communism and of the USSR has created an environment favorable to reintegrating Poland with the world economy, provided that its government stays the course of economic transformation and skillfully exploits opportunities offered by the new political realities in Europe.

EVOLUTION OF FOREIGN TRADE:
DISAPPEARANCE OF INSTITUTIONAL CONSTRAINT

Reforms of the foreign trade systems began well before the collapse of communism in 1989. Foreign trade represented an area of much experimentation during the 1980s. Different policies appeared easy to formulate, implement, and also reverse. The general approach taken by communist reformers included linking domestic prices to international prices; establishing direct contacts between enterprises and international markets, bypassing traditional foreign trade organizations; establishing a larger number of intermediaries, with a less restricted trading profile; introducing currency auctions; and reducing the number of exchange rates and devaluing them to more realistic levels. While these measures contributed to a proliferation of marketing expertise at the level of enterprises and provided incentives to boost exports, they failed to introduce "market clearing at single prices without ex post and ad hoc subsidies and levies, yielding a profit which is retained by enterprises or losses which penalize them."[2]

Thus, no matter how radical the reform measures, the foreign trade regime under central planning remained a source of enormous distortions and inefficiencies, insulating domestic producers from the impact of change in relative prices on world markets. They fell short of making foreign trade an effective conveyor of international efficiency standards. In order to achieve this end, one would have to replace the antiexport biases (i.e., import restrictions, administrative allocation of raw materials and foreign exchange, and price controls) with administrative mechanisms designed to encourage exports and discourage imports, as well as the "soft-budget" constraint that would punish inefficient producers. However, these changes were not possible without abandoning central planning and dismantling the communist political order.

Before the collapse of communism, decentralization of the foreign trade regime had made most progress in Hungary and Poland—both were highly indebted to the West and were the first to begin orienting their economies away from the CMEA. Foreign trade reforms shared two sets of features. The first included supplementing the limited financial autonomy granted to SOEs (state-owned enterprises) by central planners with discretion to conduct foreign trade. Thus began an erosion of the state monopoly over foreign trade. Trade licenses were no longer granted exclusively to dominant exporters and importers. They were made available to all firms and covered most products. In Poland, significant steps along these lines were undertaken in the early 1980s, when authorities liberalized conditions for obtaining foreign trade licenses. Between 1982 and 1985, the number of SOEs empowered to conduct foreign trade operations grew from 109 to 361. By the end of the 1980s, the state monopoly had been abrogated. As a result, the number of firms operating in international markets dramatically increased.

The second set of features included creating incentives for SOEs to expand exports through hard currency retention schemes and exchange rate policy. The latter essentially consisted of a series of devaluations toward more realistic rates. Between 1980 and 1985, the Polish real exchange rate had appreciated by 30 percent. The exchange rate policy had a more significant impact on export performance once SOEs were allowed to retain some of their foreign exchange earnings. Retention schemes amounted to limited convertibility. SOEs then became more sensitive to exchange rate policy. Polish exporters, who were allowed to retain 25 to 30 percent of their foreign exchange earnings, responded to a substantial devaluation of the Polish złoty in late 1987 by increasing exports—the 17.4 percent increase in convertible currency exports during 1988 was attributable to the devaluation.[3]

While these changes in the foreign trade regimes reduced the insulation of enterprises from international markets, an almost full protection of SOEs from international competition remained. The trade regime offered no clue as to whether domestically profitable operations had a positive or negative value added at world prices. Equalization schemes provided a buffer between domestic producers and world prices. These measures had a limited impact on foreign trade, simply because SOEs did not become full-fledged firms. They operated in an administrative environment devoid of competition, market-clearing prices, freedom of entry, and the final penalty for poor performance, namely, bankruptcy. In other words, without replacing the administrative environment in which economic actors operated, even dismantling the state monopoly of foreign trade while retaining the administrative economic system could not contribute to improvement in overall economic performance. Replacement, however, could not occur without the collapse of communism.

The collapse of communism in Poland created conditions for a swift move from a supply-constrained to a demand-constrained economy through removing political and ideological constraints to dismantling central planning (or whatever was left of it) and establishing an economic system based on market-clearing prices and competition among autonomous economic actors. The stabilization-cum-transformation program launched on 1 January 1990 liberalized prices and the foreign trade regime, unified the exchange rate, and introduced limited convertibility of the domestic currency. Firms could decide what they wanted to import and/or export, and they had the right to buy foreign currency at the official exchange rate in order to import goods or services from abroad. As a result, tariffs and the exchange rate have become effective trade policy instruments.

Transformation from an administrative economic system (a supply-constrained economy) involved a simultaneous change in macroeconomic policies and in their microeconomic foundations. Although the macroeconomic stabilization program was carried out in an institutional environment dominated by SOEs, resembling administrative units rather than full-fledged firms with unambiguously defined property rights, they responded to a new set of incentives by dramatically expanding their exports to the West. Taking into account that their organizational structures had been designed to facilitate administrative management by the state and that their capacity to compete internationally also was limited because of outdated technologies, this was truly an astounding development. On the import side, dismantling of the state monopoly over foreign trade brought about rather an unexpected change, given its scope. Import activities became dominated by private firms, which accounted for more than half the total value of imports during 1991.

That the economy was able to respond to the new incentives resulted from changes in the economic system implemented during the 1980s. In retrospect, the ability of SOEs to respond to the new incentives was clearly underrated. The various reform measures introduced in the 1980s provided fertile ground for a quick move from a supply- to a demand-constrained economy, whereas they had a rather limited impact in improving microeconomic efficiency and export performance under the earlier administrative economic system.

The changes introduced during the 1980s significantly increased SOE autonomy in conducting their domestic and foreign transactions, contributed to proliferation of marketing expertise among managers, and allowed SOEs to establish direct contacts with Western importers. Extension of licenses to other than centralized foreign trade organizations—traditional guardians of state monopoly over foreign trade—led to an increase in the number of SOEs directly responsible for their own exports. Foreign currency retention schemes, allowing exporters to retain a portion of their hard currency earnings, contributed to the proliferation of marketing skills, since they could use foreign exchange receipts to purchase imports. For instance, around half of all imports were financed from this source in 1989. The gradual dismantling of the state monopoly over foreign trade in the 1980s forced SOEs to develop contacts with Western customers and gain some expertise in marketing their products. The driving force behind Poland's export expansion in the West were the SOEs with earlier exposure to Western clients.[4]

FACTORS BEHIND THE EXPORT SUPPLY RESPONSE

To place developments in exports to the West during the early 1990s in perspective, one must examine trends during the 1980s. Polish trade with the West during the latter period can be divided into two distinct phases. The first, covering 1980-1983, witnessed a collapse accompanied by a quickly aborted attempt to cut links with the West. During the second (1984-1989) phase, a policy of expanding trade with the West was actively pursued, although the results of this effort were mixed. Among central and southern European CMEA countries, Polish export growth to Organization for Economic Cooperation and Development (OECD) markets was second to that of Hungary but the region had performed very poorly. Taking into account the virtual collapse of exports during 1981 and 1982, subsequent export growth left much to be desired. Despite progressive liberalization of the foreign trade regime and strong political pressures to boost exports to obtain much-needed hard currency revenues to service its international debt and pay for imports, Poland failed to recapture the share of OECD markets that it had held in 1980. Exports of farm products, mineral fuels, and raw materials increased, but they were not large enough to compensate for the dismal performance in manufactures. As a consequence, Poland's competitive profile shifted toward low value-added manufactures and natural-resource intensive products.

The collapse of exports during the early 1980s was reversed by exporters of coal, farm products, and manufactures who succeeded in increasing their shares of OECD markets in the second phase. In the 1984-1989 period, the ratios of the average export growth rate to OECD import growth rates were 1.12 for the total, 1.88 for foods and feeds, and 1.23 for manufactures.[5] By the end of the decade Poland had not been able to regain the share in OECD import demand that it held in 1980. As can be seen in Chart 1, the share of nonmanufactures came close to the 1980 level, while that of manufactures remained below it. In view of modernization in its industrial base during the 1970s, financed by Western credits, the shift in Poland's comparative advantage (as revealed in exports to Western markets) to natural resource intensive products demonstrated its inability to compete in markets for products whose manufacture called for more sophisticated technologies, marketing skills, and organization techniques.

Extrapolation from 1980s trends would have sketched the following picture: Poland's position in Western markets would be stagnant or improving only marginally at a hesitant pace; its export commodity composition would continue to shift toward natural resource- and unskilled labor-intensive products; and its competitiveness, in the most rapidly expanding markets for manufactures, would

Graph 10.1
**Share of Poland's Export in OECD Import Demand in the
1980-1991 period**

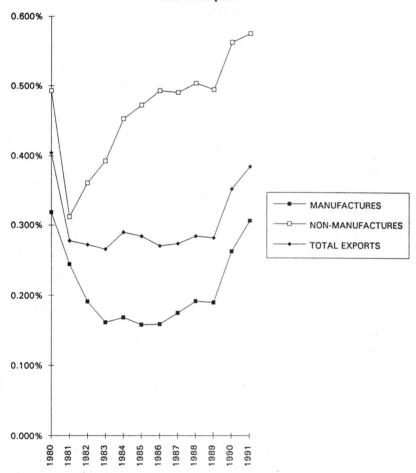

remain stagnant. In addition, symptoms of industrial decline were abundant throughout the 1980s, as many industrial sectors lacked access to resources for modernization of their aging productive capacities. Yet the pace at which exports to the OECD increased and the extent of the shift to manufactures in the export structure were astounding. What happened defied projections by both Polish and Western experts involved in the preparation of the transformation program.[6] As can be readily seen from Graph 10.1, the developments following introduction of the transformation program in 1990 were not a reversal but rather a dramatic acceleration of trends observed in the 1984-1989 period.

Export performance improved in all product categories, including manufactures during 1990-1991. Exports increased three times more than the increase in OECD total imports, while the increase in Poland's exports of manufactures to the OECD was around four times larger. The value of manufactured products exports rose by 58 percent in 1990 and 23 percent in 1991. Thus, contrary to expectations, the driving force behind the Polish export boom in the 1990-1991 period were manufactures—not farm products, energy, and raw materials, as one might have expected. Poland's share in OECD's total imports rose from 0.28 percent in 1984-1989 to 0.37 percent (a 28 percent increase) in 1990-1991, mainly due to expansion of manufactured goods' export—their share in OECD imports of manufactures rose from 0.17 percent to 0.28 percent (by 63 percent). Manufactured goods accounted for 63 percent of the increase in 1990 exports, for 90 percent of the increase in 1991, and for 71 percent of the growth in the value of Poland's exports between 1989 and 1991.

Which manufactures represented a success story in Western markets? Table 10.2 provides a list of manufactured goods that contributed most to the export upswing. It contains product categories meeting the following two criteria: first, the value of exports in 1991 was larger than U.S. $10 million; and, second, the average annual rate of growth (in current prices) during the 1990-1991 period was equal to or larger than 40 percent. The second criterion is quite restrictive, as it excludes all product categories whose value failed to almost double between 1989 and 1991. The products were selected from the breakdown of exports to the EC at a three-digit SITC (Standard International Trade Classification) level.[7]

Although based only on exports to the EC, the analysis of these product groups sheds light on developments in Polish exports of manufactures to the West in general. First, it should be noted that the EC provides an outlet for almost 80 percent of Polish products sold on OECD markets, and the EC share has been expanding. Second, the value of export items in Table 10.2 accounted for around 23 percent of total Polish exports to the EC in 1991 and for 42 percent of its exports of manufactured goods. Third, between 1989 and 1991, their value increased by more than U.S. $1 billion, accounting for more than one-third of the increase in manufactured exports to OECD countries. Thus, exporters meeting the above criteria made a significant contribution to performance in Western markets.

Not surprisingly, one cannot find high-technology products among most successful exports: Poland, like other former communist-ruled countries, missed the information-computer revolution. Sectors which stand out in their export performance are representative of the second industrial revolution, driven by chemical and steel industries. Excluding textiles and most nonmetallic mineral manufactures, they were high on central planners' investment priorities during the 1960s and to a lesser extent in the early 1970s. Capital equipment is not on the list, although the transport equipment industry—mainly thanks to shipbuilding—had a significant share.[8]

Contrary to popular perception, the factor content of manufactured products which registered the highest increase in exports to the West was not biased in favor of unskilled labor- or natural resource-intensive products, and their factor intensity did not change significantly between 1989 and 1991. The first column of Table 10.2 identifies product groups by relative factor intensities. Products responsible for the largest share of exports listed in this table are human capital-intensive goods (12 product categories). They generated export revenues of $739 million, accounting for 47 percent of exports by the "successful" group. The second largest contribution came from technology-intensive products (nine product categories)—with $458 million in exports. They accounted for 29 percent of the total in Table 10.2. Hence, the two groups at the higher end of the value-added spectrum accounted for around 76 percent of exports with above-average performance. Their share in the increase in total exports of products identified in the table between 1989 and 1991 was roughly the same. This suggests that within the "above-average-expansion" group, there was no major shift in relative factor intensities.

Products typical of a low level of industrial development accounted for the remaining 24 percent of exports. The unskilled labor-intensive group (five product categories) accounted for 18 percent, and the value of their exports was $289 million. Products belonging to the natural resource-intensive group (three product categories) were valued at $92 million. Thus, among the industrial sectors setting the pace for export expansion during 1990 and 1991, human capital- and technology-intensive products played a dominant role, and the latter represented the component changing more rapidly in the export commodity composition during 1991.

Given Poland's relatively ample endowment in some nonrenewable natural resources and its moderate climate favoring agriculture, the share of natural resource-intensive products in total exports—as opposed to a limited sample of manufactured exports—was significantly larger. The Polish export structure became less human capital- and technology-intensive during the 1980s and early 1990s. Although the share of the technology-intensive group in Polish exports increased, its EC-10 (European Community, excluding Greece and Portugal) market share remained constant and the RCI (revealed comparative index) fell slightly. The share of products characterized by high

Table 10.2

**Polish Manufactured Product Exports to the EC
and Their Relative Factor Intensities (FI)**

FI SITC (Group)	Description: Division (group heading)	Rate of Growth, 1990-1991 (in percent)	Value of Exports (1991) (U.S. $ million)
TI 512	Organic Chemicals (alcohols and phenols)	53.4	72.4
TI 523	Inorganic Chemicals (organic and inorganic compounds of precious metals)	42.8	65.9
TI 562	Fertilizers, Manufactures (mineral or chemical)	165.5	125.0
TI 598	Chemical Materials and Products (miscellaneous)	40.3	10.5
HC 641	Paper and Articles of Paper Pulp (paper/paperboard cut to size or shape)	47.1	10.5
UL 651	Textile Yarn and Fabrics (textile yarn)	46.4	15.3
NR 661	Nonmetallic Mineral Manu-factures (lime, cement, etc.)	76.6	55.5
NR 663	(mineral manufactures)	134.0	18.6
UL 664	(glass)	45.8	25.4
UL 665	(glassware)	81.1	55.2
UL 666	(pottery)	67.2	20.4
NR 671	Iron and Steel (pig iron, sponge iron, etc.)	92.5	18.3
HC 672	(ingots and other primary forms)	55.5	152.6
HC 673	(iron and steel bars, rods, etc.)	89.9	264.0
HC 676	(rails and railway truck construction materials)	151.7	17.2
HC 678	(tubes, pipes and fittings)	81.9	32.8
HC 679	(iron and steel castings)	52.4	23.6
HC 691	Manufactures of Metals (structures)	67.6	83.9

FI SITC (Group)	Description: Division (group heading)	Rate of Growth, 1990-1991 (in percent)	Value of Exports (1991) (U.S. $ million)
HC 692	(metal containers for storage and transport)	73.0	11.0
HC 697	(household equip. of base metal)	53.8	22.6
TI 728	Machinery and Equipment (machine tools)	40.0	92.1
TI 741	Industrial Machinery (heating and cooling equipment)	44.9	16.6
TI 743	(pumps and compressors)	75.2	31.6
TI 744	(mechanical handling equip. and parts)	47.1	27.4
HC 775	Household Electrical and Nonelectrical Equipment (laundry equipment)	51.9	57.4
HC 791	Transport Equipment (railway vehicles)	70.2	13.8
UL 793	(ships, boats)	48.8	172.3
UL 841	Clothing (outer garments of textile fabrics)	58.0	151.4
Total exports (US $ million)			1,729.2

Notes:

FI—relative factor intensities; TI—technology-intensive products; HC—human capital-intensive products; NR—natural resource-intensive products; and UL—unskilled labor-intensive products.

Source: Derived from data compiled from official Polish sources (Marczewski, note 7) by B. Kamiński, "The Foreign Trade Dimensions of the Market Transition in Poland" (Washington, D.C.: The World Bank, 1992), mimeographed.

human capital input declined in EC-10 imports from Poland. Polish exporters outperformed other suppliers only in low value-added production, demonstrating a significant improvement in "revealed" comparative advantage for natural resource- and unskilled labor-intensive products.

Neither in the 1980s nor during the 1990-1991 period did the factor content of exports move toward products requiring highly skilled labor and technological sophistication. The share of unskilled labor-intensive products in Polish exports significantly increased during both the 1980s and the 1990-1991 period. Part of this increase could be attributed to changes in relative prices in favor of manufactures, with the fall in the prices of raw materials and energy, in the 1980s. However, a more adequate explanation for the increased weight of unskilled-labor intensive products is that the capital stock was rapidly deteriorating. At the same time, a decline occurred in the competitiveness of products at the higher end of the value-added spectrum. The technological quality of manufactures in the 1980s was lower than in the 1970s. Therefore, the export drive could only derive from traditional sectors characterized by high capital and unskilled labor content. It could not originate with sophisticated engineering products because their production remained underdeveloped.

Too short a period of time has elapsed to make any firm prognosis whether this development presages a movement up the technological ladder in Polish exports to the West. The comparison of 1991 with 1990 points to a fall in competitiveness for exporters of technology-intensive products. Since the technology-intensive group in Polish exports consisted mainly of traditional labor- and energy-intensive products, it is likely that some of them lost their competitive edge once energy prices were no longer subsidized in 1991.

Given the relatively high quality of scientific education in Poland, there is a dissonance between the country's endowment in human capital and the move toward unsophisticated labor-intensive products in its exports. Two economists have shown a positive correlation between education in Poland (as well as other East-Central European countries) and comparative advantage in sophisticated engineering goods which, however, is yet to be revealed in its exports to the West.[9] Whether this dissonance remains only a transitional phenomenon, a legacy of the earlier misallocation of resources, will depend on whether private investors are able to exploit this potential comparative advantage and whether government creates a friendly environment for export-oriented activities.

The export expansion was initially propelled by the swift movement to a new set of institutional arrangements, revamping the existing incentive structures. Virtual termination of the supply-constrained economy in 1991, the result of decontrolling prices and restoring macroeconomic fiscal and monetary controls, combined with the introduction of current account convertibility of the Polish złoty, produced a strong export stimulus not only to the West but also to the CMEA just before its collapse.[10] Faced with collapse of domestic consumer demand, devaluation, and elimination of government subsidies, export expansion became one of the few survival options available to SOEs. During the first year of the transformation program, the rapid appreciation of the złoty (which followed devaluation regarded by many analysts as excessive) had little impact on the propensity of Polish SOEs to export. Despite the appreciation, exports continued to increase through 1990, suggesting that exporters were relatively immune to the changes in exchange rate policy. With a hardening of the budget constraint and depletion of reserves accumulated under the administrative economic system, their capacity to compete successfully in international markets may be jeopardized.

THE IMPACT OF THE CMEA COLLAPSE ON POLAND'S EXPORTS

Reorientation of trade occurred in the face of significant changes in external circumstances. The CMEA, accounting for around half of Polish trade, collapsed in 1991, leading to a fall in bloc import demand for Polish products and to a deterioration in the terms-of-trade vis-à-vis the USSR.

The export upswing toward the West coincided with the above demise. The former Soviet market which provided an easy outlet for sectors developed specifically to meet its requirements—as a rule much less exacting than elsewhere—has almost disappeared. Because of the contraction in this import demand and the gradual shift to convertible currencies in trade transactions in the late 1980s and during the 1990-1991 period, Polish exporters had already been losing preferential access to Eastern markets. By 1991, when the full change to hard currency occurred, they had to compete in former CMEA markets on the same footing as other suppliers. This put an end to the dual external environment for Polish trade activity; one subject to market forces and the other nurtured by preferential intra-CMEA arrangements. The former comprised so-called hard goods, while the latter were mostly manufactured goods and "soft" products unmarketable in the West because of high costs and low quality. This section addresses two questions: what was the extent of reorientation of Polish exports from the CMEA to the West? and, what was the extent of export diversion away from CMEA?

Although the demise of the CMEA inflicted a heavy cost on the Polish economy,[11] its trade impact was less damaging because of lower dependence than for other member countries. This dependence had decreased well before the demise of the USSR. A reorientation of Poland's trade was already under way in the 1980s. Between 1970 and 1990, the CMEA share fell from 60 to 39 percent.

The reorientation of trade away from the CMEA during the first two years of the transformation program was formidable. However, this was mainly due to expansion of trade with the OECD rather than to the collapse of import demand in the CMEA. The share of the former CMEA in Poland's exports (in current prices) fell from 49 percent in 1985 to 16.9 percent in 1991, with the Soviet Union accounting for 11 percent of Polish exports, and Czechoslovakia—the second largest trading partner in the CMEA—only 4.7 percent. The share of the EC rose from 23 percent of the total in 1985 to 47.2 percent in 1990 and to 55.6 percent in 1991. However, the decline in exports to the CMEA in 1991 was much smaller than the increase in the value of exports to the West.

Three observations can be derived from Table 10.3, presenting annual changes in the value of Poland's exports in 1990 and 1991 as well as during the period from 1988 to 1991 (when the value of intra-CMEA exports was falling) to the Soviet Union, other East-European CMEA members, and OECD countries. First, the pattern of change in trade with "small" CMEA members was different than with the USSR, especially in 1991. Following the dissolution of the TR (transferable ruble) payments mechanism in January 1991, exports to the Soviet Union increased while those to the CMEA-4 (Bulgaria, Czechoslovakia, Hungary, and Romania) collapsed. Second, the increase in exports to OECD markets more than offset the fall in exports to CMEA-4 markets. Third, the increase in Polish exports to the USSR during both 1990 and 1991 followed the earlier expansion in 1988 and 1989. The increase between 1987 and 1991 was slightly above U.S. $1 billion. Because Soviet exports had been falling since 1988, Poland ran significant trade surpluses apparently needed to pay off its debt to the Soviet Union.

It is tempting to draw the conclusion that thanks to Western trade, Polish enterprises, mainly state-owned, could more than compensate for losses in CMEA-4 markets during 1990 and 1991. This conclusion is not necessarily correct, since not all exports to the CMEA-4 could have been redirected to the West and the import demand of the Soviet Union shifted to "harder" goods. While more research is needed at the level of industrial enterprises, some preliminary observations can be obtained by comparing changes in Poland's export baskets before and after an almost complete switch to hard-currency settlements in intra-CMEA trade which took place in 1991.

The change in composition of exports by area can be used as a proxy measure depicting the extent of the switch following the dramatic opening of the economy in January 1990. Polish export baskets to CMEA and to the EC were traditionally strongly dissimilar: the former had a large component of capital equipment and electroengineering, whereas in the latter, food, raw materials, and energy dominated. The former were regarded as soft goods

Table 10.3

Changing Polish Export Orientation from CMEA to OECD, 1988-1991

	1990	1991	1988-1991
	(U.S. $ million)		Total
Soviet Union	78	335	1081
Other European members of the CMEA-4	498	-834	-6
OECD countries	2557	1110	4845
Totals	3133	611	5859
Note: Soviet Union's balance of trade with Poland	-1282	-1410	

Source: International Monetary Fund, *Direction of Trade Statistics Yearbook* (1992)

which, because of low quality, could not be sold in markets other than the CMEA; the latter were hard goods, imposing hard-currency opportunity costs for the CMEA exporters. A good measure of the resemblance is the similarity index assuming the value of zero if the two structures are entirely different, and the value of one when they are the same. There has been a convergence in the composition of export baskets, as measured by this index; its value increased from 0.6321 in 1985 to 0.6766 in 1989, 0.7345 in 1990, and skyrocketed to 0.8823 in 1991.[12] The convergence was not, however, unidirectional, as products previously dominant in exports to CMEA increased their share in exports to the EC, thus indicating redirection of exports from CMEA to EC, and vice versa.

Taking into account that the transferable ruble almost totally disappeared from commercial transactions in 1991 and that former CMEA exporters lost preferential access to one another's markets, the increased similarity of the two export structures can be explained as follows. Faced with market constraints, importers in former CMEA countries slashed soft goods in favor of hard goods, independent of their origin. They were not willing to spend scarce foreign exchange on goods produced by their trading partners from the former Soviet bloc unless they were competitive with products offered on international markets. In 1991 the change in structure of import demand became exacerbated by a steep decline in aggregate output and investment activity throughout all postcommunist countries. Therefore, some part of the decline probably was not due to the lower quality of products from CMEA, but to the fall in import demand for capital goods and other intermediate products.

Given the increase in the share of the electroengineering sector in exports to the EC during the 1985-1991 period, some part of the decline of this sector in exports to CMEA can be attributed to the reorientation away from the CMEA. For instance, between 1985 and 1990, the combined value of exports of power-generating equipment (the main product of the electroengineering sector representative of soft goods) to the Soviet Union and the EC slightly increased from $864 million to $884 million. The share for the EC increased from 12 in 1985 to 41 percent in 1990; correspondingly, the share for the Soviet Union dropped from 88 to 59 percent. Hence, the power-generating equipment loss of the USSR market was considerably offset by increased exports to the EC.[13]

A striking foreign trade-related feature of the transformation program was the increase in openness of sectors previously oriented toward domestic markets. The export orientation of sectors that had neither been nurtured by intra-CMEA specialization schemes nor exposed to Western markets increased significantly between 1989 and 1991. For instance, the export share of total sales of such sectors as wood-paper rose from 11 in 1989 to 32 percent in 1991, and of light industry from 9 to 22 percent.[14] The shares of these industries in exports to the EC increased significantly during the same period.

An interesting point emanating from this analysis is that Polish authorities were correct to ignore the Western expert advice on establishing an East European Payments Union that would promote trade among CMEA.[15] The advice failed to take into account salient characteristics of intra-CMEA trade and the impact of the shift from a demand-constrained to a supply-constrained economy. The proponents of this scheme acted on the premise that CMEA had been successful in integrating its member-countries' economies.[16] They seemed oblivious to the fact that the Soviet attempts to impose supranational planning and to increase intraindustry integration within CMEA failed. The much lower than anticipated impact that the CMEA dissolution had on the Polish economy in 1991 supports the idea that the economic dependence level was not as considerable as some earlier analyses had suggested.

The dramatic change in commodity composition of Polish exports to CMEA in 1991 mainly resulted from the exports collapse of soft goods. Extending the CMEA arrangements under the guise of an East European Payments Union would have affected the welfare of all its participants negatively. This trade would have had to be subsidized, simply because domestic production costs exceeded world prices. Thus, introduction of an East European Payments Union would have unnecessarily weakened incentives to restructure trade in line with actual comparative advantage.

PROSPECTS: EXTERNAL ECONOMIC SETTING

The end of the Cold War converted Poland's political status in the West from that of a cryptic adversary to an ally, which brought some tangible long- and short-term economic benefits. The country has become the recipient of significant financial and technical assistance from Western governments and international organizations (International Monetary Fund and the World Bank). Their assistance was instrumental in launching a radical stabilization program based on liberalization of prices. Western governments also offered some trade concessions, including extension of GSP (Generalized System of Preferences) treatment, restoration of MFN (Most Favored Nation) status with the United States, and the elimination and suspension of some quantitative restrictions by the EC.[17] Finally, the collapse of communism made possible the European Association Agreement with the EC (December 1991) and the Gothenburg Declaration (June 1990), promising a free-trade agreement, limited to manufactures, with EFTA (European Free Trade Association). In addition, the EC has significantly increased quotas for some products imported from Poland.

Changes in the external economic setting could not have had a significant impact on export performance during the 1990-1991 period, however. Products in which Poland had a comparative advantage, for example, textiles and clothing, or coal and steel, were excluded from trade concessions in 1990. The provisions for MFN treatment were expanded during 1991 to include coal and steel products through protocols with the European Coal and Steel Community. Trade stipulations by the European Association Agreement, also referred to as the Europe Agreement, went into effect on 1 March 1992. The free-trade agreement with EFTA, broadly similar to the trade section of the Europe Agreement, was signed in November 1992. Since all these developments took place mainly after the initial two years of the stabilization-cum-transformation program, the emerging external environment will provide strong stimuli to sustain the impressive expansion in trade with the West in the years to come. Thus, barring unexpected domestic and external shocks, access to Western markets in the immediate future will considerably improve in comparison to the 1990-1991 period.

The objective of the Europe Agreement is to facilitate Poland's membership in the EC. Its major provisions include: (1) the introduction of free trade in industrial goods by the year 2002; (2) improved access for agricultural products similar to that stipulated in the Lomé convention and Mediterranean association/cooperation agreements; (3) EC financial and technical assistance, albeit no specific amounts have been indicated; (4) possible introduction of free trade in services in the future. For around 60 percent of present EC industrial imports from Poland, all duties and other restrictions were eliminated on 1 March 1992. The EC will gradually reduce tariffs on other sensitive products—mainly iron, steel, and textiles—over the next five to six years, also beginning on 1 March 1992.

In the long term, the Europe Agreement will significantly expand access of Polish exporters to the EC, its largest trading partner. In the short term, expansion of Polish exports critically depends on the growth of import demand in the EC-10, especially Germany, which replaced the Soviet Union as Poland's largest trading partner in 1990. During 1991 the main engine of Polish export growth was Germany.[18] Had it not been for expanding German markets for Polish products, it is rather unlikely that the 1990 export upswing would have extended into 1991. Poland's exports in current prices to EFTA, North America, and Japan slightly contracted, and to other EC-10 countries they stagnated (increased by a mere $7 million in current prices), but they grew by more than U.S. $1 billion to Germany. Therefore, a slowdown of economic growth in Germany is likely to have serious consequences for Polish exports.

The potential impact of the Europe Agreement goes well beyond trade. The prospect of EC membership, although not explicitly mentioned in the agreement, provides guidance for institutional transformation and improves access to West European financial markets. Although transplanting institutions from a different environment is not always productive, the necessity of matching solutions concerning organization of the banking sector, development of fiscal policy instruments, setting of industrial standards, and so on, sets a clear path to be followed by Polish decision makers. Easier access to EC markets will attract foreign direct investment. The Agreement has already opened the possibility to obtain "continuous access to EIB [European Investment Bank] loans beyond the present framework."[19]

Another potential benefit from the agreement, with a foreign trade impact, is that attractiveness of Poland to foreign investors may likely increase. Thus, industries should also profit from financial resources and know-how of Western firms. As a result, the export basket should expand and become more diversified.

While the Europe Agreement is by far the most significant aspect of Poland's emergence into the international economic environment, the development of commercial relations with other neighboring countries has also been high on the government's foreign agenda. Responding to pressures from Western governments, Poland undertook negotiations with Czechoslovakia and Hungary to establish a free-trade area. Western insistence on "joint" treatment of the Central European *troika* had the positive impact of containing potential adversary tensions, produced by their initial scramble to outrace one another in joining the EC, and forced them to establish closer political and economic links. In December 1992 the free-trade agreement among the three governments was signed. Given the relatively small volume of their mutual trade,[20] its immediate impact will not be significant. It sets, however, a groundwork for future expansion of trade as well as cooperative political and economic relations.

In the east, Poland borders now on four new states that resulted from dissolution of the Soviet Union—Russia, Lithuania, Belarus, and Ukraine. The future of trade with these countries hinges critically on their ability to impose macroeconomic stability and liberalize their foreign trade regimes. In the meantime, little can be done to add vitality into their commercial relations with Poland.

Barring unexpected domestic and external political developments damaging to economic relations, the end of the Cold War and of the political division of Europe augurs well for Poland's rapid reintegration into the world economy.

NOTES

1. The CMEA was officially dissolved at its 46th General Session, held in Moscow on 28 June 1991. Its members had included Bulgaria, Cuba, Czechoslovakia, the German Democratic Republic, Hungary, Mongolia, Poland, Romania, the Soviet Union, and Vietnam.
2. D. M. Nuti, "Progress in Trade Reforms, Missing Links, Convertibility," in Michael Kaiser and Alexander M. Vacic, eds., *Reforms in Foreign Economic Relations of Eastern Europe and the Soviet Union* (New York: United Nations Economic Commission for Europe, 1991), p. 50.
3. Jan Winiecki, "Post Soviet-Type Economies in Transition," *Weltwirtschaftliches Archiv* 76 (1990).
4. H. Mueller, "Export Performance of Polish Enterprises during the Transition Process" (Washington, D.C.: The World Bank, December 1991), mimeographed.

5. Author's calculation from OECD (excluding Australia and New Zealand) mirror trade statistics, as reported in the United Nations COMTRADE data base.

6. The stabilization program, as presented in the Polish government letter of intent to the International Monetary Fund, assumed a slight increase of exports and a hard-currency trade balance deficit of $800 million in 1990. There actually was a surplus of $2.2 billion. Grzegorz Kołodko, *Polityka finansowa, stabilizacja, transformacja* (Warsaw: Institute of Finance, 1991), p. 13.

7. As compiled from official Polish statistics by K. Marczewski, "Poland's Export Performance in 1985-1991" (Washington, D.C.: The World Bank, July 1992), mimeographed.

8. Ironically, the shipbuilding industry, which the communist government wanted to close down allegedly for economic reasons, succeeded in increasing its exports by almost 50 percent in both 1990 and 1991, and accounted for 10 percent of foreign currency earnings.

9. C. B. Hamilton and L. A. Winters, "Trade with Eastern Europe," *Economic Policy* (April, 1992).

10. In contrast to otherwise stagnating intra-CMEA trade, Poland ran trade surpluses with most of its CMEA-trading partners in 1991. See B. Kamiński, "The Framework of Soviet-East Central European Economic Relations in the 1990s," in R. F. Staar, ed., *East-Central Europe and the USSR* (New York: St. Martin's Press, 1991), pp. 37-58.

11. The shrinking supply and demand in the Soviet Union and the shift to world prices resulted in a dramatic worsening of terms-of-trade, estimated at between 20 and 40 percent, and undercutting economic viability of sectors nurtured by CMEA preferential agreements. According to an estimate, the terms-of-trade loss reduced the GDP of Poland by 4 percent. M. Blejer and A. Gelb, "Persistent Economic Decline in Central and Eastern Europe," *Transition: The Newsletter about Reforming Economies* 3, no. 7 (July-August, 1992); The World Bank, Washington D.C.

12. Based on author's calculations from data in *The State of the Economy: Including Forecasts for the Future: First Half of 1992: A Brief Summary* (Warsaw: Central Planning Office, July 1992), Table 20.

13. All data taken from the United Nations COMTRADE data base, as reported by Poland. One important caveat should be made: given the high level of aggregation, this analysis cannot suggest that the same products were simply shifted from CMEA to the West or that they were manufactured by the same producers.

14. *The State of the Economy,* Central Planning Office.

15. The most vocal analysts came from the U.S. Economic Commission for Europe as well as J. Brabant, *A Central European Payments Union* (New York: Institute for East-West Security Studies, 1991); O. Havrylyshyn and J. Williamson, *From*

Soviet disUnion to Eastern Economic Community (Washington D.C.: Institute for International Economics, 1991).

16. An examination of CMEA developments between 1949 and 1988 shows that this was not the case. See B. Kamiński, "Council for Mutual Economic Assistance: Divisions and Conflicts at its 40th Anniversary," in R. F. Staar, ed., *Yearbook on International Communist Affairs* (Stanford, Calif.: Hoover Institution Press, 1989), pp. 413-431.

17. President Bush announced in March 1991 the Trade Enhancement Initiative for postcommunist Europe, expanding tariff benefits for export under GSP. In response to the Polish government's decision to launch a stabilization program, the EC eliminated on 1 January 1990 all quantitative restrictions that were not in conformity with Article XII of GATT (General Agreement on Tariffs and Trade), as applied to a Trading State (i.e., a centrally planned economy). Around 12 percent of Polish exports during 1989 had been affected by these restrictions.

18. Germany's share in total Polish exports increased from 14 in 1989 to 25 in 1990 to 29 percent in 1991. Excluding Germany, EC demand for Polish products stagnated in 1991; thus, Germany's share in Polish exports to the EC-10 increased from around half to 58 percent in 1991. *Handel zagraniczny w 1991* (Warsaw: Ministry for Foreign Economic Cooperation, 1992).

19. *World News* 4, no. 49 (15-29 January 1992): 8.

20. In 1991, Czechoslovakia and Hungary accounted for around 6 percent of Polish exports and only 4 percent of Polish imports.

11

Prospects for Regional Cooperation

*Sarah Meiklejohn Terry**

In the mid-1980s, Charles Gáti described Moscow's East European alliance system as "alive but not well."[1] At the beginning of 1993, three years after the precipitous collapse of that system, the same might be said of the status of relations among the postcommunist states in Central and Eastern Europe. As recently as mid-1991, the number of regionally focused initiatives was encouraging. In particular, prospects for an expanding "Pentagonale" grouping, an enhanced Conference on Security and Cooperation in Europe (CSCE) with mechanisms for crisis prevention and management, the emergence earlier that year of the "Visegrád Triangle"—even proposals for a "Tisza-Carpathian" group—all seemed to augur well for a vibrant regional network with several institutional pillars and with linkages both to the West European-North Atlantic communities to the west and to several of the former Soviet republics in the east.

From the perspective of early 1993, however, the commitment to regional cooperation within East-Central Europe has taken a distant third place to an introspective preoccupation with the national "self" (or "selves"), manifested most ominously by the reopening of old ethnic and territorial wounds, and to the rush to join "Europe" as represented in the first instance by the EC and NATO. To this an optimist might respond, not without reason, that Gáti's observation related to the death throes of a moribund empire, while one can

* The author is grateful to Dr. Jan B. de Weydenthal, regional analyst with Radio Free Europe/Radio Liberty, for his comments on a draft of this chapter.

still hope that what we are now witnessing are the birth pangs of a new configuration of relations both within the region and between the eastern and western halves of the continent and, thus, that we should not overreact to hiccups that occur along the way. By contrast, the pessimist would counter, also with some justification, that we are merely seeing (albeit with some new wrinkles) a repetition of old patterns of behavior on all sides that had defeated regional cooperation in the past and that left these countries vulnerable both to domestic instability and outside domination.

Already twice in this century—first in the immediate aftermath of World War I, and then in the early years of World War II—cooperation in East--Central Europe had fallen victim to some combination of four negative forces: (1) domestic instability and political fragmentation; (2) regional conflicts based on territorial, ethnic and/or economic disputes, and diverging perceptions of national interest; (3) long-standing imperial ambitions of Russia and/or Germany; and (4) the benign (or malign) neglect on the part of Western powers to which the new and fragile states in the region looked for support and protection.[2] While it would be unwise to jump to premature conclusions about the future, the last 18 months have witnessed the unraveling of the two "success stories" of post-World War I federalism—first, with the fratricidal decomposition of Yugoslavia and, more recently, with the so far "velvet divorce" of the Czechs and Slovaks. In addition, the final months of 1992 witnessed a rising tide of acrimony on many sides (e.g., between Hungarians and Romanians, Slovaks and Hungarians, Poles and Lithuanians), as well as the poisonous spread of neo-Nazi influences into Central Europe from a reunited Germany.

In assessing the balance between the optimistic and pessimistic scenarios for regional cooperation, this chapter will focus on the three (now four) core Central European states—Poland, Hungary, and the Czech and Slovak Republics—and will examine their attempts both to develop new forms of cooperation among themselves and to forge strong links with the larger European community.

In the three years since the collapse of Central Europe's communist regimes in the second half of 1989, the evolving status of relations among the successor states can be likened to changing images in a kaleidoscope, in which appealing patterns emerge, shine brightly for a moment, and then dissolve into new combinations and configurations. In this fast-changing environment, the dynamics of regional relations can best be grasped chronologically, with the years between late 1989 and the end of 1992 being broken down into three overlapping but distinct phases, corresponding roughly, if imperfectly, to the calendar years 1990-1992. Each phase was characterized by shifting perceptions both of domestic political and economic conditions within the region and of the broader international environment—in particular, the receptiveness (or lack thereof) of the West European/North Atlantic community to the rapid inclusion of Central Europe into its economic and security structures, as well as the existence or absence of potential threats from the East (whether of an economic, political, or military nature).

PHASE ONE—1990

Despite strong personal ties among a number of the new political leaders forged in earlier dissident days, 1990 was not an auspicious year for regional cooperation. The dyspeptic state of relations among the three core Central European states at the beginning of the year was evident on all sides. Poland, in particular, found itself somewhat isolated and vulnerable, while its two neighbors to the south saw themselves on a fast track toward inclusion in the European Community. In part, this was due to a deceptively benign international environment in which the Soviet Union, still intact and under the combined foreign policy leadership of President Mikhail Gorbachev and Foreign Minister Eduard Shevardnadze, was for most of the year cooperating in the controlled deconstruction of its "external empire." At least in Hungary and Czechoslovakia, this climate encouraged both a false euphoria over newly refound independence and excessive optimism over the ease and speed of their "return to Europe." The Hungarians especially were convinced that their long history of reform efforts and the fact that they were well ahead of the others in attracting foreign investment gave them preferential status. Indeed, despite official denials, there was a palpable sense of competition among the three—a race to join Europe that was perceived as a kind of zero-sum game in which, if one wins, the others must lose, "as if all were courting the same woman."[3]

But the reluctance of the Central European states to forge closer links among themselves also had deeper and more structural roots. First, four decades of forced cohabitation in the Soviet bloc had only compounded a long history of mutual grievances and mistrust. Cultural and ethnic differences had been allowed to fester under a blanket of denials and ritualized protestations of fraternal friendship, or were exacerbated by policies of overt or covert assimilation. Moreover, the shared pathology of Marxist-Leninist rule, misdirected development, and "integration" within the confines of a Moscow-dominated CMEA left all with a familiar litany of economic woes:

technological obsolescence, low productivity and poor quality, redundant capacities, excessive dependence on a disappearing Soviet market, nonconvertible currencies and cumbersome trading mechanisms. It should have come as no surprise, therefore, that they tended to see each other as inappropriate and undesirable partners, or that trade among them plummeted following the fall of their communist regimes. As a Polish journalist commented recently: "When a blind man takes the hand of a lame man, they create a pair which together can move forward more easily. Those afflicted with the same handicap do not have that chance."[4]

Other divisive factors concerned geopolitical, demographic, and economic asymmetries—especially between Poland, on the one hand, and Hungary and Czechoslovakia, on the other. As one Polish analyst put it at the time, the geopolitical concept of Central Europe "embraces the countries between Russia and Germany . . . [But] the only country truly in that unenviable position is Poland. And that is precisely one of the main reasons why other Central Europeans do not necessarily wish to associate themselves with Warsaw."[5] Indeed, through much of 1990 the Poles were perceived both by themselves and by their neighbors as uncomfortably exposed on both their western and eastern flanks. In the West, uncertainty over a reunited Germany's continued recognition of the Oder-Neisse boundary (defining Poland's post-World War II western and northern frontiers and accounting for one-third of its territory) caused Warsaw, reluctantly and temporarily, to view the continued presence of Soviet troops as a guarantee of the territorial integrity of the country at a time when Budapest and Prague were negotiating accelerated withdrawals of Soviet troops and pushing for early termination of all Warsaw Pact activities. In the East, Moscow's acquiescence in the demise of allied communist regimes in Central and Eastern Europe did not mean that it had yet accepted a total loss of influence in the region, as evidenced by concerted efforts well into 1991 to negotiate new bilateral treaties with all the countries in question, including a special security clause prohibiting them from joining alternative alliance systems that the Soviet side deemed hostile. By virtue of its size and strategic location, Poland once again became the target of unwanted attention. According to one source, "the Soviets [were] resigned to allow two separate regional confederations, one in the North, with the Baltics and Scandinavia, and one in the South, over former Hapsburg lands, but neither embracing Poland."[6] Under the circumstances, it was only natural that Prague and Budapest sought to insulate themselves from Warsaw's problems; but the latter's unease over the former's receptivity to substantial German investment—and with it, potential political as well as economic influence—was also understandable. The Poles were especially irritated when Czechoslovak President Václav Havel chose, within days of his election in December 1989, to pay official visits to Bonn and Berlin before traveling to Warsaw and Budapest.

From a demographic perspective, Poland, with a population approaching 40 million (or nearly 50 percent more than Czechoslovakia and Hungary combined), was seen as a potential heavyweight in the region, "both too large and too risky a partner for other Central European nation-states." In addition to sheer size, smaller neighbors were wary of a political style that was sometimes overbearing and condescending. "Poles are generally disliked in other Central European countries for their cockiness . . . [and] pretentious sense of self-importance."[7] Likewise, from an economic perspective, Poland was out of step with the others, not only due to the country's crushing external debt and decade-long history of political and economic instability, but also because the Poles were the first to bite the bullet of free-market austerity. Given the near-term impact of the radical reform program introduced by the government of Tadeusz Mazowiecki on 1 January 1990—to wit, deep recession accompanied by surging unemployment and inflation—Poland temporarily (and unfairly) became "exhibit A" of how not to undertake the transition to a market economy.

A final asymmetry—this one political—stemmed ironically from the April 1989 "Roundtable Agreement" that eventually led to the installation of the first noncommunist government in Central and Eastern Europe in more than 40 years. Having been the front-runner in 1989, Poland soon found itself saddled with an increasingly anachronistic compromise struck at a time when both the communists and the Solidarity opposition assumed a continuation of Soviet hegemony over the region. In the spring of 1990, as Czechs, Slovaks, and Hungarians were voting their former communist rulers out of office in fully free elections, the Poles were stuck with an unfinished house-cleaning: in particular, the "contractual Sejm," in which 65 percent of the seats in the more powerful house of parliament were reserved for parties in the old communist-led coalition; a newly established executive presidency expressly designed for General Wojciech Jaruzelski, the man who had imposed martial law in 1981; and four former communists in key cabinet posts, including defense and interior. In the new postcommunist Central Europe, Poland seemed oddly "out of synch."

Thus, in this first period, the only proposal for cooperation within the region came not from leaders of the countries concerned but from the Polish-born American academic and former National Security Advisor Zbigniew Brzeziński. Already in January, he had tried to revive the World War II concept of a Polish-Czechoslovak federation as the best way of reinforcing the independence of the two countries.[8] In light of the asymmetries discussed above—especially the political ones—the proposal was at best premature; at worst, it may have contributed to the coolness between Warsaw and Prague, where it fell on deaf ears. Instead, throughout most of 1990, attention was focused primarily on interregional and pan-European initiatives, most importantly on enhancing two existing organizations—what had been known till then as the Adria-Alpine Group and the CSCE. In addition, 1990 was a year in which playwright/President Havel seemed to emerge as the *primus inter pares* among Central European leaders, and in which he actively sought to use that image to promote Czechoslovakia as the natural leader in the region.

The original Adria-Alpine Group was a unique organization in a divided Cold War Europe. Formed in 1978, it provided a limited forum for discussion and coordination of largely nonpolitical issues among neighboring provinces of four countries in the Adriatic/Alpine region: neutral Austria, Warsaw Pact member Hungary, communist but nonaligned Yugoslavia, and NATO/EC member Italy. Joint concerns included regional planning, environmental and health issues, economic and agricultural problems, as well as cultural cooperation. Despite its apolitical character—and especially as the Cold War waned in the late 1980s—membership in the group assumed added significance for Hungary as a vehicle for pursuing its goal of gradually backing out of the Warsaw Pact (what might be called "stealth neutrality"). It was probably no accident, therefore, that it was at a meeting in Budapest in early November 1989 as Eastern Europe's communist regimes were unraveling— a meeting attended for the first time by the foreign ministers of the four member countries—that the group was reconstituted from a subnational organization to one operating at the state-to-state level. It was only a matter of time (very little time, as it turned out) before the questions of expanded membership and a broader agenda would arise.[9]

Adria-Alpine's appeal to other states in the region was obvious. As a group spanning the two alliance systems as well as the nonaligned world, membership would not imply an explicit break with Moscow (still a politically impossible, if not unthinkable, move); but it would mean formal affiliation with states outside the Warsaw Pact and a tentative first step toward the shared goal of full EC membership. For Poland, in particular, it could also have meant the first step toward realization of a long-nurtured dream of building a network of cooperative linkages along a North-South axis to offset the pressures from East and West. Both Prague and Warsaw expressed interest in joining, but only the Czechoslovak application was accepted. The reason or reasons for excluding Poland at this point remain

uncertain. Possibly the others were wary of being drawn into the uncertainties over the Polish-German boundary or the still unresolved status of Soviet
troops in the country; it is also possible that they were sensitive to Moscow's
objections to Poland's participation in any independent regional grouping.
But an element of Polish-Czechoslovak rivalry cannot be excluded. In his
speech to the summit of Polish, Hungarian, and Czechoslovak leaders
convened in the Slovak capital of Bratislava on 9 April, Havel referred to
his own country's pending admission to the "Adriatic Community" and then
turned to Poland's status:

> Our brothers the Poles know that they do not belong to the historic Danube area, but
> at the same time, they are, with reason, anxious that they could again be pushed
> aside by a rapidly forming, integrated community and take up once more their
> traditional role as the ill-starred zone between . . . [Germany and the Soviet Union].[10]

In an attempt to soften the pain of rejection, Havel suggested that Poland
belonged more to the Baltic region but in the process revealed part of his
own agenda for elevating Czechoslovakia's status:

> If we want to, and we must, think about one another in solidarity, then we all
> jointly have to do some hard thinking about the geopolitical position of Poland.
> Ideas are appearing about some kind of North or Baltic equivalent of the Adriatic
> Alliance with Czechoslovakia as the geographically logical connecting link of
> both those provisional communities.[11]

At its Venice summit held 31 July-1 August, the group, now officially
renamed the Pentagonale, set itself an ambitious agenda for the period
through 1992. Five formal working groups were either confirmed or newly
established (road transport, telecommunications, environment, small and
medium enterprise development, and culture and tourism), and plans for two
more (on energy and migrations) were announced. On a more political level,
the policy statement adopted at the summit described the Pentagonale as a
"geographically circumscribed" initiative within the broader spectrum of
European organizations (especially the CSCE and EC) which "represents a
level of cooperation which will be helpful in bringing those member countries not yet participating in—or candidates to—the EC closer to the European Community." It also foresaw "a regular exchange of views . . . on
matters of a political nature," interparliamentary cooperation, and support
for contacts among nongovernmental organizations of member countries.
While not excluding the involvement of nonmember states in specific

Pentagonale projects ("particularly those dealing with the environment"), the statement appeared to preclude further expansion, echoing Havel's speech at Bratislava by suggesting that "encouragement must be given to the creation of other regional associations to the North and Southeast, with which profitable cooperation" could be established. Small wonder that many Poles felt frustrated, even bitter, over their exclusion—especially in light of the lack of interest on the part of the Scandinavian countries in closer cooperation with Warsaw beyond the problem of cleaning up the Baltic Sea.[12]

The second major initiative of 1990, also spearheaded by Havel and his foreign minister, Jiří Dienstbier, involved a proposal to transform the CSCE into a pan-European security system that would gradually replace the Warsaw Pact and NATO alliances. In a memorandum distributed three days before the April summit in Bratislava, the Czechoslovak leaders outlined a three-stage plan for "institutionalizing our joint efforts within CSCE and creating effective mechanisms of a new type." The centerpiece of the first stage was to be the immediate creation of a European Security Commission, with headquarters in Prague, to "provide a [until now missing] permanent all-European platform for the consideration of questions relating to security on the continent, and for seeking their solution." The commission would meet regularly at the level of permanent representatives, and at least once a year at the level of foreign ministers; it would also have a subordinate Military Committee. Stages two and three foresaw the emergence, first, of a treaty-based Organization of European States (including the United States and Canada), and, finally, of a "confederated Europe of free and independent states."[13]

There can be little doubt that all former Soviet bloc states attached enormous importance to the Helsinki/CSCE process, of which they were charter members by virtue of being signatories to the 1975 Helsinki Agreement. Not only had it played a facilitating role in their liberation from Soviet domination, it was also their only formalized link to the full North Atlantic community—in particular, to a continued American military and political presence in Europe which most saw as at least a provisional guarantee of their future security in a very uncertain climate. What this meant, of course, was that not all shared Prague's idealism (even naiveté) about the obsolescence of the traditional alliance systems, and especially of NATO. The gaping hole in the Havel/Dienstbier proposal centered on the promise of "effective mechanisms of a new type." In fact, no specific amendments were offered to replace the unanimity rule in CSCE decision-making; the Prague memorandum stated only that the proposed commission would "operate on the basis of consensus." As a more somber Havel admitted a year later, "everything appeared to us to be clear and simple."[14] In the end, the CSCE's November 1990 summit in Paris—the most important result of which was the signing of the long-awaited conventional forces in Europe (or CFE) arms reduction agreement—did approve the establishment of a Secretariat in Prague and a Crisis Prevention Center in Vienna, but made no changes in the unanimity principle that hindered effective enforcement.

PHASE TWO—1991

The second year of postcommunist transformation was marked by brightening prospects for cooperation at both the regional and pan-European levels. For Poland, the most important development was the end of its quasi-isolation, first with the formation in February of the Visegrád Triangle (comprising Czecho-slovakia, Hungary, and Poland), and later with Warsaw's belated inclusion in the Pentagonale (hence, Hexagonale). It was also a year in which the Triangle states made important strides toward inclusion in the broader European com-munity. By year's end, they had reached provisional association agreements with the EC and had been included in the newly formed North Atlantic Cooperation Council—although both achievements fell well short of their hopes. On the negative side, however, 1991 was a year of nasty surprises that demonstrated in manifold ways both the tenuous nature of past achievements and the enormous difficulty of constructing a new architecture for European cooperation and security.

The reasons for the sudden rapprochement in Central Europe were again related both to changing internal situations in each of the three countries and to a substantially altered international climate. At the domestic level, the political and economic asymmetries that had weighed so heavily on relations in 1990 were considerably reduced in at least two senses. First, although its economy was still in deep recession, Poland had weathered the first year of "shock therapy" far better than many had feared, with little labor unrest and no sign of retreat from its bold reform program. At the same time, Czecho-slovakia and Hungary—both at least a year behind Poland in embarking on radical economic transformations—were beginning to feel the pinch of declining production accompanied by rising inflation and unemployment. Moreover, all three economies were staggering under the impact of slumping trade with the Soviet Union. Second, from a political perspective, the anomaly of former communists still occupying high political office in Poland had been partially resolved with the December 1990 presidential elections, in which Solidarity leader Lech Wałęsa replaced General Jaruzelski, and the appointment of an entirely noncommunist government; with the scheduling of new fully free parliamentary elections for 1991, this asymmetry would be completely eliminated.

Changes in the external environment were even more significant in ways that both pushed and pulled the three states together. On the "pull" side, the signing in November 1990 of a treaty in which a united Germany formally recognized its postwar boundaries with Poland, narrowed the gap between Warsaw on the one hand, and Prague and Budapest on the other—and not only over policy toward Germany. It also allowed the Poles—finally—to open negotiations with Moscow over the withdrawal of Soviet troops and to take a stance parallel to that of its neighbors on the dissolution of the Warsaw Pact. On the "push" side, by the beginning of 1991 all three had a more realistic appreciation of the long time frame, as well as stringent conditions in terms of domestic legal and economic adjustments, that the EC was determined to impose for admission; they also seemed to recognize that none stood to be admitted on a preferential basis and that further pursuit of competitive tactics would only be counterproductive.[15]

But the most important "push" toward closer regional cooperation almost certainly came from a renewed sense of threat from the East, fueled by the conservative backlash in the Soviet Union that first appeared in the waning months of 1990 and culminated in the abortive coup against Gorbachev in August 1991, and which shattered the perception of a relatively benign international climate that had prevailed a year earlier. Like a wounded bear, the Soviet military and communist hardliners began showing their frustration over loss of empire and privilege by bringing mounting pressure on Gorbachev's reform leadership to reverse course. In quick succession between October 1990 and January 1991, the Soviet leader: (1) abandoned the radical economic reforms (the so-called Shatalin Plan) that he had tentatively approved only two months earlier; (2) broke off negotiations (again) with reformist Russian President Boris Yeltsin on issues of reform and a new union treaty; (3) allowed the military to violate the spirit (if not the letter) of the just concluded CFE treaty by moving close to 60,000 tanks and other pieces of heavy military equipment east of the Urals, out of the area covered by the treaty; (4) replaced several key reformist officials (including his prime minister, interior minister, and vice-president) with conservatives; and (5) ordered (or permitted?) a military crackdown against breakaway Lithuania. This series of setbacks to Soviet reform was punctuated in mid-December by the dramatic resignation, amid warnings of an impending coup, of Foreign Minister Shevardnadze, the man probably most responsible for the largely peaceful implosion of Moscow's external empire two years earlier.

For the Central Europeans, Shevardnadze's resignation, the blatant attempt to evade CFE arms limits, and the use of military force in nearby Lithuania were most worrisome. In addition, all three were finding Soviet negotiators increasingly truculent over a whole range of issues related to troop withdrawals, the termination of Warsaw Pact activities, and the new bilateral treaties under preparation. Warsaw, which had reached an agreement to open withdrawal talks only at the end of 1990, was told that a large contingent of Soviet troops would have to remain in Poland until the completion of the much larger scale withdrawal from the former East Germany in the mid-1990s, an operation that also posed serious problems for Czechoslovakia; Budapest and Prague, both of which had supposedly reached final withdrawal agreements already in 1990, suddenly found themselves in testy arguments over demands for reparations for alleged building "improvements" on former Soviet bases and rejections of counterclaims for environmental damages. Finally, all three had become alarmed over the repeated postponement in the second half of 1990 of the promised Warsaw Pact meeting to discuss the time frame for dissolution of the alliance, and even more so over Moscow's repeated insistence on the inclusion of the special security clause (mentioned earlier) in the new bilateral treaties. Indeed, this last point was formalized as a core tenet of Soviet policy in a January 1991 resolution of the CPSU Central Committee that reiterated Moscow's opposition to the inclusion of any Central or East European country in West European security structures and advocated the use of economic (especially energy) leverage to maintain a Soviet sphere of influence in the region.[16]

It was this heightened threat perception, perhaps even more than the shared aspiration for early EC membership, that provided the main driving force behind the limited degree of cohesion the Triangle countries were able to develop. Finding themselves in a "security vacuum," they suddenly saw the virtue of occupying that uncomfortable space collectively—on a single sofa, so to speak, rather than in separate armchairs. This new, more sober attitude was reflected in their quick response to the Lithuanian crisis in January. Within days of the outbreak of violence, the three foreign ministers met in Budapest and issued a joint appeal for the immediate dismantling of the Warsaw Pact's military structures, as well as a stepped-up timetable for ending its political activities and disbanding CMEA.[17] On the same day, 21 January, Czechoslovakia and Hungary signed a bilateral military cooperation agreement; similar Czechoslovak-Polish and Polish-Hungarian agreements were signed on 27 February and 20 March, respectively, marking the beginning of a pattern of intensified coordination on defense and security issues. The agreements, which were all for five-year terms with automatic renewal clauses, provided for consultations on a wide range of issues from the development of new military doctrines to such practical problems as maintaining aging Soviet equipment. Other common concerns included training, inculcation of democratic values, possible coproduction of military equipment, and the threat of mass migrations from an increasingly unstable Soviet Union.[18]

At a follow-up meeting on 2 August in Kraków, the three defense ministers signed an additional "defense coordination" agreement, providing for a "system of regular consultations at all levels of their military establishments." In all these contacts, Triangle officials were scrupulous in maintaining that they had no intention of creating a new military alliance and that their cooperation was "not aimed at any other country." But, as one analyst has noted, the reaction of the three to the attempted coup in Moscow just two and a half weeks later "indicated that there might have been a greater depth to their military cooperation than they were willing to make public." At a hastily called meeting on 20 August, the day after the coup was announced in Moscow, senior Triangle officials agreed on "concrete measures regarding cooperation in the areas of immigration, border protection, and the exchange of political information." It was later disclosed that at least Warsaw had issued standby mobilization orders, and that "constant liaison" had been maintained among the three capitals throughout the crisis. Another round of postcoup consultations led to a joint appeal, issued at the Kraków summit on 6 October (moved forward from 1992), for the "direct inclusion of Poland, Czechoslovakia, and Hungary in the activities of the [NATO] alliance"—a status short of full membership, but one that presumably would have implied the extension of a security umbrella over the Triangle.[19]

It was also the perceived security vacuum that prompted Poland's admission to the Pentagonale. Already in late 1990, Warsaw (with Hungary's support) had been invited to participate in two of the working groups and to appoint a permanent representative to the organization. Now in January—again only days after the violence in Vilnius—Italian Foreign Minister Gianni de Michelis told a meeting of parliamentarians from the Pentagonale countries that, in light of "the present international situation" (a reference mainly to the deteriorating situation in the USSR), "it is impermissible for us to leave Poland between two great powers when the formation of a new pan-European security system is still quite a long way off." Polish membership was subsequently approved in May and became official with the next, now Hexagonale, summit in August. By this time, the number of working groups had grown to at least nine—the two additions being scientific research and development and information—and others had had their mandates expanded.[20]

At the broader European level, 1991 saw some forward movement in NATO-Triangle relations on both sides. By the time of his visit to Brussels on 21 March, Havel's attitude toward both NATO and CSCE had come full circle from the year before in Bratislava. Rather than seeing the former gradually dissolving into a pan-European security system built around the latter, Havel now—albeit without giving up his commitment to a more effective CSCE in the longer term—recognized that "as the only working and time-tested defensive alliance" in Europe it was NATO that must be the "nucleus" or "cornerstone" of a pan-European system.[21] This brought Prague into closer alignment with views adopted earlier in both Budapest and Warsaw and set the stage for a more coordinated approach to the Western alliance (as seen in the October appeal). For its part, NATO already in mid-1990 had invited all Warsaw Pact members to establish diplomatic relations with the alliance; now in 1991, amid growing instability to the east, NATO showed a greater willingness to expand mutual visits and consultations specifically with the Central European military establishments—a move that undoubtedly encouraged and contributed to the development of security cooperation within the Triangle.[22] Nonetheless, the alliance remained reluctant—as it had been before the dissolution of the Warsaw Pact—to establish any formal ties with Central Europe. The stated reason was that to give preference to some former WTO members over others would be an affront to Moscow that might complicate the ongoing arms control process or upset the delicate balance of power within the Soviet Union; but a second reason was obviously that NATO members, already at odds over the question of the alliance's role in "out of area" conflicts, were unwilling to accept any real responsibility for the region's defense. In November, the North Atlantic Council rejected the October appeal in favor of establishing the broader and more amorphous North Atlantic Cooperation Council (NACC) as a forum for consultations among all NATO and former Warsaw Pact states.[23]

Ironically, trilateral cooperation on political and economic issues in 1991 yielded, if anything, more mixed results than in the security area. I say ironically because the 15 February summit, held in the provincial Hungarian town of Visegrád from which the Triangle took its name, was hailed at the time as a major breakthrough in Central European cooperation. Indeed, it was a breakthrough in the sense that by comparison with the 1990 Bratislava summit, which lacked both coordination and a clear focus and which produced no agreed program of action, Visegrád ended with an ambitious agenda focused around four goals, described by the Declaration as "essentially identical":

- restoration in full of each state's independence, democracy, and freedom;
- the dismantling of the economic and spiritual structures of the totalitarian system;
- the building of parliamentary democracy and a modern constitutional state, and respect for human rights and fundamental freedoms;
- total integration into the European political, economic, security, and legislative order.

These were to be achieved through multilayered collaboration at the European, regional, and subregional levels in at least eight priority areas. In addition to their "harmonization" of relations with European institutions, these included several initiatives to foster intraregional cooperation and understanding at the social, cultural, and local government levels; free movement of capital and labor, interenterprise cooperation, and joint development of strategies for attracting foreign investment; improvements in transportation infrastructure, telecommunications and energy networks; environmental cooperation; and the creation of "optimum conditions" for ensuring minority rights.[24]

The reality proved quite different. Instead of becoming an organization promoting intraregional cooperation as well as integration at the European level, the Visegrád process became fixated almost exclusively on the latter—in effect, it became a vehicle for coordinating Central Europe's "road to Europe" while development of closer ties within the region languished on the back burner. At the European level, the Triangle's efforts were rewarded in December by the signing of association agreements with the EC, but only after very difficult negotiations (and an initial veto by France). Moreover, although they offered the prospect of full membership within ten years, with gradual lowering of trade barriers and partial protection for Central European markets in the interim, the agreements were seen by the Triangle as something of a consolation prize; particularly distressing was the EC's refusal to open its markets wider to Central European exports in the "sensitive" areas of steel, textiles, and agricultural products. The other trilateral achievement of 1991, the only major one within the region (apart from cooperation on security matters discussed above), was the agreement reached in November to begin talks on establishing their own free-trade zone; but this, too, appears to have been motivated more by the loss of markets in the East and constraints on access in the West than by a genuine commitment to regional integration.[25]

The reasons for the lack of progress within the Triangle were several. Perhaps most important at this point was the shared fear that successful collaboration at the regional level would be used as an excuse to delay or even derail integration into the EC, and that the Central European states would be left in a second-class status. French President François Mitterrand's suggestion that the Triangle should form its own regional association, rather than seek early EC membership, did nothing to calm such fears. A second set of issues concerned the emergence (or reemergence) of ethnic and interstate conflicts: between Czechs and Slovaks over the latter's demands for greater autonomy and a slowdown in the pace of economic reforms in their still common state; between Hungarians and Slovaks both over the status of the Magyar minority in Slovakia and the controversial Gabčikova-Nagymaros dam on the Danube; and, at a somewhat lower level of contention, between Poles and Czechs over cross-border trade and the status of the Czechoslovak Federal Republic's (CSFR) small Polish minority. Still a third set of issues was related to the continued presence of structural asymmetries, such as divergent approaches to economic reform that complicated free-trade talks, and the perpetuation of mutually negative social stereotypes of one another.[26]

At the official level, the response to these concerns was a joint effort to deny any intention of "institutionalizing" the Triangle; instead, it was repeatedly described as "a political club." In fact, there were serious discrepancies on this point. The Poles, in particular, were eager for closer economic cooperation. As Wałęsa told an interviewer shortly after the French veto in September:

> Each of us very much desires to link up with Western Europe. A really serious question arises here: Should we strive to make the most rational use possible of the comparable potential of comparable economies for better cooperation among the CSFR, Poland, and Hungary, and then, on this basis, attempt a more effective approach toward an integrated Western Europe? On more than one occasion experience has taught us the extent to which we are mutually dependent on each other. I think we can simultaneously continue . . . transformations oriented toward where the West is now and at the same time, utilize our existing possibilities . . . This would be perhaps perceived in the way you mentioned in your question: Training hard in the second league and then breaking through to meet the very best competition.[27]

As sensible as this point of view might have seemed—and Wałęsa would raise the issue again in expanded form a year later—it was not one shared in Prague or Budapest where the insistence on maintaining the "informal" nature of trilateral cooperation remained firm. As the year came to a close, it was also among some Polish commentators that one could detect the greatest sense of disappointment over the continuing disparities among the three and their inability to overcome the element of competitiveness in their common "road to Europe."[28]

PHASE THREE—1992

It quickly became clear that this would be a year in which the meager and hard-won gains of 1991 were jeopardized by developments both within and beyond the Triangle. First, domestic preoccupations—a complicating factor in trilateral relations from the start—now became a major stumbling block as all three countries found themselves in the throes of domestic crises of quite different sorts. In Poland, the long-awaited fully free elections in October 1991 had yielded a badly fragmented parliament, which promptly and over the express objections of President Wałęsa chose a prime minister committed to a softening of the country's rigorous austerity program. Thus, the short-lived and raucous tenure of Jan Olszewski's minority government—it lasted barely six months—was marked by legislative gridlock and a budget crisis that came close to derailing economic reforms and undermining international confidence won over the previous two years. The fall of the Olszewski government in June—in a bizarre episode over lists of alleged informers for the old regime—was followed by a two-month hiatus in which the next prime minister-designate was unable to form a government at all. Only at the end of July did Poland again have a government that was both committed to the IMF-approved reforms and generally capable of mustering a parliamentary majority. The new prime minister, Hanna Suchocka, an able and pragmatic conciliator, also had the good sense to bring back a number of seasoned officials from the earlier Mazowiecki and Bielecki governments. Other important steps toward renewed stability were the signing in early November of the so-called Little Constitution, regulating several contentious aspects of presidential-parliamentary relations, and the adoption of a tough new plan for restructuring the deficit-ridden coal and steel sectors. By year's end, the Suchocka government had weathered several waves of labor unrest, the economy was experiencing the first postcommunist upturn in industrial production in the region, and Poland again looked like a credible partner.[29]

As Warsaw was emerging from its crisis, however, Prague and Budapest remained mired in theirs. In Czechoslovakia, the issue of full independence for Slovakia versus maintenance of a looser federation was effectively decided by the June 1992 elections which saw the victory in each republic of the party most determined to split the federation—the acerbic Václav Klaus's rigorously free-market Civil Democratic Party in Prague and the mercurial Vladimír Mečiar's populist-nationalist Movement for a Democratic Slovakia in Bratislava. Indeed, although the issue of Slovak sovereignty was initially forced by Mečiar and resisted by then President Havel, it was Klaus who in the wake of the elections seized the opportunity to unburden the Czech Republic from the obligation of supporting inefficient Slovak industries, which implied both an easing of economic reforms and possibly a slower pace of integration with the EC. In addition, he was eager to distance himself from rising tensions between Slovakia and Hungary. Thus, the second half of the year found Prague and Bratislava preoccupied primarily with negotiating the terms of their "velvet divorce."[30]

The situation in Hungary was again quite different and specific to the country's circumstances. As the economic recession deepened and popularity ratings of Prime Minister József Antall's ruling Hungarian Democratic Forum continued to drop (to a humiliating 8 percent by year's end), public attention became fixated increasingly on issues surrounding the national psyche—that is, not only on the status of Magyar minorities in neighboring countries, but also on the equally volatile issue of "Hungarianness" at home with all of its anti-Semitic and xenophobic overtones. Already on his election in 1990, Antall's claim to be the "spiritual leader" of all 15 million Hungarians rankled with Bratislava and Bucharest. Now, two years later, relations had become increasingly inflamed by encroachments on linguistic and cultural rights of the Hungarian communities in Slovakia and Romania on the one hand, and counterdemands (staunchly supported by Budapest) for recognition of their "collective rights" and autonomy on the other.[31]

The situation recently has been exacerbated by developments on all sides: in Slovakia, both by the imminent breakup of the CSFR, which the Hungarian minority sees as leaving it exposed to even greater discrimination, and by the Danube dam which the Slovaks rushed to finish in November, and which Budapest regards not only as a violation of its territorial integrity but also as a looming environmental disaster; in Romania, by the repeat electoral victory of the ex-communist National Salvation Front of President Ion Iliescu in September, and by a rising tide of anti-Hungarian Romanian nationalism in Transylvania. On the Hungarian side, Antall's repetition in August of his claim to speak for all Hungarians was less than helpful, as was the signing in November of a joint Russian-Hungarian statement on minority rights. The latter, in particular, caused a fire-storm of protest in Bucharest and Bratislava, where it was perceived as an attempt to enlist Moscow's support for Budapest's position that the principle of "collective" (in addition to individual) rights be accepted as the international standard for protecting ethnic minorities. Until it is satisfied on this point, the Antall government has refused to give explicit guarantees of existing borders, resulting in a standoff in bilateral talks with both Slovakia and Romania. Finally, as 1992 closed, the creeping spread of "ethnic cleansing" into the Voivodina region of Serbia threatened to draw Hungary into the Yugoslav imbroglio.[32]

Disarray at a number of levels beyond Central Europe also impacted relations within the Triangle. The Hexagonale, renamed the Central European Initiative at the beginning of 1992 to accommodate the growing number of post-Yugoslav states, disappeared from view for most of the year, resurfacing only in late November. Already in 1991, there had been no evidence of high-level political activity after the August summit at which Poland was formally admitted—something that could be explained by the fact that the designated chair for the year was Yugoslavia, then in the process of disintegration. The reasons for the organization's dormancy through most of 1992, when the chairmanship passed to Austria, were less obvious; nor was it clear if the technical working groups continued to function.[33] As for the CSCE, to which Havel had attached so much importance two years earlier, the combination of an expanding membership (from 34 to 52 states with the breakup of the USSR), its nascent and essentially toothless crisis-prevention mechanisms, and the absence of a back-up commitment from NATO, left the organization paralyzed in the face of the escalating Yugoslav crisis. The "Helsinki II" program, which was adopted in July 1992 and which gave a high profile to such activities as seminars on tolerance and nondiscrimination, offered little hope for the effective interventionist agenda that Havel had envisioned.

In addition, the breakup of the USSR following the failed August coup had a differential impact on the Triangle countries. While all shared both a sense of relief over the collapse of the Soviet center as well as heightened anxiety over potential mass migrations from former Soviet territories, only Poland found itself bordering on four post-Soviet states: Russia (in the form of the highly militarized Kaliningrad *oblast'*), Lithuania (with which relations were strained over the status of the Polish minority), plus Belarus and Ukraine (both of which also have sizable Polish minorities). By contrast, Hungary and Czechoslovakia bordered only on one, Ukraine, and the Czech Republic alone on none. This discrepancy not only left the Poles more exposed in the event of wide-scale disorder in the east, but also gave Warsaw a greater incentive to build a network of political, economic, and security ties with its new neighbors as one means of fostering stability and cooperation. In both official and unofficial commentaries, there was a growing awareness based on historical precedent that Poland had a choice between providing a bridge between East and West with strong links in both directions, or risk seeing that bridge built over them and, most likely, again at their expense.[34]

A final external factor affecting trilateral relations was the unexpected disarray in the European Community. The December 1991 Maastricht Treaty, which was supposed to inaugurate the final stage in the creation of a single market by the end of 1992, instead ushered in a year of wrangling over everything from monetary policy and interest rates to agricultural trade and larger subsidies for the EC's poorer southern tier. In part, differences over specific policy issues reflected the general economic slowdown in the community, aggravated by the continued drain on Germany, where the dislocations of reunification were fueling an upsurge of neo-Nazi violence against foreigners. In brief, the much anticipated "Europe 1992" was not going to happen on schedule and, as defined by Maastricht, might not happen at all; in the interim, complications in the process of "deepening" EC integration could only postpone a "widening" of the community. Under the circumstances, prospects that Brussels would step up the pace of trade liberalization with Central Europe (especially in the three key "sensitive" areas of steel, textiles, and agriculture) were slim. In addition, two other factors clouded EC-Triangle relations. First, the queue of aspiring members, mostly the small and prosperous EFTA countries, was already long; moreover, while they would add significantly to EC coffers, even their entry seemed likely to be delayed until the existing Twelve had an agreed set of rules among themselves. Second, the least developed of the Twelve (Spain, Portugal, and Greece) had already indicated that they would oppose EC expansion to the east—to countries that inevitably would impose a heavy long-term burden on the EC budget—until their own development needs had been more fully met.[35]

The combined effect of all these developments on the Triangle was to sharpen the differences among them on the question of deepening their own cooperation, even as they continued to coordinate relations with the EC, NATO, and CSCE. Again, the critical dividing line was over the question of whether to institutionalize relations within the Triangle—and, if so, how far. As before, Warsaw was the lone proponent of institutionalization, proposing both a deepening and a widening of cooperation as the best means of promoting greater stability and faster economic recovery in the region until full integration at the European level could be achieved. At the other extreme, and especially after leadership passed from Havel to Klaus following the June elections, Prague remained steadfastly opposed and, as the year closed, increasingly intent on "jumping the queue" to the EC at whatever cost. Thus, 1992 was a year of decidedly mixed results in trilateral relations, with important achievements in some areas offset by setbacks or lack of progress in others.

Not surprisingly, the most progress was made in cooperation on security matters, where the pattern established in 1991 of regular consultations among the three military establishments continued unabated. Even the security implications of the pending breakup of Czechoslovakia and the creation of an independent Slovak army, the main topic of a meeting of the defense ministers in September, were handled smoothly. In addition, at this and subsequent meetings in November and December, new areas for consultation were agreed on. These included cooperation in areas of common concern such as air defense, as well as several confidence-building measures among the three in the framework of the CFE treaty and the "Open Skies" agreement. (The latter were partly in response to rising tensions between Slovakia and Hungary and Mečiar's repeated charges in the second half of the year, denied by both Budapest and Prague, that Hungary was holding large-scale maneuvers near the Slovak border.)[36]

The most serious discrepancy in approaches to regional security, however, arose shortly before the September defense ministers' meeting, when Warsaw floated the idea of a "NATO-2," comprised not only of the Visegrád countries but also several post-Soviet states (the Baltics, Belarus, and Ukraine), as well as Romania and Bulgaria. The concept, which was quickly and summarily rejected by Prague and Budapest, reflected both Poland's greater exposure to potential instability in the East and a growing conviction that the CSCE and NACC were too "passive" and "symbolic" to be of practical significance. As presented by Wałęsa's top security advisor, Jerzy Milewski, the rationale was not to create a new alliance system as an alternative to NATO; indeed, he specifically stated that a guarantee of eventual NATO membership would be a precondition of any new regional alliance. Rather, Milewski foresaw NATO-2 as a transitional organization to defuse conflicts in the region and prepare the way for more rapid entry into NATO-1. On the latter point, he noted that

> we will be welcome in NATO to the extent that NATO reaps an advantage from our membership, and . . . [that] we show that our relations with the East are good. . . . our trump card will be well-established cooperation with the countries

of our region, as is the case within the "Visegrád Triangle." . . . What we want
is the formation of active mechanisms genuinely capable of preventing an open
conflict or dispelling tension.

Thus, members of this transitional alliance would be required to renounce
all territorial claims and contribute to the formation of a joint peacekeeping
force. In any event, Prague and Budapest rejected the idea of a military pact
either within the Triangle or on a broader regional basis.[37]

On the economic front, trilateral cooperation remained focused, as it had been
in 1991, on the joint effort to speed up the pace of access to Western markets
and set a timetable for full integration with the EC. That effort yielded limited
success with the March 1992 decision to put the gradual trade liberalization
features of the association agreements into effect, pending required ratification
of the agreements by all 12 EC members. Beyond that, however, repeated appeals
by Triangle countries for a clear commitment to early entry into the community
met with repeated rebuffs, first at the London meeting of the EC and Visegrád
leaders in late October and later at the EC's Edinburgh summit in December.[38]
In light of its own internal economic difficulties, the EC's reluctance to take on
the burden of a more rapid absorption of Central Europe was understandable.
On the other side, however, hard-pressed governments feared that the ten-year
time frame for integration foreseen in the association agreements was undermining their fragile stability and sapping popular support for closer ties with the
West. As Prime Minister Suchocka told a German interviewer in early November, "Most people here want to realize their chances in the EC in the next one or
two years."[39]

The one promising new dimension of EC-Triangle relations—especially
in light of the West's inaction in the face of the Bosnian tragedy—were signs
of the EC's willingness to play a mediating role in regional affairs. This
involved, in the first instance, an attempt to defuse the Danube dam dispute
(at this writing still under investigation by an international team of experts).[40]
In the second instance, the West was apparently successful in bringing
pressure to bear on the Czechs not to pull out of negotiations on the trilateral
(now quadrilateral) "free- trade" zone, already almost a year behind schedule. The agreement, finally signed in late December and scheduled to come
into effect in March 1993, was hailed at the official level as a major
breakthrough that would promote intraregional trade and attract more foreign
investment; unofficially, however, it was widely recognized that the phased
reduction of tariffs (mostly on industrial goods) would have little impact in
the presence of nontariff barriers left untouched by the agreement and
provisions for the continued protection of agricultural markets.[41]

Frustration over the slow pace of trade liberalization, both with the EC and within the Triangle, led the Poles to float a second trial balloon. A year after Wałęsa had first spoken of the potential advantages of "training hard in the second league" before taking on the main competition, a group of his closest advisors proposed a "Central European Trade Initiative"—in effect, a kind of "EC-2" as the economic counterpart of "NATO-2." Like the latter, EC-2 (which would also embrace countries beyond the Triangle) was not intended as a long-term alternative to full EC membership but as a transitional arrangement "to fill the vacuum left by the collapse of CMEA . . . that will exist until Poland (and similar countries) are integrated with the [EC]."[42] The potential benefits of such an arrangement for Poland were obvious; not only were Polish exports the most adversely affected by the remaining nontariff barriers within the Triangle, but a restoration of trade ties with neighboring post-Soviet states was increasingly seen as vital to the country's continued economic recovery. However, the idea fell on deaf ears, especially in Prague, where, with the approaching separation of the Czech and Slovak republics, Klaus was making it increasingly clear that cooperation even within the Visegrád group would henceforth be "no more important" to the Czechs than bilateral relations with other countries.[43]

One of the few positive developments as 1992 came to a close was the surprise reappearance of the "Central European Initiative" (CEI) with a meeting at the foreign ministers level on 20-21 November in the Austrian city of Graz (with the former Yugoslavia now being represented by Slovenia, Croatia, and Bosnia-Herzegovina). According to a Polish source, its working groups had continued to function during the year-long hiatus in high-level meetings and had elaborated more than 100 projects. A major constraint on CEI activities had been a lack of financial resources, but by the time of the Graz meeting the group had apparently reached an understanding with the European Bank for Reconstruction and Development (EBRD) for assistance with at least seven infrastructure projects. Just what prompted member countries to call attention to the CEI at this point is not clear. But on the basis of the limited information available, there were at least three agendas at work—one overt and two hidden or less obvious. One purpose clearly shared by all was to coordinate their responses to the Bosnian crisis and the danger of a spillover of "ethnic cleansing" into Hungarian enclaves in the Voivodina; in fact, exactly a month after the Graz meeting, four of the foreign ministers traveled to New York to appeal directly for United Nations intervention. A second, less explicit Polish agenda may have been to gain acceptance in a different forum for their vision of broader and more institutionalized regional cooperation embodied in the earlier EC-2/NATO-2 proposals. Hence, Foreign Minister Krzysztof Skubiszewski's emphasis on the need for the CEI to be "open for cooperation with all interested states"; hence, also, the significance of the presence, for the first time, of observers from Bulgaria and Romania as well as Ukraine and Belarus. Still a third agenda, this one specifically Hungarian (and in all probability not one articulated at Graz), appears to have been Budapest's intention to use a reenergized CEI, of which it would be the chair in 1993, as a forum for bringing pressure to bear on Slovakia on both the Danube and minority issues. In an interview shortly after the Graz meeting, the Hungarian foreign ministry official designated as coordinator of CEI activities for 1993 singled out "cooperation along the Danube" as Budapest's priority; other intriguing points in the interview were a less than subtle hint that Hungary might try to use the breakup of Czechoslovakia as leverage by forcing the successor states to apply for readmission, his emphasis on the increasing salience of political issues, and his reference to the "special problem" of national minorities.[44] Only time will tell whether the CEI can withstand the strains of conflicting interests among its members.

A BALANCE SHEET—JANUARY 1993

So far this century in this part of Europe, political stability and national autonomy have proven fragile and short lived in the absence of a broader framework within which to both mediate contentious territorial, ethnic, and economic issues left fallen by empires and focus energies on common needs and interests. Two years after the Visegrád summit, which was supposed to mark the beginning of their coordinated road to Europe, the discordant notes are again hard to ignore. To return to Gáti's analogy, cooperation within what is now the Quadrangle may be "alive" but it is definitely "not well." The Czech Republic will likely remain in the group in the near term, if only nominally and under duress; the Czechs may also find their apparent economic edge over the others eroded as painful realities of industrial restructuring take hold. Slovakia, the weakest of the four and suddenly more on its own than it may have anticipated, is groping to define both its domestic and foreign policies.[45] Hungary, increasingly fearful that the seemingly intractable tensions over its diaspora will hinder integration with Europe, now laments the collapse of cooperation at the narrower regional level.[46] And Poland, increasingly constrained by the limited nature of the Visegrád process, is actively pursuing its own agenda of building a network of economic and security ties with its new neighbors to the east while simultaneously adapting its economic and legal structures to the requirements of eventual EC integration.[47]

None of this provides much basis for optimism over the future of Central European cooperation. But neither is it cause to jump to fatalistic conclusions about the political immaturity of these countries or their incapacity to put their collective house in order with a modicum of encouragement and support. All things considered, the Visegrád countries have weathered the first three years of their postcommunist transitions no worse—and perhaps somewhat better than expected. And where they have faltered—as with the reemergence of old fault lines obscured by four decades of Cold War—they have plenty of company among their more prosperous Western neighbors. What all of this does suggest, however, is that Central Europe's prospects revolve around two questions: first, the extent of Western support that can be anticipated in the foreseeable future; and, second, in the absence of that support, the willingness and capacity of the Central European countries to pursue alternative strategies.

On the first count, the outlook is not good. The most the Central Europeans can hope for is that the EC and NATO will continue to engage them as the most deserving of the postcommunist states, and that they will not be pushed to the back burner in the West's preoccupation with the deepening crisis in the former Soviet republics. Prospects for early integration into the EC are nonexistent; moreover, in light of recent gyrations in EC currency rates, the Visegrád countries might ponder whether they want their economies held hostage to Germany's egocentric focus on the cost of reunification. Beyond that, hopes for accelerated trade liberalization are slim, especially in the areas that might be of immediate benefit to Central Europe's exports, but where Western Europe is also hurting.[48]

In light of these barriers, the Quadrangle countries have two viable options. First, they can drop their reluctance to "deepening" and institutionalizing cooperation within the Central and East European region; and, second, they can seek membership in the European Free Trade Association (EFTA) as a "constructive halfway house" en route to eventual EC membership. The two strategies could be pursued simultaneously and would be mutually supportive; indeed, it could be argued that such combined strategy would facilitate admission to the EC. A deepening of regional cooperation would have to begin with a commitment to reduce the remaining nontariff barriers to trade within the Visegrád "free-trade" zone and to expand the zone to other former CMEA states (much as Warsaw's "EC-2" proposal envisaged). Not only would this stimulate trade within the region, but equally important, would provide a more attractive environment for foreign investment.[49] The EFTA option, proposed in a new study by the Centre for Economic Policy Research in London, could have several advantages. It "would counter the economic and political marginalization implicit" in the bilateral agreements the Visegrád Four now have with the EC; it would also help enterprises in Central Europe "develop business ties in a market with enormous growth potential." In addition, an enlarged EFTA would find its bargaining powers vis-à-vis the EC enhanced.[50]

NOTES

1. Charles Gáti, "The Soviet Empire: Alive But Not Well," *Problems of Communism* 34, no. 2 (March-April 1985): 73-86.

2. For an analysis of these earlier false starts, see Sarah Meiklejohn Terry, *Poland's Place in Europe: General Sikorski and the Origin of the Oder-Neisse Line, 1939-1943* (Princeton, N.J.: Princeton University Press (1983).

3. Joanna Solska, "Grupa Wyszehradzka," *Polityka* (1 January 1993), p. 3.

4. Ibid.

5. Grzegorz Górnicki, "Is Poland Really in Central Europe?" *East European Reporter* 4, no. 2 (Spring/Summer 1990): 57.

6. Ibid., p. 58. Górnicki cited a Pentagon source, which obviously cannot be confirmed; but it is a position reminiscent of the Soviet attitude toward regional organizations during World War II (see Terry, *Poland's Place in Europe,* especially pp. 315-34), and one reflected in a resolution adopted by the CPSU Central Committee in January 1991 (see Note 16 below).

7. Górnicki, "Is Poland Really in Central Europe?"

8. See, for example, Jan Obrman, "Czechoslovakia Overcomes Its Initial Reluctance," *RFE/RL Research Report* 1, no. 23 (5 June 1992): 20.

9. For background on the Adria-Alpine Group, see Johnathan Sunley, "Alpe-Adria," *East European Reporter* 4, no. 2 (Spring/Summer 1990): 65-66.

10. For the text of Havel's speech at Bratislava, see ibid., pp. 59-61.

11. Ibid.

12. Concerning expansion of the Pentagonale and its new agenda, see *East European Reporter* 4, no. 3 (Autumn/Winter 1990): 54-56. For a candid expression of the feeling of rejection in Warsaw, see the interview with Polish journalist Grzegorz Musiał, "An End to Solidarity?" in ibid., pp. 59-60. Concerning possible reasons behind Poland's exclusion and the unlikely prospects for a Baltic equivalent to Pentagonale, see Robert Sołtyk, "Penta, hexa czy wcale?" *Gazeta wyborcza,* 11 July 1991.

13. The text of the memorandum is translated in the same issue of *East European Reporter* as Havel's speech (see Note 10 above), pp. 62-63.

14. See Havel's speech at NATO Headquarters, 21 March 1991, in *East European Reporter* 4, no. 4 (Spring/Summer 1991): 65. Concerning his continuing commitment to the "futurological" promise of CSCE, see the abridged text of his opening address to the Conference on European Confederation, held in Prague, 12-16 June 1991, in *East European Reporter* 5, no. 1 (January/ February 1992): 42-46.

15. On this more realistic approach to EC integration, see, for example, Grzegorz Górnicki, "Visegrád: The Three-Cornered Umbrella," *East European Reporter* 4, no. 4 (Spring/Summer 1991): 68-69.

16. See especially Rudolf L. Tökés, "From Visegrád to Kraków," *Problems of Communism* 40, no.6 (November-December 1991): 104-107. The resolution of the CPSU CC, "On the Development of Conditions in Eastern Europe and Our Policy in this Region," dated 22 January 1991, was published in *Izvestiia TsK KPSS*, no. 3 (1991), pp. 12-17.

17. Both Foreign Minister Skubiszewski (in his January 1991 speech at the Royal Institute of International Relations) and Havel (at NATO in March) used the term "security vacuum"; see their respective speeches in *East European Reporter* 4, no. 4 (Spring/Summer 1991): 61-68. Concerning the 21 January foreign ministers meeting, see Jan B. de Weydenthal, "The Visegrád Summit," *Report on Eastern Europe* 2, no. 9 (1 March 1991): 29.

18. See Douglas L. Clarke, "Central Europe: Military Cooperation in the Triangle," *RFE/RL Research Report* 1, no. 2 (10 January 1992): 42-45.

19. Ibid.; concerning the October summit, see Jan B. de Weydenthal, "The Cracow Summit," *Report on Eastern Europe* 2, no. 33 (25 October 1991): 27-29; also "The Triangle," *East European Reporter* 5, no. 1 (January-February 1992): 44.

20. See, for example, Józef Wiejacz, "Grupa Pentagonale i miejsce Polski," *Polska w Europie*, no. 5 (June 1991): 79-88. Sołtyk, in "Penta, hexa, czy wcale?," lists 12 working groups—the new ones being statistics, tourism (now apparently separated from culture), and cooperation in disaster assistance; he also notes that Poland had proposed creation of a thirteenth working group for agriculture and food processing.

21. For the text of Havel's speech, see *East European Reporter* 4, no. 4 (Spring/Summer 1991): 65-68. Concerning his more realistic appraisal of the near-term potential of the CSCE, see the abridged text of his opening address to the Conference on European Confederation held in Prague, 12-16 June 1991, in *East European Reporter* 5, no. 1 (January-February 1992): 42-46.

22. Tökés, "From Visegrád to Kraków," pp. 108-109. The most important demonstration of Western concern over Central European security was NATO Secretary General Manfred Woerner's appearance at a Prague conference on the "Future of

European Security" on 25 April, at which he expressed the need for "a new modern and comprehensive concept of security."

23. Concerning the formation and implications of the NACC, see Christopher Jones, "The Security Policies of the Former Warsaw Pact States" in *Postcommunist Eastern Europe: Crisis and Reform,* Andrew Michta and Ilya Prizel, eds. (New York: St. Martin's Press, 1992), pp. 112 and 125-26; the author also covers the final dissolution of the Warsaw Pact in mid-1991. For the relevant NATO statements concerning relations with former Warsaw Pact states and the founding of the NACC, see *NATO: Communiqués 1991* (Brussels: NATO Office of Information and Press, 1992), pp. 26-39.

24. For commentaries on the summit as well as translations of the Visegrád Declaration, see de Weydenthal, "The Visegrád Summit"; and *East European Reporter* 4, no. 4 (Spring/Summer 1991): 68-70.

25. For details of the Association Agreement signed between Poland and the EC on 16 December 1991, see Mieczysław Nogaj, "New Principles of Trade with EC Countries and Changes in Customs Regulations in Poland," *Polish Foreign Trade,* nos. 3-4 (March/April 1992); similar agreements with the CSFR and Hungary were signed the same day. For background on the free-trade talks within the Triangle, see Károly Okolicsányi, "The Visegrád Triangle's Free-Trade Zone," *RFE/RL Research Report* 2, no. 3 (15 January 1993): 19-22.

26. Concerning the various structural, economic, and psychological obstacles to closer cooperation among the Triangle countries, see, for example, Rafał Wiśniewski, "Po Wyszehradze—Środkowoeuropejskie perspektywy," *Polska w Europie* no. 5 (June 1991): 66-78; and Stanisław Pużyna, "Trójkąt środkowoeuropejski—wyzwanie i szansa," *Polska w Europie,* no. 6 (September 1991): 82-88. See also the comments by Jerzy Marek Nowakowski, et al., in the summary report of a conference held at the Center for International Studies of the Senate in October 1991, *Polska w Europie,* no. 7 (January 1992), 53-58. Nowakowski mentions still another disincentive to closer trilateral relations, namely "friendly" advice from Moscow, at least to the time of the August coup attempt, not to "spoil" relations with the East. For an overview of the first year of Triangle cooperation from the perspectives of all three countries, see the special section on "The Central European Triangle," *RFE/RL Research Report* 1, no. 23 (5 June 1992): 15-32.

27. As quoted in Tökés, "From Visegrád to Kraków," pp. 110-11.

28. See the Polish articles cited in Note 26 above, especially the summary of the October conference.

29. For running analyses of the roller-coaster course of Polish politics in 1992, see the following articles in *RFE/RL Research Report*: Louisa Vinton, "Poland: Government Crisis Ends," 1, no. 3 (17 January 1992): 14-21; Anna Sabbat-Świdlicka, "Poland: Weak Government, Fractious Sejm, Isolated President" in 1,

no. 15 (10 April 1992): 1-7; Louisa Vinton, "Poland's Government Crisis," in 1, no. 30 (24 July 1992): 15-25; Louisa Vinton, "Poland's 'Little Constitution,'" in 1, no. 35 (4 September 1992): 19-26; and Anna Sabbat-Świdlicka, "Poland: A Year of Three Governments," in 2, no. 1 (1 January 1993): 102-107.

30. On the prelude to the breakup of Czechoslovakia, see, for example, Jan Obrman, "Czechoslovakia: Stage Set for Disintegration?" *RFE/RL Research Report* 1, no. 28 (10 July 1992): 26-31; and Jiří Pehe, "Czechoslovakia: Toward Dissolution," *RFE/RL Research Report* 2, no. 1 (1 January 1993): 84-88. See also Klaus's adamant statement, during a joint news conference with Mečiar on their return from the 28 October EC-Visegrád summit in London, that the Danube dam dispute "is not a Czech affair"; in *Foreign Broadcast Information Service: Eastern Europe Daily Report* [hereafter FBIS-EEU], no. 211 (30 October 1992), p. 5.

31. For an overview of political developments in Hungary during 1992, see Judith Pataki, "Hungarians Dissatisfied with Political Changes," *RFE/RL Research Report* 1, no. 44 (6 November 1992): 66-70. Concerning the rise of right-wing nationalism, see Edith Oltay, "A Profile of István Csurka," *RFE/RL Research Report* 1, no. 40 (9 October 1992): 26-29; also Ernest Beck, "Hungary Fears Right-Wing Violence," *The Wall Street Journal,* 29 December 1992. Concerning the status of the Hungarian minorities in Slovakia and Romania, see Alfred A. Reisch, "Mečiar and Slovakia's Hungarian Minority," *RFE/RL Research Report* 1, no. 43 (30 October 1992): 13-20; and Michael Shafir, "Romania: Toward the Rule of Law," *RFE/RL Research Report* 1, no. 27 (3 July 1992): 34-40.

32. On József Antall's claim to speak on behalf of all Hungarians, see report of the joint news conference with Klaus, 17 August 1992, in FBIS-EEU-92-160 (18 August 1992), pp. 12-14. For conflicting views of the dam issue, see Mečiar's charge during his 29 October news conference (Note 30 above) that tensions had been "artificially created" by the Hungarians as an excuse for demanding changes in the Trianon borders; for Budapest's response, see the interview with Foreign Minister Géza Jeszenszky in FBIS-EEU-92-226 (23 November 1992), p. 23. The text of the 11 November Russian-Hungarian statement on minority rights is in FBIS-EEU-92-230 (30 November 1992), pp. 23-24. For Romanian President Ion Iliescu's response, see the report of his 26 November news conference, in FBIS-EEU-92-229 (27 November 1992), p. 15. For other signs of rising ethnic tensions in Transylvania, see several commentaries and official Romanian statements in FBIS-EEU-92-213 (3 November 1992), pp. 20-23.

33. See, for example, Katarzyna Kołodziejczyk, "Inicjatywa środkowoeuropejska," *Rzeczpospolita,* 21-22 November 1992, p. 7. It is worth noting that, in his wide-ranging review of Poland's foreign policy priorities to the Sejm in June 1992, Foreign Minister Skubiszewski made no mention of the Central European

Initiative; see his "Droga do Europy 1992," *Polska w Europie,* no. 9 (July-September 1992): 5-12.

34. See, for example, excerpts from former Prime Minister Jan Krzysztof Bielecki's talk delivered at the Institute of Economic Affairs in Brussels (9 March 1992), and Jerzy Marek Nowakowski, "Polska i Europa środkowa," both in *Polska w Europie,* no. 8 (April 1992): 5-8 and 20-26, respectively; also Skubiszewski's June 1992 report to the Sejm (see Note 33 above) and Edward Wende, "W europejskiej tradycji," *Polska w Europie,* no. 9 (July-September 1992): 13-15.

35. Concerning the burden that the East-Central European countries would impose on the EC, see *Is Bigger Better? The Economics of EC Enlargement* (an annual report of the Centre for Economic Policy Research), London, 1992; for a summary of the implications for Central and Eastern Europe, see Eugeniusz Możejko, "Między pogłębieniem a poszerzeniem," *Życie gospodarcze,* 17 January 1993, p. 20. According to CEPR estimates, the early integration of the Visegrád states would cost the wealthier EC states 8 billion ECUs (approx. $10 billion) annually, Bulgaria and Romania would add another 5 billion ECUs.

36. Concerning cooperation on security matters during 1992, see, for example, FBIS-EEU-92-188 (28 September 1992), pp. 6-8; Alfred A. Reisch, "No Plans for a Military Pact," *RFE/RL Research Report* 1, no 40 (9 October 1992): 55; *Rzeczpospolita,* 21-22 November 1992, p. 7; and FBIS-EEU-92-237 (9 December 1992), p. 1.

37. See the interviews with Milewski in *Rzeczpospolita,* 8 September 1992 (in FBIS-EEU-92-177 [11 September 1992], pp. 14-16), and 28 October 1992 (reported in *RFE/RL Research Report* 1, no. 44 [6 November 1992]: 61). For the Czechoslovak and Hungarian positions, see the first two items in Note 32 above. Despite Milewski's references to the NACC and CSCE as "passive" and "symbolic," the Poles remained committed to taking maximum advantage of the opportunities offered by the former and to strengthening the crisis-prevention potential of the latter. See, for example, Skubiszewski, "Droga do Europy"; the report of the foreign minister's statement at the December 1992 CSCE meeting in Stockholm, in FBIS-EEU-92-246 (22 December 1992), p. 1; and an interview with the deputy defense minister on Poland's defense goals and relations with the NACC, in FBIS-EEU-92-192 (2 October 1992), p. 22.

38. The most important initiative was the submission of a joint memorandum to the EC, in anticipation of the London and Edinburgh meetings, in which the Visegrád countries appealed for further trade concessions (especially in the "sensitive" sectors), an agreed timetable for beginning negotiations on full EC membership, expanded political dialogue at all levels, and more financial aid especially for small- and medium-size enterprises; as reported by *Rzeczpospolita,* 12-13 September 1992, in FBIS-EEU-92-183 (21 September 1992), pp. 23-24; also the follow-up report from the Polish Press Agency (PAP), in FBIS-EEU-92-206 (23 October 1992), p. 3.

For a brief comment on the Edinburgh summit's failure to act on the Visegrád appeal, see Marek Ostrowski, "Po szczycie w Edynburgu," *Polityka*, no. 51 (19 December 1992): 2; the writer concludes that the whole edifice of European cooperation—not only Visegrád-EC relations, but also Maastricht—is standing "on weak legs."

39. Markus Ziener, "Warsaw Calls for More Western Commitment," *Handelsblatt* (Düsseldorf), 5 November 1992, p. 14; in FBIS-EEU-92-220 (13 November 1992), p. 12.

40. See, for example, Nicholas Denton and Anthony Robinson, "Danube dam threatens to open floodgates of hostility," *The Financial Times,* 29 October 1992; and Károly Okolicsányi, "Slovak-Hungarian Tension: Bratislava Diverts the Danube," *RFE/RL Research Report* 1, no. 49 (11 December 1992): 49-54.

41. For details of the agreement as summarized in *Gazeta wyborcza* (23 December 1992), see FBIS-EEU-92-250 (29 December 1992), p. 32; also Okolicsányi, "The Visegrád Triangle's Free-Trade Zone." Neither source mentions the issue of remaining nontariff barriers, although Okolicsányi does note Western pressure on Klaus not to bolt the Visegrád group; on this point see also Klaus's final remark at the 29 October news conference (Note 30 above) to the effect that "we do not see any major reason why the EC should force us to create a free-trade zone. . . ." For press commentaries that took a less favorable view of the agreement than official statements, see Solska, "Grupa Wyszehradzka" (Note 3 above); Leszek Mazań, "Trójkąt biedy," *Polityka*, no 47 (21 November 1992): 19; and Zsuzsa Regös, "Forced Integration—What Is in the Visegrád Covenant?" *Népszabadság,* 9 December 1992, in FBIS-EEU-92-240 (14 December 1992), pp. 27-28.

42. Arkadiusz Milewski, "Nostalgia za CEMA?" *Nowy świat,* 15 September 1992; in FBIS-EEU-92-183 (21 September 1992), pp. 24-25.

43. See Klaus's statement at Vienna on 15 December 1992, in FBIS-EEU-92-244 (18 December 1992), p. 9. This was the first time he had stated this position so bluntly, but hardly the first time he had presented the Czech Republic as more qualified for rapid integration into the EC than the other Visegrád countries; see also FBIS-EEU-92-215 (5 November 1992), pp. 10-11. On the issue of nontariff barriers, the most serious tensions were between Poland and the CSFR over the latter's tight border controls to prevent Poles from buying up subsidized Czech goods following the adoption of free-market reforms by Warsaw. As former Foreign Minister Jiří Dienstbier recently commented, he went along with this policy against his will: "It was terrible . . . The borders went down with the West and up in the East"; quoted in William Echikson, "Falling from grace in Eastern Europe," *The Boston Sunday Globe,* 31 January 1993, p. 66.

44. For general coverage of the Graz meeting and Skubiszewski's remarks, see Kołodziejczyk, "Inicjatywa środkowoeuropejska"; for the interview with the Hungarian official, András Szabó, see FBIS-EEU-92-239 (11 December 1992),

pp. 16-17. Szabó's approach to broadening CEI cooperation was also more cautious than Skubiszewski's; referring specifically to the four observer states, he noted, "this does not mean the expansion" of the CEI, only that they could participate in some working groups. The subsequent appeal to the United Nations is reported in FBIS-EEU-92-246 (22 December 1992), p. 1.

45. See, for example, Jan Obrman, ed., "Roundtable: Relations with the Czech Republic and Hungary," and his, "Uncertain Prospects for Independent Slovakia," *RFE/RL Research Report* 1, no. 49 (11 December 1992): 33-42 and 43-48.

46. A meeting of Hungarian and German parliamentarians in early November yielded a warning to this effect; see FBIS-EEU-92-217 (9 November 1992), pp. 22-23.

47. See, for example, EM, "Stowarzyszenie z EWG," *Życie gospodarcze, 20-27 December 1992, p. 30.*

48. In the most obvious area, the steel industry, see Andrew Hill, "EC maps a path for the steel industry's contraction," *Financial Times,* 15 February 1993; and Anthony Robinson, "Europe's other steel industry reels," *Financial Times,* 19 February 1993.

49. For an analogy to the benefits of liberalizing trade within Latin America, see James Brooke, "Latin America's Regional Trade Boon," *The New York Times,* 15 February 1993.

50. See Anthony Robinson, "Eastern European countries should join EFTA before EC," *Financial Times,* 9 November 1992.

12

National Security Relations

*Arthur R. Rachwald**

In 1989, Poland began to examine its national security objectives in light of unfolding developments in Europe. Newly elaborated priorities were confined to five distinctive goals that define Poland's *raison d'état* in the period of transformation from socialism to democracy and a free-market economy, and the departure from Cold War animosities. These objectives of Polish policy are the following:[1]

- To incorporate the country in the comprehensive network of political, military, and economic relations among the states of Western Europe, including active involvement with the CSCE process and NATO security system
- To develop, on the basis of the recent Polish-German treaty, a community of interests, especially the management of movement across borders and coordinating policies toward Russia and other successor states of the former USSR
- To normalize bilateral relations with Russia on principles of equality and respect, with special emphasis on the rapid and complete withdrawal of Russian troops from Polish territory
- To pursue regional, political, and economic integration with countries east and south of Poland

* The writer wishes to thank Professor Condoleezza Rice of Stanford University for her comments on a draft of this chapter.

- To establish special links with the United States to further American involvement in the political and military affairs of Europe in general and Poland in particular, including U.S. investment in the Polish economy

EUROPE

The policy to integrate with the states and international organizations of Western Europe is driven by political and economic calculations as well as the prevailing attitude that Poland's historically rightful place is among the other members of Western civilization. The identification with Western cultural and political tradition has symbolic meaning for the Polish nation, which prides itself on being an outpost of Catholicism against Eastern Orthodoxy and autocracy. Its post-World War II status as a Soviet satellite insulted cultural lineage and attempted to reverse the course of an entire millennium of Polish history.

Painful experience has taught the Poles about the hazards of relying exclusively on another state for national security needs. Whether it was France, Britain, or the USSR, Polish basic security guarantees were neglected or exploited, and the country became an easy target of conquest. Neither satellite status nor a bilateral security arrangement had worked well. Located between two much larger neighbors, the Poles had to search for distant allies who maintained only remote interest in Polish affairs.

The outcome of the Cold War was fortunate. Not only did the Soviet Union disintegrate, but the German Reich was not resurrected. The Poles are not threatened by military aggression, and their territory is not claimed by any neighbor. The end of the Cold War terminated political and military pressure from both geographic sides. The most significant development, however, was that Poland found itself on the threshold of a dynamic supernational structure which would redefine traditional international politics in Europe. The country is not pressured to side with France or Russia to support its security against Germany. Such former configurations had always reduced the international status of Poland to that of a French or Russian dependent, and aroused anti-Polish attitudes in Germany, and both allies proved to be of dubious quality. France remained too weak as protector, while Russia habitually conspired with Germany against Poland and extracted a heavy price for its patronage. Today, the Poles have the prospect of joining a large international community in partnership with all major European nations, which terminates the need for sectarian coalitions to achieve bilateral solutions.

Membership in a pan-European security system has become the paramount international priority for Poland since its emancipation from the Soviet bloc. The country is now outside NATO and the European Community. The most immediate by-product of the communist demise was the political, economic, and military isolation of Poland. Under such circumstances, the Euro-Atlantic security framework, prosperity of the European Community, and stability of Western democratic institutions became natural attractions for the emerging Third Polish Republic. This pro-Western orientation now enjoys strong popular support in Poland. However, the Polish-German border is now a line of continental division between the affluent, secure West and the poor, weakened East. The Odra-Nysa (or Oder-Neisse) borderline has become the European Community's external boundary. Full integration of Europe is yet to come, so the main task facing Polish statesmen is how to gain access to the Western institutional framework, that is, how to convince NATO states that their security is inseparably tied to the security of Poland and other East-Central European countries.

The practical question related to membership in Western security and economic organizations is that of finding a credible sponsor for the Polish cause. Inspired by its historical fascination with France, Warsaw's initial choice was to approach Paris and to solicit benevolent understanding in Washington. However, Poland soon rediscovered that the French way to Europe was not a viable option. To begin with, France's "empty chair" policy relegates the country to only partial NATO membership and, thus, Poland's close association with France would not expedite its cause. Moreover, France is known to be a maverick within the Western alliance, famous for its own regional, even global, aspirations and its eccentric, if not clever, political style. Next, the Poles quickly learned that they had not been one of the top French priorities in Europe, despite public attention to democratization in Poland. Finally, the international balance in Europe has changed substantially over the four years since the conclusion of the Roundtable Agreement in April 1989. A unified Germany has overshadowed France as the central state in Europe and the immediate neighbor of Poland. In consequence, the Polish road to Europe is through the new Germany. Any attempt to circumvent its Western neighbor would only complicate and delay implementation of Polish objectives. At the same time, German preference for "widening," as opposed to France's inclination toward "deepening," the European Community is complementary to Polish objectives.

The Poles have also determined that the decision regarding their membership in Western organizations does not depend on the favoritism of a single state, but rather on the expectation that NATO would adopt a view favoring the formation of a single, uniform security zone for Western and East-Central Europe. Poland decided that it should avoid excessive association and dependence on one or another member of NATO and the EC. As a result, Warsaw adopted a two-pronged, French-German approach.

With the French, the Poles focus on matters of military integration. Although not prepared to give up on joining NATO, Poland is fully aware of the difficulties associated with this objective. The North Atlantic Treaty Organization is a closed military coalition, with an Atlantic orientation and a legacy of defense against the East. Incorporation of a former Soviet-bloc state does not appear to be natural, at least not at this time, when the future purpose and scope of NATO is still under discussion. After all, NATO members have little to gain from offering membership to a country that has a long way to go before its political and economic stability can be taken for granted.

Another risk associated with membership in NATO involves the future profile of Polish foreign policy, specifically its attitude toward the smaller states of East-Central Europe and the danger of nationalist strife among the former republics of the USSR. Consequently, premature membership in NATO would result in unilateral Polish advantages without corresponding gains on the NATO side. At this point in time, the West would assume a considerable obligation for Poland's security without any tangible benefits for the security of its own allies. In fact, such a step could diminish Western security, possibly inciting Ukraine, Russia, and other countries east of Poland. The Western fear of becoming involved in protracted local conflicts similar to the civil war in former Yugoslavia lies at the root of NATO's current reluctance to accept new obligations. In order to give partial recognition to the security concerns of East-Central European states, NATO formed in December 1991 a special organization, the North Atlantic Cooperation Council (NACC), to manage mutual relations. Hence, the NATO-2 concept must await its time.

This situation forced Polish authorities to "stop kicking the closed door," and to look for a gradual approach to full integration with the security system of the West. The guiding principle of this policy is that Poland first must become a stabilizing factor in East-Central Europe, perhaps the most important state in the region. It means that the major causes of Polish internal instability, including the low combat efficiency of its armed forces, must be overcome to make the country capable of dealing with its own security matters. As the foreign minister pointed out:[2]

> The objective of Polish foreign policy is integration with West European structures and institutions. Our strategic objective in the security sphere is to join

NATO. This long-term goal will not be easy to attain. Therefore, it requires small, gradual steps, one step at a time, whereby each step must be successful.

This gradual alignment of Poland with Western political and defense standards is to be facilitated by cooperation and eventual full membership in the West European Union (WEU), which is seen in Poland as the military component of a future political union. It is expected that, following ratification of the Maastricht Treaty, the WEU will gain importance, especially because France attaches great hopes to this organization. Since the WEU is exclusively European in scope, it is not threatened by the withdrawal of American troops from Europe, and would withstand a rupture in transatlantic relations.

Furthermore, the idea of the "Eurocorps," like the one established by French and German governments, is particularly appealing to a Poland looking for avenues of integration with Western states. A Polish-German military corps is not anticipated at this time, although Warsaw has a good chance to become an observer or an associate of the WEU. Poland is determined to continue developing close contacts and cooperation with NATO on specific security issues, purchases of modern military equipment, and training of Polish officers. During 1991, in addition to joining the North Atlantic Cooperation Council, Warsaw established bilateral cooperation, consultation, and exchanges at the general staff level. For the time being, NATO and the WEU complement each other, and membership in WEU is seen as a stepping-stone to membership in NATO.

Along the German track of its European policy, Poland places an emphasis on membership in the European Community. For the Poles, membership in EC is a perfect setting for solving the so-called German problem. Instead of facing its mighty western neighbor alone, Poland would rather entangle Germany in a complex network of multilateral relations. The official position, however, is that the principal reason behind Poland's interest in the EC remains neither to contain Germany nor to gain economic advantage. Instead, in the words of its foreign minister, Poland

> . . .wishes to guard against any risk of a return of totalitarianism and to guarantee the permanence of the democracy which was recently regained. It is also seeking a definitive and stable place in Europe.[3]

To constrain Bonn's inherent advantages, Warsaw invited the united German state to serve as Poland's gateway to the West. Since Polish economic difficulties have a direct impact on Germany, which is highly vulnerable to a flood of job-hunting Poles, the Germans promised in the 1991 treaty to assist the Polish government in gaining admission to the European Community. This way, Poland acquired a powerful and strongly motivated champion of its European cause. Admission to the EC, however, is not a simple task, especially at a time when the European Community is undergoing momentous changes. The Poles are now aware that full membership in the EC must wait, probably until the end of this decade. And yet, the country is hurriedly preparing for this occasion. All social, legal, and economic legislation is designed to harmonize the Polish system with West European standards and to comply with legal guarantees of human rights and freedoms.[4]

Poland has already become a member in the Council of Europe and has concluded an agreement on associate membership with the EC. Continuing progress toward full membership in the EC is uncertain, however, as the Poles see declining interest by the West to support their accession. As Jacques Delors, president of the EC Commission, explained, stretching out the "engagement period" is a necessity:[5]

> There is no point in trying to hurry the marriage. In this way, Poland's marriage to the European Community will be more successful and stable. This is all the more important since divorces in an integrated Europe are extremely costly.

It is important to realize, however, that the question of Poland's association with the EC is the subject of intensive internal debate. Anxiety over the political vulnerability, high economic prices, and social dislocation that would result from competition with Western industrial democracies drives some Polish politicians to the conclusion that economic protectionism, political neutrality, and responsibility for their own security are the best alternatives for Poland. Some opponents of Polish membership in the European Community go so far as to argue that Poland is volunteering to become a German colony or a satellite of bureaucrats in Brussels. The feeling that "we barely dug our way out from under the Soviet boot, and now we have crept under the elegant patent-leather pump of Brussels," is the prevailing one among Polish isolationists.[6]

Left outside of NATO, Poland and other East-Central European states have become de facto a convenient buffer zone between the West and the former republics of the USSR, where the probability of divisive ethnic conflict is very high. According to the opinion of militant nationalists, Poland should give up hopes of partnership with the West. Its historical position has been between the East and West, always at the edge of Western civilization, and on the western rim of the Slavic group of nations. In the Western world, Poland will always be a second class member and a European pariah, easy to manipulate, exploit, and abuse.

Geographic proximity, combined with a similar level of economic and political development, qualifies Poland for partnership with its eastern and southern neighbors. Membership in NATO, according to this perspective, would not contribute to Poland's security, since the danger of another "great European war" is not likely to appear in the near future. Poland could be threatened only by some relatively small local conflicts, and the country must be prepared to handle these confrontations with its own resources. Poland's anxiety to join NATO is only an expression of the nation's weakness and a source of exacerbation in relations with its eastern neighbors, especially Russia.

GERMANY

The legacy of Polish-German relations is exceedingly painful and impossible to survey without bias. For Poland, the Third Reich was an embodiment of the ultimate in evil, a threat to the physical existence of the Polish nation. Poland's hope that the results of World War II had provided a permanent solution to the German problem, by dividing and deindustrializing the country, failed to materialize. Now, less than 50 years after the war, the Poles again are facing a united Germany as the leading economic power in Europe. Polish public opinion is presented with the perplexing dilemma of how to comprehend modern Germany. "Traditional" opinion, rooted in historical experience, favors vigilant and isolationist policies, while "Europeanists" stress the far-reaching changes in German political culture and Germany's potential to become Poland's bridge to Europe.

The key element of the German problem, as perceived by Poles, is that of the western border. Despite treaties with the German Democratic Republic (1953) and the Federal Republic of Germany (1970), Poland's first task once freed from Soviet hegemony was to make sure that a united Germany would abide by agreements of its two predecessors. From the moment of its conception, united Germany was unequivocally contained within the international borders of its two constituent states. Poland's rather symbolic presence at the "two-plus-four" talks, permitted only when territorial issues were placed on the agenda, served the purpose of internationally recognizing the Odra-Nysa border. It also resulted in a commitment by both German governments on behalf of the future united Germany to promptly conclude a treaty with Poland recognizing this border as permanent according to international law.

The 1990 Moscow agreement on the unification of the two German states, in its first paragraph, states that "united Germany shall comprise the territory of the Federal Republic of Germany, the German Democratic Republic, and the whole of Berlin . . . The confirmation of the definite nature of the borders of the united Germany is an essential element of the peaceful order in Europe." The second paragraph obligated Germany and Poland to "confirm the existing border between them in a treaty that is binding under international law." This treaty was concluded in November 1991, just one month after German unification. It also stated that the "existing border between them is inviolable now and in the future" and that "both parties to the treaty declare that they have no territorial claims whatsoever against each other and will not assert such claims in the future."[7]

Settling the border question enabled both parties to look into current problems, such as economic relations, issues related to border crossing and transit through Polish and German territories, cultural, scientific, and other forms of bilateral exchange, and the status of minorities in both countries. The June 1991 "Treaty on Good-Neighborliness and Friendly Cooperation" had addressed these issues, as well as normalized mutual relations following the 1963 pattern of reconciliation between Germany and France. Moreover, in this treaty Germany pledged to promote Poland's objective to enter the European Community. The Poles concluded that the road to Europe led through Germany.

As a result, Poland's relations with Germany were accorded a very special status. Although not as pervasive, this relationship is almost as distinctive as the link with Moscow during the communist period. All consequential foreign policy decisions made by Poland had to be scrutinized from a European, in practice, German, perspective. To accomplish this objective, Warsaw established a special ministry on relations with the European Community. Polish authorities are aware of the lopsided dependence on their western neighbor. Like the Soviet Union under communism, Germany is Poland's principal trading partner. In 1991, over 30 percent of Polish foreign trade was directed toward Germany, but Poland accounted for only 1 percent of Germany's foreign trade.[8]

To offset their special ties with Germany, and to avoid the impression of being a German satellite, the authorities in Warsaw are diversifying Poland's international ties by establishing an extensive network of bilateral relations with other European states. The Poles are also opposed to the idea of rewarding Germany with global status and can see no need to amend the UN charter to allow Germany and Japan to enter the Security Council as permanent members. However, owing to Poland's geostrategic location, its plans to join Western Europe, and Germany's commanding position on the continent, there is no other single country that could counterbalance Poland's reliance on Germany. The former Eastern Europe is transforming itself into Central Europe.

One of the lessons of Polish history is that the country could stand up to its western neighbor as long as Germany was acting alone. Extremely tragic consequences resulted when Germany allied itself with Russia, another of Poland's archenemies. The breakdown of the Soviet Union opened new options for Germany, including an anti-Polish coalition with Ukraine and the Baltic States. To prevent another Rapallo or Nazi-Soviet agreement at the expense of Poland and the entire East-Central European region, Warsaw's diplomatic effort is focused on an agreement with Germany that would coordinate the eastern policies of both countries. This way, Poland can obtain assurance that Germany would not act behind its back and against Polish interests, and that some measure of symmetry would be applied to mutual relations. German leverage over Poland's western policy would be balanced by Poland's voice in Germany's eastern policies.

The issue of minorities is now the most sensitive and potentially explosive dilemma in mutual relations. The November 1991 treaty regulates minority status according to the norms of international law, encouraging the German minority in Poland to identify itself and demand political and cultural rights. The number of Polish citizens who claim German ethnic origin does not exceed 700,000, which is less than 2 percent of the population in Poland. However, they represent a well-organized and active group, enjoying generous support from private and public financial sources in Germany. In view of economic difficulties in Poland, many ethnic Germans express an intention to remain in Poland and to "participate in building the European house."[9]

This "Europeanization" of Poland, beginning in Silesia and with the assistance of the German minority, represents a real long-term threat to Polish sovereignty over the Odra-Nysa territories. Some politicians in Germany argue for a special status in Silesia. As Dietmar Bremer, a German activist in Poland, has stated,

. . .the center of gravity for the process of integrating Poland with Europe and for Polish-German relations is shifting to Silesia. The German government will try to keep the German minority in Silesia; to this end, it will support them materially. Meanwhile, the Polish government should give the German minority more attention, seeing it as an element to aid in the process of Poland's integration into Europe.[10]

One example of such integration is the concept of creating the Oderland-Nadodrze Euroregion, extending about 100 kilometers east and 50 kilometers west of the Odra and Nysa rivers, with a population of about five million.[11] This project would stimulate economic prosperity along the border. However, in light of Germany's economic and managerial superiority, the political status of this region also would have to change. Implementation of this economically attractive idea is likely to alter the ethnic and social character of the entire region. Poles would contribute an inexpensive labor force, while the German side would provide technical and organizational know-how as well as private and public financial resources. Many in Poland see the Oderland Euroregion concept as a disguised plan for the Balkanization of Poland. In the long run, Warsaw's sovereignty over these territories may degenerate into a "Polish administration."

On the other hand, the Poles in Germany are the least influential and most poorly organized minority group, despite their strength of about two million. They represent one of the largest concentrations of immigrants in Europe, and only in 1992 did they finally create a Polish-German Congress. Poles find the Western standard of living highly appealing and eagerly accept Germanization. The *Polonia* in Germany is deeply divided and likes to conceal its ethnic identity. In contrast to Germans living in Poland, the Polish minority in Germany exerts hardly any political influence, perhaps even less than the Turks or Arabs.[12]

Lack of balance is evident in Polish-German relations today. There are few positive assets that Poland can offer, emphasizing instead negative consequences of Germany's failure to improve the Polish economy and to integrate Poland with the European Community. The most frequently repeated threat is that of allowing eastern refugees to pass through Poland and inundate Germany. Only revision of this approach can help the country to adopt the attitude of a partner, rather than that of a client, and to formulate bilateral relations on a more equal footing. The question is whether Poland will be able to generate within itself enough vitality to reach a socioeconomic level that would make the country an attractive partner for Germany and other Western nations.

RUSSIA

While Polish-German relations have already stabilized on a businesslike level of negotiation, the emotions and legacy of the past continue to adversely affect the normalization of ties between Poland and Russia. For some Poles, postcommunist Russia is just another reincarnation of the dreadful tsarist

Russian and Soviet empires, assuming the regional and global place of the former USSR. The United States, Western Europe, and other regions treat the Russian state as a superpower, creating the impression that Russian objectives will continue to prevail over the aspirations of East-Central European states. Weakened by its domestic turmoil and economic confusion, the Russian state does not present any immediate threat to Poland or the other nations of the region. This situation may change dramatically in the future, when Russia succeeds in turning around its economy.

Stimulated by nationalism and a sense of pride, as a result of shaking off Soviet hegemony, Poles are frequently accused of adopting a shortsighted "bear-baiting" attitude toward Moscow. Poland's advances vis-à-vis NATO and the EC, as well as its assertive bilateral relations with former republics of the USSR, cause serious concern in Moscow. Equally agitating for Russia is Poland's "eastern policy" of close economic and security ties with the Baltic States, Ukraine, and Belarus. This follows the traditional pursuit of influence in the area between Poland and Russia, to drive Moscow away from European affairs. It also assumes that the only threat to Polish national sovereignty originates from Russia. This policy, labeled by Russians as the "Parys Doctrine,"[13] assumes that Russia is a "bucket of ashes" left after the disintegration of the Soviet Union. As such, it should be left outside European politics. In this view, the proper role of Poland and other East-Central European states is to become a buffer zone against an essentially non-European Russia.

This tight knot of prejudice, however, is not only a bequest from historical experience. There are also three direct reasons for the generally unhappy state of Polish-Russian relations. First is the slow withdrawal of Russian forces from Poland and Germany. Second, Warsaw is seeking a guarantee from Moscow to supply raw materials, especially oil and natural gas, which are critical to the economy. Last, Poland wants to maintain Russian markets for its defense industry products as well as secure an uninterrupted supply of spare parts for its armed forces. Thus, despite dissenting feelings toward Russia, the Polish leadership fully understands the significance of normal relations, including the fact that symptoms of friction with Russia would further prejudice Polish hopes for integration with Western Europe.

The most significant recent development in Polish-Russian relations involved the May 1992 visit by President Lech Wałęsa to Moscow. It was the first arrival in the Kremlin by the head of an independent Polish state. Two previous visits, those of Prime Minister Władysław Sikorski in 1941 and Prime Minister Tadeusz Mazowiecki in 1989, were at lower-ranking levels.[14]

Besides historical symbolism, President Wałęsa's trip to Moscow was intended to become a "great opening" for mutual relations, a reversal of some 500 years of Polish-Russian animosity. Despite forceful criticism at home, the Polish delegation set no preconditions for negotiations and did not advance demands that a preamble to the treaty must include a condemnation of both Stalinism and the 1939 Molotov-Ribbentrop Pact. In the joint declaration issued by the two presidents, both sides condemned Stalinism and totalitarianism. In this respect, Poland rejected a counterproductive "score-settling" strategy and instead decided to continue a pragmatic policy designed to settle issues and to set the stage for productive future relations.

The Wałęsa-Yeltsin agreement brought several tangible benefits. The most significant compromise involved withdrawal of Russian troops, which had been stationed on Polish territory for almost half a century. Both sides adopted the zero-option formula for military disengagement, favored by Warsaw, whereby the Russians would pay transportation costs while the Poles renounced claims regarding ecological and other damage. Only in this way could Poland secure Russian agreement to the complete withdrawal of combat units by 15 November 1992. The remaining 4,124 Russian military personnel are expected to leave by the end of 1993. However, Poland assumed the responsibility of providing housing for the withdrawn soldiers and to subsidize their retraining for civilian professions.

In addition, Polish-Russian negotiations produced an agreement for long-term economic cooperation. In exchange for supplies of oil and gas, Poland will deliver electrical machinery, foodstuffs, and pharmaceutical supplies. However, these relations are far from balanced. In 1991 Poland imported $1.8 billion worth of goods but exported only $875 million.[15]

Equally urgent was an understanding on the Kaliningrad (formerly Königsberg) region, the only area where both countries share a common border. Cooperation in this region is of special sensitivity, as Poland remains concerned about the troop concentration there. Russian plans to convert the district into an economic free zone also means that it could quickly become dominated by Germany. A draft agreement between Poland and Russia on cooperation in the Kaliningrad region was prepared in June 1992. For current issues, both countries established a "Roundtable" to discuss Polish investments and cooperation in transportation, energy, trade, and the environment.[16] Both sides failed, however, to agree on military cooperation. Although Warsaw accepted the view that a system of common security in Europe cannot be implemented without Moscow's participation, it decided to wait until the withdrawal of Russian combat troops had been implemented.

The treaty gave Polish-Russian relations fresh momentum. Both countries, however, cannot live in harmony until the legacy of the past receives full public exposure and honest evaluation, as has already happened in the case of Polish-German relations. Moscow's reluctance to review tsarist and Soviet crimes against the Polish nation fosters an atmosphere of doubt and suspicion against the long-term objectives of Russia. "They will pounce on us again," say politicians in Warsaw, who fear that Russia's proclivity to make concessions to Poland and other countries is just another *peredyshka,* or breathing space, before Moscow is ready again for another round of aggression.

For the time being, however, Poland has stabilized relations with its former archenemy and has even placed itself in the position of broker between Moscow and Kiev. It only appears to be a *ménage à trois* international arrangement in East-Central Europe, where all three partners are friendly toward one another. In essence, however, it is a "marriagelike" relationship between Poland and Ukraine to curb a revival of Russian hegemony throughout the region. The desire to keep some distance from Russia is clear from Poland's enthusiasm to conclude military agreements with Latvia, Ukraine, Hungary, France, as well as the Czech and Slovak republics. This has restricted Polish-Russian military contacts to politically inconsequential sports contests between soldiers of both armies.[17] This example of Poland's "twin-track" eastern policy, inclusive of ties with immediate neighbors, and temperance in relations with Russia, will prevail at least until all Russian troops stationed in Poland have withdrawn.

For this reason it is now premature to conclude that the historical rivalry between Poles and Russians is over, as has already happened between France and England or between France and Germany. Whether a new chapter in Polish-Russian relations has been opened will not be known until the domestic transformation in Russia is completed and the foreign policy objectives of Moscow are clearly defined.

For the time being, the balance of power in the entire East-Central European region is far from settled, as domestic evolution continues to unfold. At this historic juncture, Poland appears to be free from the Russian threat. The Polish model of transition from communism to democracy and a free-market economy is being emulated by its neighbors. In the east, Poles enjoy respect and sympathy while, after two centuries as an occupying power, Russians are viewed with anger and distrust. However, the contest for a *primus inter pares* in the region is not yet over. The final equilibrium in the region may eventually be decided, not so much by Poland or Russia, but rather by policies formulated in Kiev or Berlin.

OTHER NEIGHBORS

Polish relations with its eastern neighbors have had a promising start. The democratic government of Poland acted quickly and with determination during the final days of the USSR. Unintimidated by Moscow, Warsaw became a model for liberation from communist rule, and the government of Prime Minister Tadeusz Mazowiecki acted promptly to recognize the independence of the former Soviet republics. On 19 October 1990, Poland signed a joint declaration recognizing Ukrainian sovereignty. Political gains from this policy included the credibility of democracy as well as goodwill toward the Polish nation and its government.

Polish relations with Ukraine constitute a critical element of the country's eastern policy. As with all other neighbors, Polish-Ukrainian history is saturated with tragic incidents, injustice, and distrust. Yet, perhaps for the first time in history, both nations succeeded in inaugurating mutual relations on the basis of equality, looking to the future rather than trying to disentangle a difficult past.[18] The Polish-Ukrainian rapprochement was a cultural breakthrough and formed a solid foundation for an eventual alliance among 90 million people.

A treaty of good-neighborliness, friendly relations, and cooperation between Poland and Ukraine was signed in Warsaw on 18 May 1992. Both countries renounced the use of force and pledged not to allow an attack against the other country to proceed from their territory. Also, they pledged to cooperate in European structures and work toward a continent without borders. This is, in consequence, a partnership between two of the largest East-Central European states, aimed directly against Moscow and its former order based on supremacy. As President Leonid Kravchuk stated, "After my visit to Warsaw, the degree of cooperation between Ukraine and Poland will be greater than with any other Commonwealth of Independent States country, including Russia." He also added that "Poland is an equal partner for us, whereas Russia is trying to speak to us from the position of 'elder brother' and is proceeding from [an] imperial position."[19] Thus, Ukrainian interest in Poland in part may be due to Kiev's desire to tell Moscow that three centuries of Russian hegemony are over.

The anti-Russian orientation of Polish-Ukrainian ties has a long historic tradition, extending back to the end of the fourteenth century. The Poles conquered western Rus', and followed this with a Lithuanian alliance. The contemporary Polish-Ukrainian axis has the same implications as the Polish Commonwealth of Nations once had. For more than 400 years, it contained Russian expansionism as well as Turkish, German, and Swedish pressures.

The same objective is apparent in the new understanding, because only by acting jointly can Poland and Ukraine resist Russia. It is important, however, to avoid the impression of a *cordon sanitaire* between Russia and Europe. Such a provocation would fuel Russian xenophobia and might prompt Moscow to act hastily. The fact remains that Poland is no longer feared in Eastern Europe as a potential oppressor or a spearhead of Catholicism against Orthodox nations. Instead, Poles are welcomed as a coequal and democratic nation, a mainstay of independence for the entire region, and a primary link to the West.

An independent Ukraine needs Poland more than Poland needs Ukraine. The country is involved in territorial, military, and other disputes with Russia. Ukraine has no effective armed forces despite the 176 intercontinental ballistic missiles (ICBMs) located on its territory and future ground troops potentially larger than Germany's. However, its economy is in deep crisis and the political system is "still run by an old-comrade network, instinctively reverting to authoritarian ways." The Ukrainian economy has not left the prereform stage and the country has yet to experience the trauma of hyperinflation, privatization (96 percent of the economy is still owned by the state), and other repercussions of transition to a market economy. The country is "seduced by Mr. Kravchuk's siren song" of nationalism and fear of Russia, while the old *nomenklatura* continues to apply methods of the old planning system and argues that "authoritarianism is better than anarchy."[20] However, Poland also has its vital interests at stake. Warsaw must be on guard against the possibility of a Ukrainian-Baltic States, Ukrainian-German, or Ukrainian-Russian alliance.

Ukraine is vulnerable to Russia's military and political pressure, and its future hinges on the direction of Russia's domestic and international policies. It has considerable potential to mature into a prosperous and politically stable country, and Poland is well advised to encourage these trends. In the near future, internal weakness and international constraints make it unlikely that Russia would attempt to coerce Ukraine. However, confrontation between these two nations cannot be ruled out, especially since nationalism and structural weakness in both countries may drive them into hazardous international ventures. Fluctuations in the tension between Ukraine and Russia represent an early warning for Poland about Russian designs vis-à-vis East-Central Europe, though Ukraine is likely to be victimized before Poland. These considerations have persuaded Poland to depart from a policy of maintaining equal distance from all states in the region, and instead throw additional weight behind Ukraine to discourage Russia from usurping land at the expense of East-Central European states.

Lithuania, another cornerstone of the old Polish Commonwealth, also has been one of Poland's top international priorities, though Warsaw did not hurry to recognize its independence. Eventually, Warsaw's advances toward Vilnius excluded territorial pretensions and avoided pressure tactics regarding the status of a large Polish minority, which constitutes a majority of inhabitants in two administrative districts. Lithuanian nationalism has strong anti-Polish overtones, as the country is searching for a self-identity autonomous from Polish culture and a common political or religious heritage. Warsaw's patience and understanding paid off, for on 16 January 1992 both countries signed a declaration of friendly relations and good-neighborly cooperation to plant seeds for a fresh start. To nobody's surprise, a large portion of the treaty centers on minority affairs. "The Parties are confident," states the Declaration, "that persons belonging to both minorities are and will remain loyal citizens of the states in which they live, while at the same time preserving and developing their national identity, and that they will promote a genuine rapprochement between the Lithuanian and Polish peoples."[21]

Political reality, however, is far more complicated. With a numerical strength of approximately one-sixth of the population, the Polish minority manifests anti-Lithuanian attitudes, supports Moscow, prefers to speak Russian instead of the much more difficult Lithuanian language, and possesses the general attitude that it "belongs" there. This resulted in a situation where "two Lithuanian antipathies, anti-Polish and anti-Russian, converged suddenly at one point."[22] Arbitrary acts, instituted by the Lithuanian government against its Polish minority, include electoral gerrymandering in order to deprive Poles of the opportunity to have a representative in Lithuania's parliament.[23] Conflict with Poland has provided a focus for Lithuanian xenophobia and diverts public attention from economic problems.

Yet the basic fact of life is that Poland and Lithuania are closely related, have identical objectives in Europe, and the independence of one state is a precondition for the independence of the other. Neither side should forget that Russia has approximately 40,000 troops still deployed in Lithuania, in addition to some 80,000 in the Kaliningrad district. A Polish-Lithuanian feud would leave Moscow the winner or could facilitate German penetration of the Baltic region. Another negative by-product of excessive nationalism in Lithuania could be seen in the return to power of former communist leaders. At the beginning of December 1992, voters elected Algirdas Brazauskas, former communist boss of the republic and more recently head of the so-called Lithuanian Democratic Party, as chairman of their parliament and president of the state. It is expected that the neocommunist leadership in Lithuania will halt implementation of economic reforms and ally the country with Moscow rather than the West, including Poland.[24] Neither a return to autocracy nor restoration of Russian influence in Lithuania can be ruled out, and a prolonged Polish-Lithuanian dispute is an open invitation for third-party involvement to the detriment of both nations' vital interests.

Polish relations with Hungary as well as the Czech and Slovak republics are less burdened by unpleasant historical experiences, and common international objectives of all four nations promote close cooperation. Hopes for membership in the European Community draws them together, and in 1991 they formed the "Visegrád Triangle." It will coordinate domestic and foreign economic policies, especially toward dismantling trade barriers and eventually establishing a free-trade zone. The main objectives formulated by the governments of the Visegrád Triangle are "a further liberalization of trade, a harmonization of legal rules, an expansion of political cooperation, and a definition of the criteria Poland, Czechoslovakia, and Hungary should meet before entering into negotiations on membership in the EC." Stabilization of national currencies, making their rates of exchange realistic, and maintenance of fiscal discipline are the first steps toward developing links with the European monetary system. The ministers of foreign economic relations from Poland, Hungary, the Czech Republic, and the Slovak Republic signed in Kraków on 21 December 1992 the Central European Free-Trade Agreement (CEFTA), setting up a free-trade zone among these four states. This first major step of the Visegrád countries is designed to remove or to lower barriers such as tariffs and quotas on numerous products other than agricultural goods to enhance regional cooperation and to facilitate integration with the European Communities.[25]

Eventually, Poland expects a two-tier relationship within the Visegrád group, political and economic. This explains reluctance to invite Ukraine. Kiev was told to wait, since the gap dividing Ukraine and Western Europe is deeper than in the case of these three East-Central European states. Division of the Czech and Slovak Republic into two separate states on 1 January 1993 did not complicate relations within the Visegrád Triangle, since it was a friendly divorce and has had little effect on the processes of economic integration.

Three years of Poland's Eastern policy have produced numerous tangible results. In addition to Ukraine and Lithuania, Poland has normalized relations with several other former republics of the USSR. Warsaw has established itself as a power broker. Poland also continues to be an "experimental laboratory" for the transition to democracy and a free-market economy throughout the entire region as well as its political and economic window to the West. The pro-Western predisposition of East-Central Europe placed Poland in a leadership position during the long march toward the West. Polish success may indeed be decisive in the transformation even of Russia.

THE UNITED STATES

Polish-American relations are traditionally long on good intentions and lofty statements but short on substance. Poland expected to reap dividends for its sacrifice in becoming the pioneer to emancipate East-Central Europe from Soviet domination and for its initiatives toward transplanting democracy. In terms of *Realpolitik,* however, Poland's special status as the Achilles' heel of the Soviet empire evaporated together with the demise of the USSR. Warsaw expected to be rewarded in the form of a unique relationship with Washington.

Polish politicians calculated that the United States would see in Poland a reliable partner for all European security matters. Unification of Germany and traditional French animosity toward the American presence in Europe could encourage the United States to look for new allies, and Poland was more than eager to volunteer to strengthen the transatlantic link of European security. The end of the Cold War, however, caused the United States to curtail its global commitments, and distant Poland did not appear to be a defense priority in Washington. Even high-level contacts between defense establishments of both countries resulted in no more than an exchange of opinions on security-related matters and insignificant deliveries of American military equipment. Poland is not a factor in the United States' global scheme, known as the "new world order."

American security guarantees are not relevant for the independence of Poland or any other East-Central European state. The United States is of the opinion that the only real threat to the safety of these countries is their internal instability and economic disarray. Moreover, Polish and other regional issues are not of global significance and thus require no direct American involvement. These are regional affairs that should be of prime concern only to the European members of NATO. The United States supports broadening diplomatic and political links between NATO and Warsaw, but it has no urge for bilateral security arrangements with Poland or any other country in the region.[26] Under conditions of domestic instability, Polish-American security ties would not accomplish more than strengthening the Warsaw government against its domestic opposition. This means that once Poland's internal conditions are in order, the United States could be inclined to support a Polish request for membership in NATO.

American economic assistance did not reach the massive proportions of $10 billion first requested by Warsaw. Except for initial humanitarian aid, the United States has channeled its resources via the International Monetary Fund and the World Bank. Both of these institutions exercise detailed supervision over disbursement of monies within the context of general Polish economic conditions. A budget deficit of less than 5 percent and a low rate of inflation are the two main prerequisites for release of credits. American economic assistance thus has become an instrument of control over implementation of economic reform.

Perhaps Poland has failed to achieve a unique place in American foreign policy, but it did manage to secure a status commensurate with its international weight, size, and location in Europe. Also, the scope of Polish-American relations is likely to unfold in proportion to the progress of building a stable and democratic state. At this moment, the United States has given Poland a chance to earn its place among the Western family of nations.

CONCLUSION

Three years of independence have produced a reorientation of Poland's foreign policy. The international status of the country has been transformed from that of a Soviet satellite to a recognized actor on the entire continent and the key element of stability and democratization at Europe's eastern edge. Without delay, independent Poland proceeded to formulate and implement new foreign-policy goals that were compatible with post-Soviet realities in Europe, and so far the country has been successful in advancing its international objectives in all five areas. Despite the euphoria of revolution and liberation, Poland did not lose a sense of proportion of the purpose of its mission abroad. Realistic assessment of national capabilities and international opportunities, as well as enormous talent to compromise and sacrifice the less significant and temporary for tangible and long-term gains, represent core values of modern Polish foreign policy. Equally important is Warsaw's ability to calibrate its policies in view of emerging exigencies of the international situation, including a willingness to scale down its ambitions without becoming discouraged or drifting away from the adopted course.

However, Polish accomplishments can be measured only in terms of initiating trends and sorting out priorities. In three years, Poland has established legal and political infrastructures for its new foreign policy. However, fulfillment of national objectives cannot be achieved without many years of persistent and tedious effort. This continuity of purpose serves as a shield against placing foreign affairs at the mercy of domestic disagreements (actually, external policy has assumed a stabilizing role in domestic affairs) and has been provided by the extraordinary diplomatic talents of Foreign Minister Skubiszewski. The basic tenets of his foreign policy include the ideas that:

- Central Europe (the Visegrád Four, or the area between Germany and the Commonwealth of Independent States) is a component part of

Western Europe, with identical economic and security concerns, and a common cultural heritage
- Philosophical underpinnings of Polish foreign policy must be free from nationalistic ambition and an isolationist proclivity, and that Polish espousal of the West should enrich rather than destroy Polish cultural identity
- In harmony with the CSCE process in Europe, Poland approached all neighbors on the basis of inviolability of existing borders, but also with an expectation that successful integration will render all European frontiers obsolete
- Rights of national minorities must receive full legal and political recognition to stress the ethical nature of Polish foreign policy, to protect Poles living abroad, and to accelerate integration of Europe
- Poland must be prepared to absorb rapid international change and setbacks without negating its commitment to join Western Europe, since Warsaw can "earn its place" only through a positive attitude and self-improvement to match Western levels
- Polish security is enhanced by foreign political and economic ties with all countries in the world. Poland has already become an indispensable regional player and achieved global presence through its participation in international organizations and such global initiatives as environmental programs and scientific research

Since 1989, Poland has constructed an elaborate network of bilateral agreements with all neighbors, supplemented by overlapping circles of various regional economic and security structures. This is a platform for the second stage of Polish foreign policy: entry into the European Community by the year 2000.

NOTES

1. Statement by Foreign Minister Krzysztof Skubiszewski to the parliament. *Życie Warszawy,* 18 March 1992.
2. Interview with Skubiszewski in *Polska zbrojna,* 19-21 June 1992. For the military component of foreign policy, see interview with National Security Bureau chief Jerzy Milewski in *Wprost,* 26 April 1992; JPRS-EER-92-067 (28 May 1992).
3. Krzysztof Skubiszewski, "Poland Faced With the Changes in the EC," *Le Monde,* 22 May 1992; FBIS-EEU-92-103 (28 May 1992).

4. Katarzyna Jędrzejewska, "Half a Year of Liberalization in Trade With the EEC," *Rzeczpospolita* (Economy and Law supplement), 28 August 1992; JPRS-EER-92-138 (25 September 1992).

5. *Dziennik Bałtycki,* 4 September 1992.

6. Jerzy Narbutt, "Is Brussels Running Warsaw?" *Ład,* 23 February 1992; JPRS-EER-92-040 (1 April 1992).

7. *Gazeta wyborcza,* 14 November 1991.

8. *Rynki zagraniczne,* 26 March 1992, p. 3.

9. *Rheinischer Merkur,* 22 May 1992; JPRS-EER-92-085 (7 July 1992).

10. Quoted in *Wprost,* 19 January 1992, p. 28.

11. Wojciech Krawczyk, "Odra jako Rio Grande, jako Oderland Euroregion," *Glob,* 9 April 1992.

12. Piotr Cywiński, "Podanie rąk," *Wprost,* 15 March 1992.

13. Poland's defense minister, Jan Parys, in an interview entitled "Then the Conflict Will Come to Germany," *Frankfurter Rundschau,* 23 March 1992; FBIS-EEU-92-058 (25 March 1992).

14. Andrzej Romanowski, "Polski Prezydent na Kremlu," *Tygodnik powszechny,* 31 May 1992.

15. Zdzisław Lasota, "Dobrosąsiedzki business," *Polska zbrojna,* 21 May 1992.

16. Yurii Stoganov, "Russia-Poland," *Rossiiskaia gazeta,* 11 September 1992; FBIS-SOV-92-182 (18 September 1992).

17. Wojciech Staszewski, "Łotwa i Ukraina, tak," *Gazeta wyborcza,* 22 September 1992.

18. Władysław A. Serczyk, "Odkrywamy Ukrainę," *Polityka,* 1 February 1992.

19. Quoted in *Izvestiia,* 20 May 1992; FBIS-SOV-92-100 (22 May 1992).

20. *The Economist,* 3 October 1992. Also see Wojciech Pieczak, "Poland and Ukraine Share a Common Fate," *Tygodnik powszechny,* 31 May 1992; JPRS-EER-92-083 (30 June 1992).

21. *Ekho Litvy,* 16 January 1992; FBIS-SOV-92-019 (29 January 1992).

22. Jerzy Marek Nowakowski, "Zagmatwany problem," *Rzeczpospolita,* 11-12 April 1992.

23. Warsaw Radio, 21 August 1992; FBIS-EEU-92-164 (24 August 1992).

24. *Elita News Bulletin,* Vilnius, 8 December 1992; FBIS-SOV-92-238 (10 December 1992).

25. *Rzeczpospolita,* 12-13 September 1992, p. 1. See also, *Rynki zagraniczne,* 1 April 1992, p. 3; Warsaw Radio, 21 December 1992, in FBIS-EEU-92-246 (22 December 1992), p. 25.

26. Commentary on Prime Minister Jan Olszewski's visit to Washington, D.C., over Warsaw Radio, 13 April 1992; FBIS-EEU-92-072 (14 April 1992).

INDEX

abortion, 3, 54, 55
  and John Paul II, 53
accountability, of local government officials, 91-3
Act on Employee Self-Management (1981), 124
Act on State-Owned Enterprises (1981), 124
"adaptive expectations" theory, 170, 171
Adria-Alpine group, 6
  appeal to Poland by, 208-10
affirmative rights, 106
agricultural land ownership, 116-17
agricultural policy, 150-1
agriculture
  and political power, 112
  in private sector, 5, 150
Alliance of the Democratic Left (*Sojusz Lewicy Demokratycznej,* SLD), 2, 29
All Polish Trade Unions, *see* OPZZ
  and Suchocka coalition, 32
"alternative local élites," as opposition, 81-82
Antall, József, 219-20
armed forces, question of control, 66
asset-stripping, 130

balanced budget, 173
  and gold standard, 176
  and tax adjustment, 174
Balcerowicz, Leszek, 35, 68
Balcerowicz plan, 21, 59

  and economic transformation, 140, 145-6
  and fiscal policy 146
  and Olszewski, 63
"Balkanization," of Poland, 244
banks, 137
  and SOEs, 149
  see also central bank
Bartosiński, Stanisław, 106
Bartoszcze, Roman (PSL candidate), 24
basic law, 4, 45
Bielecki, Jan Krzysztof, 63, 68, 218
  and Olszewski, 63
  as prime minister, 35, 59
bilateral treaties, with Moscow, 206
bilateral relations (Poland), 242-3
border issues, Poland, 220-1
  see also Odra-Nysa
"bounded rationality," 178
Bowen, Catherine Drinker, 107
Brazauskas, Algirdas, 10, 250
Bremer, Dietmar, 243
Brzeziński, Zbigniew, 207-8
budget
  deficit, 6, 42
  and pensions, 161
  priorities change in, 162
  see also balanced budget, state budgets
Bujak, Zbigniew, 28
Business Center Club, 43
business infrastructure need, 141

cabinet selection, problems of, 62-63

capacity utilization, 157

Carpathian Euro-Region Pact (1993), 7

Catholic Church, 3, 51-55
  changes in, 51, 52
  and elections, 22, 24
  influence of, 46, 52, 139
  and the intelligentsia, 51
  and public opinion, 69
  public role of, 53-4

Catholic Electoral Action (*Wyborcza Akcja Katolicka,* WAK), 54
  seats of, 61, 62
  and ZChN, 29

CEI, *see* Central European Initiative

Center Accord (*Porozumienie Centrum,* PC), 22, 28

Center Alliance, 63, 68, 74
  and "group of five," 68
  seats of, 61, 62
  and Wałęsa support, 59, 60

Central Planning Office, unemployment forecast, 158

Central Statistical Office, unemployment survey of, 161-2

Center for Public Opinion Research, 47

Center for the Study of Public Opinion (CPSO), 69
  on democracy, 75

central bank, 6, 173, 176-7

central government, 13, 89, 93
  role in local government, 85-86, 91, 92-93

Central European Free-Trade Agreement (CEFTA), 251

Central European Initiative (CEI), 220, 224-5
  EBRD funding of, 224

Central European Trade Initiative, as EC-2, 224

Centre for Economic Policy Research (London), 227

CFE, *see* Conventional Forces in Europe

change, *see* reform; transformation; transition

Charter of Rights and Freedoms, 4, 34, 105, 106-7

Christian Democratic Forum (*Chrześcijańsko-Demokratyczne Forum,* ChDF), 32

Christian Democratic Movement, 21

Christian Democratic Party (Partia *Chrześcijańsko-Demokratyczna,* PChD), 29, 53

Christian National Union (*Zjednoczenie Chrześcijańsko-Narodowe,* ZChN), 24, 63, 67-68
  leaders of, 29-31
  orientation of, 22, 27, 28
  supporters of, 31

Christian Peasant Party (Stronnictwo *Chrześcijańsko-Ludowe,* SChL), 29

Chrzanowski, Wiesław, 31, 67, 70

Chrześcijańsko-Demokratyczne Forum (ChDF), see Christian Democratic Forum

church-state relations, 54

Cimoszewicz, Włodzimierz, 24, 25

citizen vouchers, *see* voucher plan

Citizens' Committees (*Komitety Obywatelskie,* KO), 20, 23, 24, 60

Citizens' Movement for Democratic Action (*Ruch Obywatelski Akcja Demokratyczna,* ROAD), 24, 29, 35

CMEA
  collapse of, 182, 213
  impact on exports of, 148, 193-7
  and trade vacuum, 224

CMEA and East Central Europe integration, 205-6

CMEA markets, 149, 181, 183
  and the złoty, 192

coal mines, 149
  and privatization in Russia, 114-15

"coalition of seven," 67-69

collective bargaining, *see* labor relations

command economy, 118, 121-2

communalization, 3, 83-84

communism, demise of, 78-80, 90, 99, 182, 184, 204

    results of, 154

communist influence

    and Mazowiecki government, 139

    and state-owned assets, 84

    in workers' relations, 155

communists

    in government, 3, 23, 24, 25, 61, 207, 211-12

    Moscow assistance of, 64

    in Poland, 2, 9-10, 21, 23-4

compensation system, 121

competition

    and economic growth, 114-115, 117

    international, and politics, 119

    Western, 148

Confederation for an Independent Poland (*Konfederacja Polski Niedpogległej*, KPN), 21, 63, 67, 74

    opposition role of, 31

    seats of, 61,

Conference on Security and Cooperation in Europe, see CSCE

Congress of Self-Governing Republic (party, May 1991), 88

Conservative Party (*Partia Konserwatywna*), and UD, 29

constitution, 3-4, 51, 69, 107

    amendments to, 4, 99

    of 1952, 70-71

    writing of, 70, 98-101

    see also basic law

constitutional committees, 99

constitutional courts, 104

constitutional deadlock, 62, 75

constitutional democracy, 107-8

constitutional reform, 57-8

    amendments, 99

    impasse of, 63

    and Sejm, 69

    and Wałęsa's draft, 6

Constitutional Tribunal (1985), 72, 103

    criticism of, 105

    and parliament, 104-5

Constitutional Tribunal Act, 104

"contractual Sejm," 207

Conventional Forces in Europe (CFE), 9, 211, 222

Council of Europe, 3

    Poland's membership of, 240

Council of Ministers, and local government reform, 86, 89

Council of Mutual Economic Assistance, *see* CMEA

CSCE, 208

    paralysis in, 220

    symbolic value of, 222

CSPO, *see* Center for the Study of Public Opinion

currency (domestic), *see* złoty

Czechoslovakia, split in, 219

debt (SOEs) restructuring, 136

decentralization, 78-80, 83

    advantages of, 79-80

    local conditions for, 85

    and market-based democracy, 78-79

    as privatization tool, 125

    useful methods of, 139

decree rule, 34, 71

    and cabinet, 6

    and economic policy, 118

    and Olszewski, 65

    and Sejm, 102

"deétatization," 77, 78

Delors, Jacques, 240

demand-constrained economy, 184-5

de Michelis, Gianni, 214
democracy
 benefits of, 111-12, 121-22
 commitment to, 60
 emerging pattern in Poland, 57, 62, 90-1
 local conditions for, 90
 poll on attitudes, 75
 problems in, 50-51, 112
 and property rights, 117
 in Russia, 122
Democratic Left Alliance (SLD), 61, 62
 and the Little Constituton, 100
Democratic Union (*Unia Demokraty-czna,* UD), 16, 20, 28, 48, 49, 62-3, 67, 68, 102
 economic liberalism of, 22
 and Parys, 66
 pivotal role of, 29, 36, 59, 75
 seats of, 61, 62
Democratic Social Movement (*Ruch Demokratyczno-Socjalny,* RDS), 28
demonopolization, 117, 148-9
Demoskop, opinion poll, 47, 48, 49
 on government, 45-46
Dienstbier, Jiří, 210
domestic policy (Polish), and Visegrád Triangle, 218

East Central Europe relations, 204-5, 207
eastern policy (Polish), 247, 248
 coordination with Germany of, 243
 results of, 251-2
 and Russia, 245
East European Payments Union, 196
EBRD, and CEI, 224
EC
 changes in, 221, 240
 Edinburgh summit (December 1992), 223

 as Poland's trading partner, 18, 182, 188
 regulations of, 6
EC markets, and Visegrád Triangle countries, 211, 216-17, 221, 223, 224
EC membership
 associate, 151
 competition for, 222
 conditions of, 212
 desire for, 203, 239, 240, 254
 German support of, 239-40
 prospects of, 7, 9, 198, 226
 timetable for, 223
EC-10, 189, 191
EC-2, 224-25, 226
economic tranformation, 4, 42-44, 145, 146-7
 and microfoundations, 78
education, 48-9
 scientific, 192
EFTA, *see* European Free Trade Association
EIB, *see* European Investment Bank
elections, 10, 22-26
elections, local (May 1990), 3, 23-4, 90
 and Solidarity, 23
elections, national (June 1989), 1, 2, 3, 22-3, 41
elections, parliamentary (October 1991), 22, 62, 100, 218
 legislative provisions for, 26
elections, presidential (November 1990), 1, 3, 20, 24-26, 211-12
 voter participation in, 2-3, 24-25
electoral campaign, 47
electoral law, 26, 60-61
electorate, disenchantment of, 58-9, 62, 69
electro-engineering sector exports, 196
employee council, 123
 sidelining of, 128, 129, 140

and state-owned enterprises (SOEs), 123

and Western advisors, 131

employee involvement

in privatization process, 135

SOEs, 140, 141

employee management, and Ministry of Privatization, 129

employee ownership, 138

Employee Stock Ownership Plan (ESOP), 128-9

employment distribution, 42, 43, 152

categories of, 49

decline in, 156-7

in private and public sector, 158

and wages, 152

see also human capital, labor market

energy extraction sector, 149, 150

energy prices, Russia, 113

entrepreneurs, 43

ESOP, *see* Employee Stock Ownership

ethnic minority conflicts, 7, 203-4, 21

and ethnic cleansing, 220

in Russia, 240

"Eurocorps," 239

European Association Agreement (December 1991), 197, 198, 199

European Charter of Local Self-Government (Council of Europe, 1985), 3, 83

and Polish local government, 84

European Community, *see* EC

European Convention of Human Rights, 104

European Free Trade Association (EFTA), 197

of Quadrangle countries, 226, 227

European Investment Bank (EIB) loans, 198

"Europeanization" of Poland, 243-4

European Security Commission, 210-11

"Euro-region," 8

executive-legislative relations, 33-34, 35

see also presidential-parliamentary relations

executive branch, and "Little Constitution," 71, 73

see also president, powers of

export

agricultural, increase in, 151

to CMEA markets, 193, 194

decline of, 148

external economic setting, 197-9

improvement in, 188, 192

to the OECD markets, 186, 187-8

products, change in, 186, 189-90, 194-6, 196-7

to Soviet Union, 194

transformation program of, 182

to the West, 182, 185, 186, 189, 193, 194, 195

Falandysz, Lech, 74

farmerization policies, 151

Finance Ministry, 87

and local government reform, 89

and "small privatization," 127

foreign investment law, modification of, 127

foreign policy (Polish), 57

assessment of, 253-4

foreign trade, 119-20

evolution of, 183-85

liberalization of, 186

reorientation of, 181, 183, 193-4

free-market, pioneering of, 207

free trade agreement (December 1992), 199

free trade zone, 199, 223, 226, 251

French constitutional model, 65, 67, 69

Friedman, Milton, 6, 169-70, 171

and "adaptive expectations theory," 170

advice of, 168
growth rule of, 173
1968 article by, 169
simple rules of, 178
friendly divorce, *see* velvet divorce
friendly relations and good-neighborly
    cooperation declaration, 250
fuel and energy production, 148

Gabčikova-Nagymaros dam issue, 217,
    219
Garlicki, Leszek, 105
Gáti, Charles, 203, 225
GDP, *see* gross domestic product
Generalized System of Preferences, 197
Geremek, Bronisław, 35, 102
    defense of "Little Constitution," by,
    75
    and parliamentary elections, 60, 63
Germany
    border treaty (November 1991), 242
    German Minority Party, seats of, 61
    and Poland, 7, 8, 212, 241-4
        post-reunification problems of,
        221
    as trading partner, 198, 242
gminy
    autonomy of, 83
    and central government, 92
    and inter-*gmina* cooperation, 84
    as prototype of local government, 81
    and public services, 92
gold standard, 175-7
Gorbachev, Mikhail S., 205, 212, 213
Gothenburg Declaration (June 1990), 197
government, 6, 71, 72-73
    budget constraints, 173
    decrees, and the "Little Constitution,"
    71
    financing, options of, 120
    paralysis, 34, 58

gross domestic product, 81
gross national product (GNP), 43
"group of five," portfolios of, 68
group ownership, 126
GSP, *see* Generalized System of Prefer-
    ences,

Hall, Aleksander, 29
hard currency debt, renegotiation of,
    127
Havel, Václav, 222
    and Adria-Alpine Group, 209
    Central European leadership of, 208
    and Czech-Slovak split, 219
    and European Security Commission,
    210
    Moscow visit of, 207
    NATO/CSCE attitude of, 215
Helsinki Agreement (1975), 210
Helsinki II program, 220
Hexagonale, 211, 222
    summit (August 1992), 214-15
    see also Adria-Alpine Group; Pen-
    tagonale
housing, 113-14
human capital, 189-91
    see also employment; labor force;
    labor market
Hungarian Democratic Forum, 219
Hungary, 208, 219-20

Iliescu, Ion, 219
IMF, *see* International Monetary Fund
independents, in local elections, 23
industrial development, 189, 218
industrial relations, chaos in, 154
industrial sector (private), increase of,
    148-9
industry decline
    and exports, 186-7
    and state control, 117

see also manufactured products
inflation, 6, 172
   forecasts, 170-1
   and monetary policy, 172-3
   and unemployment, 169-70
intelligentsia, 20, 36
   and the Catholic Church, 51
   political orientation of, 28
   and reform, 3, 50
interest rates, 151, 171-2
International Monetary Fund (IMF), 31,
   59, 197, 218, 252
Interstate Commerce Commission, 117

Jankowski, Gabriel, 68
Jaruzelski, Wojciech, 1, 10, 19, 24, 207
   and employee councils, 140
   replacement of, 211-12
Jefferson, Thomas, 108
Jerzy Regulski, 88
John Paul II (pope), 51, 53
joint stock companies, 126, 128, 135-7
   ownership of, 125, 127
joint ventures, 137, 149

Kaczyński, Jarosław, 74
   and Wałęsa, 34
Kaliningrad *oblast'*, 220
   draft agreement on (June 1992), 246-7
Keynes-Kalecki effect, 156
Kiszczak, General Czesaw, 34
Klaus, Václav, 219, 222
   and Visegrád Triangle cooperation,
   224
KLD, 20, 22, 27, 28, 68
   support for, 48, 49
   see also Liberal Democratic Congress
KO, *see* Citizens' Committee
Kokoshin, Andrei, 8

Kołodziejczyk, Piotr, 65
Komitet Obywatelski (KO), *see* Citizens'
   Committee
Konfederacja Polski Niepodłeglej (KPN),
   see Confederation for an Independent
   Poland, KPN
Kongres Liberalno-Demokraticzny
   (KLD), *see* Liberal Democratic
   Congress, KLD
Koseła, Krzysztof, 53
Kozakiewicz, Mikoaj, 60
KPN, 24, 48, 49
   see also Confederation for an Inde-
   pendent Poland
Kravchuk, Leonid, 9, 57, 249
Kuroń, Jacek, 68

labor code, and wages, 155
labor force, 152, 157, 189
   hoarding of, 151
   shortage in, 162
Labor Fund, 159, 163
labor-intensive products, 192
labor market, 151-63
   freedom of, 152, 155
   liberalization of, 5-6
   transformations in, 164
   see also employment, human capital
labor relations, 155, 163
Labor Solidarity, 28
labor unions, 2, 43
labor unrest, 218
   see also strikes
Law on Privatization, 130
law, rule of, 103-5
Leadership, 32-36, 89
"legalized parasitism," 125
legislative rule, 58, 71, 73-74, 118
Lepper, Andrzej, 44, 51
Lętowska, Ewa, as ombudsman, 103
Lewandowski, Janusz, 68, 125

Lewandowski-Szomburg proposal, 131
Liberal-Democratic Congress (*Kongres Liberalno-Demokratyczny*, KLD), 20, 63, 67, 68
    and Krzysztof Bielecki, 31
    seats of, 61, 62
    see also KLD
liberalization (of large firms), 163
liberals, 28
Lipton, David, 131
liquidation, 127, 128, 129, 137-8
Lithuania, 250-1
"little coalition," 68
Little Constitution, 101-3, 69-71
    approval of, 2, 4, 16, 34, 70, 100-1, 218
    and budget plan, 218
    compromise of, 70-71, 74, 100, 102-3
    criticism of, 58, 74, 102
    and division of power, 74, 218
    importance of, 73, 75, 103
    and political gridlock, 34
    provisions of, 33, 34, 71, 72-3, 101-2
    Senate amendments to, 100
    and special powers, 102; *see also* decree rule
    as temporary solution, 45
    and Wałęsa, 74
local government, 81-2, 87-8
    autonomy of, 91-93
    economic needs of, 79-80, 92-3
local government officials, 90, 91-3
local government reform, 88-9
    power struggles of, 89
    progress in, 88, 90-91, 93-4
    resources of, 88-89
Local Self-Government Act (22 March 1990), 83, 86, 87, 88, 91
    and central government support, 84
    criticism of, 85-86
    and *gminy* services, 92

and property rights delineation, 83
Local Self-Government Assemblies, 86-87
local self-governments, "institutional" environment of, 85-89
London Club, 6
Lutkowski, Karol, 65, 68

Maastricht Treaty (December 1991), 221
Macierewicz, Antoni, 31, 32
Main Statistical Agency, 43
manufactured products, export of, 186, 188-9
market-based democracy, 80-1
    and decentralization, 78-79
market economy, 164
    and taxes, 118-19
    Wałęsa support of, 59
marketization (industrial), decline of, 149
martial law, lessons of, 19
mass privatization schemes, 131-33
    and liquidation, 127, 128, 129, 137-8
    politics of, 130
Mazowiecki, Tadeusz, 1, 43, 61, 66, 99, 218
    appointment of, 44
    and the intelligentsia, 20
    in Moscow, 245
    and parliamentary elections (1991), 29, 60
    and presidential race, 24, 25, 58-59
    and wage freeze, 120
    and Wałęsa, 34-35
Mazowiecki government, 70, 99, 129
    economic program of, 59, 141
    radical reform of, 127, 207
Mečiar, Vladimír, 219, 222
Merkel, Jacek, 24
MFN, *see* Most Favored Nation
Mikołajczyk, Stanisław, 22
Milewski, Jerzy, 67

and NATO-2, 222-3
military agreements (Polish), 247
military cooperation agreements, 9, 206,
 213-14
Ministry of Finance
 and local government funding, 83
 and *nomenklatura* profits, 130
 and Pact on SOEs, 136
Ministry of Ownership Transformation,
 4, 129
 central authority of, 128
 privatization plan of, 128
 and SOE transformation, 135
 work pace of, 134
Ministry of Privatizatation
 see Ministry of Ownership Transformation
minorities issue, 219-20, 243, 244
Mitterrand, François, 217
Moczulski, Leszek, 24, 74
Molotov-Ribbentrop Pact (1939), 243,
 246
monetary policy, 168, 169, 177-8
 and economic system, 178-9
 and foreign exchange, 175-6
 and government debt, 6, 167, 173,
 176
 and inflation, 172-3, 174
 influence of, 174
 and interest rates, 171-2
 and seigniorage, 174
 and unemployment, 169-71
monetary policy operations, 168-71
monetary stability, 120
money supply, 120
monopoly, 117
Most Favored Nation (MFN) status,
 197
Movement for the Third Republic
 (*Ruch dla Trzeciej Rzeczpospolitej*,
 RTR), 32

NACC, *see* North Atlantic Cooperation
 Council
National Commission on Education
 (Polish, 1774), 108
national investment funds, 5
national investment trusts, 131
 and SOEs, 132
National Local Self-Government Assembly, composition of, 87
 see also Local Self-Government Assembly
National Security Bureau, secret plan of,
 66-67
national security concerns, 235-6
 and NATO membership, 7, 234
National Salvation Front (Romania), 219
NATO
 and Poland, 203, 235, 241
 and the Visegrád group, 215, 226
NATO-2, 222-3, 224, 238
natural resources, and export, 189
"natural unemployment rate theory,"
 169-70, 171
"negative rights," 105, 106
neoliberalism, and transition, 17
Neutrum, 55
nomenklatura, Polish, 9-10
 administrative control by, 126, 130
 entrenchment of industry by, 129, 130
 in government positions, 18, 140
 and *nomenklatura* capitalism, 125
 see also communists
nomenklatura, Russian, 9
nomenklatura, Ukrainian, 249
non-cooperation, as political strategy, 17
non-*popiwek* wage regulations, 163
non-tariff barriers, 226-27
non-voters, 22
North Atlantic Cooperation Council
 (NACC), 7, 215, 238, 239
 see also NACC

North Atlantic Treaty Organization, 222, 238
  see also NATO
NSZZ "Solidarność" (*Niezależne Samorządne Związki Zawodowe*), 43

Oderland-Nadodrze Euroregion, creation of, 244
Oder-Neisse, *see* Odra-Nysa
Odra-Nysa border issue, 8, 206, 214, 243
OECD, *see* Organization for European Cooperation and Development
Office of Local Government Reform, and service association, 92
Ogólno-Polskie Związki Zawodowe, see OPZZ
Olechowski, Andrzej, 65
Olszewski, Jan, 42, 59, 70
  and authority conflict, 64-65, 72
  Center Alliance candidate, 63
  and ChDF, 32
  and communists, 35, 64, 66, 67, 218
  government of, 35, 62-65, 68
  mass privatization schemes, 132
  and no-confidence vote, 67
  and the "Parys Affair", 66, 67
  and reprivatization, 134
  and SOEs, 135
  supporters of, 29-30, 64, 65
Ombudsman, role of (1987), 103
Onyszkiewicz, Janusz, 68
"Open Skies," agreement, 222
opinion polls, *see* public opinion polls
OPZZ (*Ogólno-Polskie Związki Zawodowe*), 2, 43, 46, 155
Organization of European States, 210
Organization for Economic Cooperation and Development (OECD), 5, 152
  exports to, 186
  imports from, 188

trade with, 194
Osiatyński, Jerzy, 68
ownership transfer, *see* privatization

Pact on SOEs (October 1992), 134, 136, 140, 163
  and employee involvement, 135
  and trade union participation, 136
pan-European security system, 210
Paris Club, 6
parliamentary elections (October 1991), 60-62
Partia Chrześcijańsko-Demokratyczna (PChD), see Christian Democratic Party
Partia Konserwatywna, see Conservative Party
party ideology, 22
"Parys Affair," 65-67, 72
"Parys Doctrine," 245
Parys, Jan, 32, 63, 67
Pawlak, Waldemar, 32, 62, 63
  as prime minister, 35, 67-8
PC, *see* Center Accord
PChD, *see* Christian Democratic Party
Peasant Alliance, 63
Peasants' Accord (*Porozumienie Ludowe*, PL), 29
peasants and workers, views of, 20
pensions, 121-2, 161
Pentagonale, 203, 209
  and EC and CSCE, 209
  membership of, 209-10
  and Poland's admission, 214
  renaming of (Hexagonale, May 1992), 214
  working groups of, 214-15
  see also Adria-Alpine Group
"people's capitalism," 128
Phelps, Edmund S., 169-70
Phillips curve, interpretation of, 169-70

Piłsudski, Józef, 10
PL, *see* Peasants' Accord
Poland, 206-7
    as transition model, 247
    and Western Europe, 236
Polish Economic Alliance, 29
Polish Economic Program, 67, 68
Polish-German Congress, 244
Polish National Bank, nominating
    president for, 72
Polish Peasant Party (*Polskie Stron-
    nictwo Ludowe,* PSL), 20, 27, 31,
    63, 67, 68, 100
    election results, 24, 62
    support of, 32 , 48, 49
Polish Peasant Party "Solidarity", 31,
    48, 49
Polish United Workers' Party (PZPR),
    10
political conservatism, 26-27
political council, and Wałęsa, 59
political culture, 20, 90, 93
political oppositon, 44
political parties, 22, 26-32, 48
    common features of, 26
    competition by, 16
    ephemeral identity of, 22
    fragmentation of, 16-19, 26,
    33, 61
    orientations of, 28
    professionalization of, 26
    and programs, 19-20
    values of, 2
political reform, and economic reform,
    18-19
politics, 2, 17, 49-50
political *skansen,* composition of, 17
Polonia Reconstituta, 36
Polska Miedź, 149
Polskie Stronnictwo Ludowe (PSL), 31
    see also Polish Peasant Party

*Polskie Stronnictwo Ludowe
    "Solidarność"* (PSL "S"), *see* Pol-
    ish Peasant Party "Solidarity"
popiwek tax, 154-5
populist capitalism, 125-6
Porozumienie Centrum (PC), *see* Cen-
    ter Accord
Porozumienie Ludowe (PL), *see* Peas-
    ants' Accord
postcommunist leadership, 16-17
power
    balance, 33
    devolution of, 83
    struggle, in government, 66-7
prejudice, 48-9
president 71-2
    powers of, 58, 71-2, 73, 102
presidential-parliamentary powers,
    issue of, 99-100
    see also executive-legislative powers
president-parliament relations, 59, 62,
    63, 66
    see also executive-legislative relations
price control, 113-14
    and price liberalization, 112-14, 184,
    197
    in Russia, 112-13
price stabilization, 177
price support, 112-13
private capital, 114-16
private enterprise, and SOEs, 125
private ownership, and government pro-
    tection, 119
private sector, 5, 43
    and employment, 43, 157
privatization, 3-4, 42, 125-7, 139
    in agriculture, 5, 150
    assessment of, 42, 44, 122-3, 129,
    138-9, 140, 141
    and local government management,
    84
    and market economy, 123

policy results of, 137-38
Privatization Council, 138
Privatization Law (1990), 127-131
Privatization Ministry, *see* Ministry of
    Owership Transformation
privatization strategies, 131, 133-4
    of industry, 121
    via liquidation, 127, 128
    Western, 123
production decline, 146-7, 161, 165
product markets, 5, 145-51, 163
property rights, 3, 117-18
Przeworski, Adam, 16
PSL, *see* Polish Peasant Party
public finance, and local government, 82
public opinion polls, 2, 3, 24, 46, 90
    and the Catholic Church, 3, 55
public sector, and employment, 158
public services, central control, 82-83
purchasing power parity, 175
PZPR, *see* Polish United Workers' Party

"quantity theory of money," 174
    version of, 172

Rakowski, Mieczyłsaw, 146, 150
"rational expectation" hypothesis, 170-1,
    172, 178
RDS, *see* Democratic Social Movement
recession, 42, 158-9
reform, and education, 48
regional cooperation, 6-7
    and external factors, 212, 221
    prospects of, 203-4, 205, 225-6
    and Soviet Union break-up, 205
religion, 51-3
    changes in, 52-53
    and economics, 53
    and the intelligentsia, 53
    revival in, 51-52

see also Catholic Church
reprivatization, 134
restructuring, 3
    regional, 163-4
    see also reform; transformation; tran-
    sition
rights, and interpretations, 105-7
ROAD, *see* Citizens' Movement for
    Democratic Action
Roman Catholic Church, *see* Catholic
    Church
Roundtable agreements (April 1989), 22,
    98
    and communist power, 99-100
    compromise of, 44, 207
    and transition, 60-1, 41, 154, 155
RTR, *see* Movement for the Third Re-
    public
Ruch Demokratyczno-Socjalny (RDS),
    see Democratic Social Movement
Ruch dla Trzeciej Rzeczpospolitej
    (RTR), *see* Movement for the
    Third Republic
Rural Solidarity, 62
Russia, 9-10
    perceived threat of, 244-5
    and Poland, 8-9, 244-7
Russian forces, withdrawal of, 245, 246
    see also Soviet troops

Sachs, Jeffrey, and employee councils, 131
Samoobrona (self-defense), 43
Samuelson, Paul, 169
Sargent, Thomas J., 174
SChL, *see* Christian Peasant Party
SdRP, *see* Social Democracy of the Re-
    public of Poland
sector privatization, 133-4
"security vacuum," 213-14
security policy, 238-9
seigniorage, 173, 174

Sejm, 24, 62
    "Sejmocracy," 74, 102
self-management, 123, 126
Shatalin plan, 212
Shevardnadze, Eduard, 205, 212-13
"shock therapy," 4, 8, 102, 127, 211
    in agriculture, 151
Sikorski, Radosław, 66
Sikorski, Władysław, 245
simple rules (Friedman), 178
Skubiszewski, Krzysztof, 63, 68, 225
SLD, 32
    see Alliance of the Democratic Left
Slovak-Hungarian tensions, 217, 219
Slovakia, 219
"small privatization," 84, 127, 137-8
Social Assistance Law (1989), 162
Social Democracy of the Republic of
    Poland (*Socjaldemokracja Rzecz-*
    pospolitej Polskiej (SdRP), 10, 28,
    49
    electorate and OPZZ, 46
    local election results, 23-24
Socjaldemokracja Rzeczpospolitej Pol-
    skiej (SdRP), *see* Social Democ-
    racy of the Republic of Poland
"social pact," 155-6
social security guarantees, 4, 164
    and poverty, 162
SOEs
    autonomy of, 181
    and collective bargaining, 155
    division of authority in, 123 155
    employee stock shares, 128, 132
    and foreign trade, 183-4
    and joint ventures, 149
    management of, 126, 129, 134-7
    ownership, 132
    and privatization, 127-8, 137, 138
    problems of, 140, 146-7, 149
    revenues from, 92

    transformation of, 4-5, 125, 128, 130,
    135, 185
    and the złoty, 184, 193
Sojusz Lewicy Demokratycznej (SLD),
    see Alliance of the Democratic Left
Solidarity, 2, 46, 126
    activists of, 136
    and "alternative" local élites, 81-82
    and austerity policies, 18
    and elections (1989), 1, 23, 98; *see*
    also Citizens' Committees (KO)
    fragmentation of, 58, 61, 99, 126
    and management of the economy,
    125
    post-election role of, 4
    and SOEs, 124, 126
    struggle of, 139
    and voting patterns, 21
"Solidarity '80," 28, 43, 155
Solidarity trade union, 126, 155
"Solidarność '80," see "Solidarity '80"
Solidarność Pracy, see also Labor Soli-
    darity
Solow, Paul, 169
Soviet coup, 212, 220
Soviet troops, in Poland, 206, 212, 213
Soviet Union
    and CFE arms limits, 211, 212, 213
    and consequences of break-up, 220
    trade with, 194
    see also Russia
special security clause (Moscow), 206
    and regional cooperation, 213
"spontaneous privatization," 125
stabilization program, 184-5, 197
Standard International Trade Classifica-
    tion (SITC), 188
state budget, and SOEs, 149
state capital, 114, 115
State Electoral Committee, 61
state farms, and privatization, 150

state monopoly, erosion of, 182, 183-4, 185

state-owned enterprises, *see* SOEs

state-owned property, inefficient use of, 115

State Treasury, as SOE owner, 125, 127, 128, 132

State Tribunal (1982), role of, 103

stock exchange, 125, 129, 130-1, 132

strikes, 156, 162, 163

Stronnictwo Chrześcijańsko-Ludowe (SChL), *see* Christian Peasant Party

Suchocka government, 29, 62, 218
    and local government reform, 94
    and privatization, 3, 4-5, 132, 141
    and SOEs, 134, 140

Suchocka, Hanna, 3, 9, 10, 68, 100
    background of, 2, 35-36
    cabinet of, 2, 68-9
    on EC membership, 223
    and "social pact," 155

Supreme Administrative Court (1980), 103

Szermietiew, Romuald, 66

Szomburg, Jan, 125

taxes, 6, 118-19

technology, Polish, 185, 186, 188-9

technology-intensive products, 192

Third Republic, emerging features of, 36

Tisza-Carpathian group, 6, 203

trade
    and external environment, 197
    liberalization of, 221, 224

trade unions, 155
    and communist past, 136
    and Solidarity, 136

transferable ruble (TR), 194, 195

transformation
    electoral politics of, 15
    fear of, 18, 19, 24

political problems of, 16-18
transition to democracy, 251
    difficulties of, 17, 77-78
    public view of, 44, 48, 49
    state role in, 77
    see also reform; transformation

Treaty on Good Neighborliness and Friendly Cooperation (June 1991), 242

Tymiński, Stanisław, candidacy of, 3, 17, 24, 25, 51, 58

U.S.-Polish relations, 252-3

U.S-NATO consensus, 252

UB, *see* Urząd Bezpieczeństwa

UD, *see* Democratic Union

Ukraine, 248-9

Ukrainian-Polish relations, 247

unemployment
    and education, 160
    and inflation, 169-70
    and privatization, 42
    rise in, 158
    statistics of, 6, 160
    of women, 159

unemployment benefits, 6, 121, 158-9, 162
    assessment of, 159-60
    and monetary policy, 170
    provisions of, 159

unemployment compensation, *see* unemployment benefits

Unia Demokratyczna (UD), *see* Democratic Union

Unia Polityki Realnej (UPR), *see* Union of Political Realism

Union of Political Realism (*Unia Polityki Realnej,* UPR), 27

UPR, *see* Union of Political Realism

Urząd Bezpieczeństwa (UB; secret police), 34

vacancies, and labor demands, 157

"velvet divorce," 204, 219

Visegrád Quadrangle
  assessment of, 225-26
  and EFTA membership, 226, 227
  and free trade zone expansion, 226
  and Poland, 225-6

Visegrád Triangle, 6, 203, 211, 215-16
  competitiveness in, 218
  cooperation issues, 221-2, 223
  Declaration of, 216
  and defense coordination (August 1991), 214, 222
  and EC, 6, 211, 216, 217, 251
  and ethnic conflicts, 217
  Kraków summit (6 October 1991) and NATO alliance, 214
  and NATO-2, 222
  and North Atlantic Cooperation Council, 211
    and Poland, 225-6, 251
    and progress, 217, 218

Voivodship Assembly of Local Governments, 86-7

voivodships, autonomy of, 81

voters, 19-22, 61,
  benefits for, 20
  concerns of, 20, 21
  and party ideology, 21
  percentages of, 19, 47
  preferences of, 47
  views of parties, 20
  see also electorate

voucher plan, 131, 132

Wachowski, Mieczysław, 34, 66

wage indexation, 152-3

wages, 120-1, 154, 156

WAK, see Catholic Electoral Action

Wałęsa, Lech, 1, 8, 10, 98, 211-12
  and "Agent Bolek," 34, 35
  constitutional model preference of, 65, 67, 69
  and elections, 24, 34, 58, 60
  leadership of, 21, 33-4, 211-12
  and the "Little Constitution," 101, 103
  Moscow trip of, 8, 245-6
  and prime minister relations, 23, 34-35, 63-5, 70
  and Solidarity leaders, 33, 35
  Visegrád Triangle cooperation, 217-18

Wałęsa-Yeltsin agreement (May 1992), 246

Wallace, Neil, 174

"war at the top," 33, 58, 62, 70

Warsaw Pact, 206, 208
  dismantling of, 57, 212, 213, 115
  Warsaw Stock Exchange, see stock exchange

West, and Polish exports, 182, 185, 197

Western advice, 131
  and CMEA trade, 196
  and exports, 197

Western European Union (WEU) and Poland, 239

World Bank, 197, 252

Woytyła, Karol Cardinal, see John Paul II

Wyborcza Akcja Katolicka (WAK), see Catholic Electoral Action

Yeltsin, Boris, 9, 212, 246
  and decree rule, 118
  price reforms of, 112-13

ZChN, see Christian National Union

Zjednoczenie Chrześcijańsko-Narodowe (ZChN), see Christian National Union

złoty, 184-5, 192